ESSAYS ON CONRAD

Ian Watt has long been acknowledged as one of the finest of post-war literary critics. *The Rise of the Novel* (1957) is still the landmark account of the way in which realist fiction developed in the eighteenth century and Watt's work on Conrad has been enormously influential. *Conrad in the Nineteenth Century* (1979) was to have been followed by a volume addressing Conrad's later work, but the material for this long-awaited second volume remains in essay form. It is these essays, as Frank Kermode points out in his foreword, which form the nucleus of *Essays on Conrad*, Watt's own philosophy, as well as his insight into Conrad's work, was shaped by his experiences as a prisoner of war on the River Kwai. His personal and moving account of these experiences forms part of his famous essay '"The Bridge over the River Kwai" as myth' which completes this essential collection.

IAN WATT is Professor Emeritus at Stanford University. He is author of *The Rise of the Novel: Studies in Defoe, Richardson and Fielding* (1957), *Conrad in the Nineteenth Century* (1979) and *Myths of Modern Individualism* (1996). Born in 1917, he was educated at Dover County School for Boys and St John's College, Cambridge. In the Second World War he was a lieutenant in the Fifth Battalion of the Suffolk Regiment. Captured by the Japanese at the fall of Singapore, he was a prisoner of war on the River Kwai for three and a half years. His subsequent teaching career took him from Cambridge to the University of California at Berkeley (1952–62), the University of East Anglia (1962–4) and Stanford University, where he has been Professor of English since 1964.

ESSAYS ON CONRAD

IAN WATT

Stanford University

CAMBRIDGE
UNIVERSITY PRESS

PUBLISHED BY THE PRESS SYNDICATE OF THE UNIVERSITY OF CAMBRIDGE
The Pitt Building, Trumpington Street, Cambridge, United Kingdom

CAMBRIDGE UNIVERSITY PRESS
The Edinburgh Building, Cambridge CB2 2RU, UK   www.cup.cam.ac.uk
40 West 20th Street, New York, NY 10011–4211, USA   www.cup.org
10 Stamford Road, Oakleigh, Melbourne 3166, Australia
Ruiz de Alarcón 13, 28014 Madrid, Spain

This collection first published by Cambridge University Press 2000

Printed in the United Kingdom at the University Press, Cambridge

Set in 11/12.5 pt Baskerville No. 2   [GC]

A catalogue record for this book is available from the British Library

Library of Congress cataloguing in publication data
Watt, Ian P.
Essays on Conrad / Ian Watt.
p.   cm.
Includes index.
ISBN 0 521 78007 1 – ISBN 0 521 78387 9 (paperback)
1. Conrad, Joseph, 1857–1924 – Criticism and interpretation.   I. Title.
PR6005.O4 Z9232   2000
823′.912–dc21   99–056318

ISBN 0 521 78007 1 hardback
ISBN 0 521 78387 9 paperback

Contents

Contents

Foreword

Frank Kermode

Readers of the final chapter of this book may find it surprising that the man who spent years labouring on the River Kwai should have returned after the war to an inconceivably different way of life and immediately embarked on a distinguished academic career. Little more than a decade later he published *The Rise of the Novel: Studies in Defoe, Richardson and Fielding* (1957). After the war years many of Watt's contemporaries, even if they had not spent them in painful captivity, found it difficult to adjust their lives to more sedate civilian routines. What readers of this collection as a whole will observe is that the strength of mind – the character – displayed in the final chapter also informs Watt's critical writing. The persistence of this quality goes some way to explaining Watt's devotion, over many years, to Conrad – an honourable stoicism that shuns illusion without being an enemy of pleasure, especially the pleasure of fine technical and aesthetic discriminations.

In *The Rise of the Novel* Watt maintained that realism, as he defined it, was the quality that distinguished the work of the early eighteenth-century novelists from all previous fiction. Before that period there were of course thousands of fictions, but the novel, as we know it, became possible only when the general acceptance of certain social, economic and philosophical assumptions, and the coming into existence of a literate, middle-class and predominantly Protestant audience, made possible such extraordinary works as Samuel Richardson's *Clarissa* (1748). Watt discriminates between the kind of realism exemplified by Defoe, with his unmatched power to persuade readers by minute presentation of detail that what they are reading is true, and a richer realism that concerns itself also with personality and civilized values generally. This variety of realism is essential to the kind of writing that we agree to call the novel. It is not merely a matter of making the narrative seem authentic as to local and period detail; it is also a matter of establishing the authenticity, the complex art and humanity, of the work as a whole.

Watt's view of the rise of the novel has often been contested, most recently and most emphatically by Margaret Anne Doody in her vast book *The True Story of the Novel* (1996). Her title itself indicates dissent from Watt, whose version of that story is, she claims, untrue. Her argument is that the novel has a continuous history of 2,000 years; that form of fiction for which Watt reserves the appellation 'novel' cannot, by his own criteria of realism, or indeed by any other criteria, be distinguished from the romance, a category into which most of that earlier writing is conventionally placed. That the English invented the novel in the eighteenth century is 'a literary lie'. Ms Doody is a strong feminist, and might want to add that the claim is also a masculine lie. The interest of her remarkable book, in the present context, is that she needs to tell the whole history of fiction in the West, and assert that its genius is entirely female, in order to undermine the forty-year-old contentions of Watt. I do not believe she succeeds.

It is not a simple coincidence that Doody's book belongs to the modern era of 'magic realism'. It seems unlikely that works in that mode, much admired of late, would meet Watt's criteria, and although I am only guessing I will say I believe he would not admire them. Doubtless it should be admitted that more permissive notions of realism now prevail both in practice and in literary theory, and it would not be beyond the wit of man (or woman) to devise reasons to show that this alteration of focus has been brought about by the social and economic changes in our world since 1957. Nevertheless *The Rise of the Novel* is a landmark, one of the very few works of modern literary criticism that may be said to have achieved classic status. As early as 1951 Watt published an important and provocative essay stressing the economic significance of *Robinson Crusoe*, so it can be said that for the better part of half a century practically any serious discussion of this book, and the eighteenth-century novel, has had to establish a relationship, even if questioning or dissenting, with Watt's work.

After resuming his interrupted career, he taught at UCLA and Harvard, at Cambridge and at the new University of East Anglia, before settling at Stanford, where he eventually became the first Director of the Stanford Humanities Center. A good deal of his published work has been on the period considered in his first book, but a vital supplement to Watt's bibliography is his work on Joseph Conrad, which culminated in *Conrad in the Nineteenth Century* (1979). This exemplary work was to have been followed by another treating Conrad's writings in the twentieth century, but it now appears, most regrettably, that we shall not see this second volume. However, the present collection contains a number of essays and lectures on Conrad, most of them on the later part of the novelist's career.

Watt has long been acknowledged to be among the finest and most learned of Conrad's expositors. The long and carefully researched chapter on Conrad's first novel, *Almayer's Folly*, is a fine example of his powers as biographer and critic. His observations on Conrad's early influences, and on his command of English (a topic that still requires attention) has not, I think, been bettered. Always attentive to what other critics have to say, he can here be seen adjudicating between angry commentators, himself perfectly composed and conspicuously true to his own Conradian idea of virtue.

When Conrad writes of Singleton, in *The Nigger of the 'Narcissus'*, that 'he steered with care', Watt comments: 'It is the climactic recognition of our utter and yet often forgotten dependence, night and day . . . on the labors of others' – and he adds that 'there is perhaps a moral for the critic here: for, in making us look up, briefly, to Singleton at the wheel, Conrad gives us a moment of vision in which, from the height of our modish attachment to ever-developing discriminations, we are compelled to affirm our endless, intricate, and not inglorious kinship with those who cannot write'. Another such exemplar is MacWhirr in *Typhoon*, a character both funny and admirable, and an instance of 'the paradoxical fact that superiors who are in many respects inept can nevertheless be very good at the job; indeed, their very lack of interest or skill in conversation and books, the main values of verbal culture, may even have left them freer to do in a more single-minded way the one thing that they have trained themselves to do'. One might say without much fear of contradiction that Watt learned this Conradian moral when in uniform or in the prison camp.

His fidelity to the spirit of the author, whom he tells us he first admired at the age of twelve, enables him, in the chapter on *Heart of Darkness*, to speak temperately on complex issues of colonialism, and, in the chapter 'Conrad, James and *Chance*', to settle the question of how the two great men stood on the vexed problem of James's disapproval of *Chance*. What is most striking is Watt's ability to *think* with Conrad, and he has that ability not only by reason of his literary intelligence but also from his conviction, strengthened at Kwai, that human society, horribly imperfect though it is, depends, if it is not to be even worse, on the devotion and courage of people honestly doing their jobs, whether commanding or commanded, whether writers or not.

And here one must glance with admiration at the chapter on the River Kwai. Watt is interested in the truth of that matter, but also in the myth that has been developed from it. What the world now thinks about the building of that bridge depends on a film that depends on, and departs from, a novel which is itself far from describing things as they really were. It seems that the Japanese had more prisoners than they could handle, and so the prisoners themselves took over the business of disciplined production. It is recorded that their lives were painful and close to desperation, but the point is made without reference to the writer's own discomforts, save in that he was one of them. They had to settle for the kind of life available. There was no chance of escape. They organized their own police force, conscious of a need for order of some kind. One officer, especially efficient, found ways to make their lot easier, and, inevitably, also expedited the building of the enemy railway bridge.

By chance a French writer came to hear about this episode, and based a novel on it. He seems to have represented it as primarily a comment on the way modern technology 'destroys human meanings and purposes'. And he began the transformation of the actual efficient officer into the character played by Alec Guinness in David Lean's movie. The film was wholly false to the situation of the prisoners; it was colonialist, it misrepresented the kind of bridge involved, and, contrary to the facts, blew it up. Watt was there; and he has since that bad time gone back to the bridge, and can say what happened subsequently to the railway. He prefers reality to myth, unlike the movie-makers and unlike their audiences.

Why did the myth take over? The answer is Conradian: 'the deep blindness of our culture both to the stubbornness of reality and to the continuities of history'. That blindness encouraged the public to accept the movie-fantasy of Nicholson's unconquerable British individualism, his triumph over his powerful but racially inferior captors. Watt believes our whole society is prone to distort the truth by such mythical thinking. It fails to observe that the world will not do its bidding, that the best and only decent form of conduct for the prisoners, as now for us, was 'work and restraint – two of Conrad's imperatives'. These imperatives have always operated powerfully in Watt's world, and are the enemies of self-indulgent myth. It is to be noted that he nowhere dwells on his own work and suffering; his concern is entirely with facts and false interpretations.

His interest in myth, and its part in the creation of undesirable social and individual fantasy, led to the writing of his most recent book, *Myths of Modern Individualism* (1996), a study of Faust, Don Quixote, Don Juan and Robinson Crusoe as myths that have acquired a special resonance in modern culture. Of course they did not have that function originally, but were recreated to suit a more modern and individualist sensibility than they at first possessed. One could read this new collection of essays as a sober and unillusioned defence of the principle of unmythicized reality as it can be studied in the novels of Conrad. He too has his fantasizing individualists – his Haldins, his nihilist professors, his corrupt anarchists – but he has also his MacWhirrs and Singletons, the men without conversation, who don't write and rarely read, but who command and are commanded, and do the work of the world. Like Conrad, Watt admires such men. Rarely has a critic shared so fully the virtues of his author.

Acknowledgements

Copyright in all essays rests with Ian Watt. His essays are reproduced from the following sources: 'Joseph Conrad: alienation and commitment' (Cambridge University Press); the introduction to *Almayer's Folly* (ed. Ian Watt, Cambridge University Press); 'Conrad criticism and *The Nigger of the "Narcissus"*' (*Nineteenth-Century Fiction*); 'Conrad's *Heart of Darkness* and the critics' (*North Dakota Quarterly*); 'Comedy and Humour in *Typhoon*' (Murisa International); 'The political and social background of *The Secret Agent*' (The Macmillan Press); the introduction to 'The Secret Sharer' (The Limited Editions Club); 'Conrad, James and *Chance*' (Methuen & Co.); 'Story and idea in Conrad's *The Shadow-Line*' (*Critical Quarterly*); 'The decline of the decline: notes on Conrad's reputation' (*Stanford Slavic Studies*); 'Around Conrad's grave in the Canterbury cemetery – a retrospect' (Radopi, Amsterdam); '"The Bridge over the River Kwai" as myth' (*Berkshire Review*).

CHAPTER I

Joseph Conrad: alienation and commitment

The doubts of the critics about the whole history-of-ideas approach are understandable enough: one way of not experiencing *King Lear* is to underline a few passages containing recognizable ideas, and to make the gratifying reflexion that the Great Chain of Being is really there. The search for such portable intellectual contents as can be prised loose from a work of imagination is likely to deflect attention from what it can most characteristically yield, in exchange for a few abstract ideas whose natures and inter-relationships are much more exactly stated in formal philosophy. And if we cannot base our literary judgements on philosophical criteria, we must be equally on our guard against the criteria of the historian of ideas, which naturally place most value on literary works which are ideologically representative; whereas the greatest authors actually seem not so much to reflect the intellectual system of their age as to express more or less directly its inherent contradictions, or the very partial nature of its capacity for dealing with the facts of experience. This seems to be true of Chaucer and Shakespeare; and it tends to become truer as we come down to the modern world, in which no single intellectual system has commanded anything like general acceptance.

All these are familiar objections; and as regards criticism of modern literature they have been reinforced by a new form of philosophy's old objections to the cognitive validity of art – by the symbolist aesthetic's rejection of all forms of abstraction and conceptualization. The ancient notion was that ideas were the natural and proper inhabitants of man's mind; T. S. Eliot's resounding paradox that 'Henry James had a mind so fine that no idea could violate it' transformed them into dangerous ruffians threatening the artist with a fate worse than death.

The alarm, we can now agree, was exaggerated; indeed, the recent tendency for much literary criticism to add moral to formal analysis might well proceed further, and make inquiry into intellectual backgrounds an essential, though not a dominating or exclusive, part of its critical procedure. For instance, an understanding of Conrad's intellectual attitudes, and of their relation to the various ideological battlegrounds both of his own and of our time, seems to me to illuminate several literary problems which have not yet been satisfactorily answered, despite the increasing critical attention which his works have lately received. At the same time, the consideration of these problems seems to indicate that it is not in ideology as such, but in the relationship of systems of ideas to other things, things as various as personal experience or the expectations of the audience, that we are likely to find answers to literary questions.

The position of Joseph Conrad (1857–1924) among his great contemporaries is unique in at least three respects. First, he has a much more varied audience: one finds his admirers not only in academic and literary circles, but among people in all stations of life. Secondly, Conrad's reputation, after a relative decline following his death in 1924, seems to have grown steadily ever since the Second World War; and it continues now, just as one detects a certain mounting impatience, just or unjust, against most of Conrad's literary peers – mainly against Joyce, Pound, and Eliot, but also, to some extent, against Yeats. The reasons for these two features of Conrad's literary appeal seem to be connected with a third and equally wellknown matter – his obscurity. For although the charge of obscurity against modern writers is not novel, it takes a very special form in the case of Conrad. E. M. Forster expressed it most memorably when he asked whether 'the secret casket of [Conrad's] genius' does not contain 'a vapour rather than a jewel', and went on to suggest that the vapour might come from 'the central chasm of his tremendous genius', a chasm which divided Conrad the seaman from Conrad the writer:

Together with these loyalties and prejudices and personal scruples, [Conrad] holds another ideal, a universal, the love of Truth. . . . So there are constant discrepancies between his nearer and his further vision, and here would seem to be the cause of his central obscurity. If he lived only in his experiences, never lifting his eyes to what lies beyond them: or if, having seen what lies beyond, he would subordinate his experiences to it – then in either case he would be easier to read.[1]

The continual contradiction which Forster describes between the seer and seaman, between philosophy and experience, seems to offer a key to the three literary problems I have posed. For whereas Conrad's 'further vision' was very similar to that of his great contemporaries, his 'nearer vision', his actual range of experience, was not; and in his works the two perspectives combine in a way which seems directly related to the varied nature of his audience, to the renewed topicality of his view of the world, and to the unresolved conflict of attitudes which underlies his obscurity.

Conrad's further vision was dominated by the characteristic despair of the late Victorian world-view, which originated in all those developments in nineteenth-century geology, astronomy, physics and chemistry which combined with industrialism to suggest that, so far from being the eternal setting created by God for his favourite, man, the natural world was merely the temporary and accidental result of purposeless physical processes. In one letter, written in 1897, Conrad used an appropriately industrial metaphor to express this notion of the universe as a determinist mechanism denying all man's aspirations towards progress and reform:

There is a – let us say – a machine. It evolved itself (I am severely scientific) out of a chaos of scraps of iron and behold! – it knits. I am horrified at the horrible work and stand appalled. I feel it ought to embroider – but it goes on knitting. You come and say: 'This is all right; it's only a question of the right kind of oil. Let us use this – for instance – celestial oil and the machine will embroider a most beautiful design in purple and gold.' Will it? Alas, no! You cannot by any special lubrication make embroidery with a knitting machine. And the most withering thought is that the infamous thing has made itself: made itself without thought, without conscience, without foresight, without eyes, without heart. It is a tragic accident – and it has happened. . . .

It knits us in and it knits us out. It has knitted time, space, pain, death, corruption, despair and all the illusions – and nothing matters. . . .[2]

In such a meaningless and transitory universe, there is no apparent reason why we should have any concern whatever with the lives of others, or even very much concern with our own:

The attitude of cold unconcern is the only reasonable one. Of course reason is hateful – but why? Because it demonstrates (to those who have the courage) that we, living, are out of life – utterly out of it. . . . In a dispassionate view the ardour for reform, improvement, for virtue, for knowledge and even for beauty is only a vain sticking up for appearances, as though one were anxious about the cut of one's clothes in a community of blind men.[3]

What has been considered man's most precious gift, consciousness, is really, therefore, a curse:

What makes mankind tragic is not that they are the victims of nature, it is that they are conscious of it. To be part of the animal kingdom under the conditions of this earth is very well – but as soon as you know of your slavery, the pain, the anger, the strife – the tragedy begins.[4]

In *Lord Jim* (1900), Stein contemplates a butterfly, and discourses like a discouraged version of the great evolutionist Alfred Wallace, on whom he was in part based:[5]

'. . . so fragile! And so strong! And so exact! This is Nature – the balance of colossal forces. Every star is so – and every blade of grass stands *so* – and the mighty Kosmos in perfect equilibrium produces – this. This wonder; this masterpiece of Nature – the great artist!'
'. . . And what of man?' [Marlow asks]:
'Man is amazing, but he is not a masterpiece,' he said. . . . 'Perhaps the artist was a little mad. Eh? . . . Sometimes it seems to me that man is come where he is not wanted, where there is no place for him.'[6]

Man, in fact, is Nature's permanent alien; he must create his own order if he can. This, of course, was how the Victorians had come to think of human destiny; the religion of progress, in Tennyson's words, called on man to

> Move upward, working out the beast
> And let the ape and tiger die.

But that was not so easy, as Freud was to show; and also, at much the same time, Joseph Conrad in *Heart of Darkness* (1899).

Kurtz begins as a representative of all the highest aspirations of nineteenth-century individualism; he is an artist, an eloquent political speaker on the liberal side, an economic and social careerist; and his story enacts the most characteristic impulse of Victorian civilization, combining the economic exploitation of Africa with the great moral crusade of bringing light to the backward peoples of the world. But the jungle whispers 'to [Kurtz] things about himself which he did not know, things of which he had no conception till he took counsel with this great solitude' (p. 131). His 'forgotten and brutal instincts' (p. 144) soon lead Kurtz to outdo the other colonial exploiters in sordid rapacity; he enslaves and massacres the surrounding tribes; and he ends up being worshipped as a God to whom human sacrifices are offered.

At the back of the great nineteenth-century dream was the assumption that man could be his own God. But to Disraeli's question 'Is man an ape or an angel?', Kurtz's fate seems to answer that we are never less likely to 'let the ape and tiger die' than when we imagine we are angels. Kurtz thought that 'we whites . . . must necessarily appear to [the savages] in the nature of supernatural beings – we approach them with the might as of a deity'. But he ends his report to the International Society for the Suppression of Savage Customs: 'Exterminate all the brutes!' (p. 118).

For Conrad, then, man's hope for progress ignores the fact that the ape and tiger are not merely part of our evolutionary heritage, but are ontologically present in every individual. This goes beyond the usual assumptions of the most sceptical of Victorians, and it makes impossible the faith in the development of man's intellectual potentialities through education which characterized the main spokesmen of the Victorian and Edwardian periods. Thus, when his reformer friend Cunninghame Graham wrote that his democratic ideal was the heroic sailor, Singleton, in *The Nigger of the 'Narcissus'* (1898), but a Singleton who has been educated, Conrad retorted:

I think Singleton with an education is impossible. . . . Then he would become conscious – and much smaller – and very unhappy. Now he is simple and great like an elemental force. Nothing can touch him but the curse of decay – the eternal decree that will extinguish the sun, the stars, one by one, and in another instant shall spread a frozen darkness over the whole universe. Nothing else can touch him – he does not think.

Would you seriously wish to tell such a man 'Know thyself! Understand that you are nothing, less than a shadow, more insignificant than a drop of water in the ocean, more fleeting than the illusion of a dream?' Would you?[7]

Knowledge merely makes the individual more conscious of the terrible disparity between actuality and aspiration: nor does man's love of his fellows afford any more secure a foundation for political and social reform. Such reform represents no more than – as Conrad put it in *Victory* (1915) – the conflict between 'gorge and disgorge' (p. 384); and man's own nature dooms his longing for fraternity; as Conrad asked: 'Frankly, what would you think of an effort to promote fraternity amongst people living in the same street, I don't even mention two neighbouring streets? Two ends of the same street. . . . What does fraternity mean? . . . Nothing unless the Cain–Abel business'.[8]

Conrad, then, shared with the Victorians their rejection of the religious, social and intellectual order of the past, but he also rejected, as completely as Yeats, Pound, Eliot, Joyce, Lawrence or Thomas Mann, the religion of progress with which they and the Edwardians had replaced it. This alienation from the prevailing intellectual perspectives both of the past and of his own time naturally did much to colour Conrad's picture both of his own selfhood and of his role as an author. I use the word 'alienation' because it seems to me the most comprehensive term to describe the two aspects of the process we are concerned with – the external or public, and the internal or private. We have already considered the public, the external ideological vision; but it would, from a literary point of view, remain merely 'notional', as Newman put it, unless it were internalized: that it was in Conrad, we shall see.

The word 'alienation' has been used in a wide variety of ways,[9] but its derivation and early usage make its main meaning reasonably clear. From *alius*, 'another', Latin developed the forms *alienus*, 'belonging to another country', and *alienatus*, 'estranged'. Our word 'alienation' thus bears the constant notion of being or feeling a stranger, an outsider. Alienation, as a translation of the German *Entfremdung*, was given philosophical currency early in the nineteenth century by Hegel, who used it to denote what he thought to be characteristic of the individual in the modern world, his sense of inward estrangements, of more or less conscious awareness that the inner being, the real 'I', was alienated from the 'me', the person as an object in society. Later, Marx transferred the idea to the economic plane; for Marx, man only loses his isolation and realizes himself as a person through his activities, through his work; but under capitalism, since the commodity and its cash value are primary, the individual, no longer in personal control of his labour, feels alienated from his work, and therefore from society and from himself.[10]

Conrad, I need hardly say, was neither a Hegelian nor a Marxist; but all his writings, and especially his letters, make it clear not only that his mind completely rejected the social and intellectual order of the day, but that his whole inner being seemed to have been deprived of meaning. There can surely be few expressions of such total estrangement from the natural world, from other people, from the writing process, and from the self, to equal this Conrad letter to Garnett:

I am like a man who has lost his gods. My efforts seem unrelated to anything in heaven and everything under heaven is impalpable to the touch like shapes of mist. Do you see how easy writing must be under such conditions? Do you see?

Even writing to a friend – to a person one has heard, touched, drank with, quarrelled with – does not give me a sense of reality. All is illusion – the words written, the mind at which they are aimed, the truth they are intended to express, the hands that will hold the paper, the eyes that will glance at the lines. Every image floats vaguely in a sea of doubt – and the doubt itself is lost in an unexplored universe of incertitudes.[11]

But alienation, of course, is not the whole story: Conrad also gives us a sense of a much wider commitment to the main ethical, social and literary attitudes, both of the world at large and of the general reader, than do any others of his great contemporaries.

'Commitment' I take to be the secular equivalent of what prize-giving speakers call 'dedication' – a binding engagement of oneself to a course of action which transcends any purely personal advantage. And the question inevitably arises as to how a man with the general intellectual perspective sketched above can possibly commit himself to anything larger than his own personal interests.

The beginnings of an answer are probably to be found in Conrad's life, which made alienation not an endless discovery demanding expression, but merely the initial premise. The initial premise because Conrad was, to begin with, an orphan; his mother died when he was seven, and his father when he was eleven. Then there was his nationality: as a Pole he belonged to a country which no longer existed, and whose people, Conrad wrote, had for a hundred years 'been used to go to battle without illusions'.[12] Adolescence brought further estrangements: in France from 1874 to 1878, Conrad tried to realize his dream of a career at sea, but he achieved only failure, debts, an unhappy love affair, and, it now seems virtually certain, an attempt at suicide. But when, at the age of twenty, Conrad joined the crew of the English freighter *Mavis*, the premise of total alienation began to be undermined. Conrad's successful struggle, under conditions, for the most part, of unbearable physical and psychological hardship, to rise from able-bodied seaman to captain, must have given him a sense of the unexpected possibilities and rewards of individual participation in the ordinary life of humanity. Conrad's years at sea were everything for his career as a writer. Not because they gave him a subject – Conrad would surely be a major novelist quite apart from the sea stories; but because to the earlier perspective of every kind of alienation there was added a foreground of immediate experience which featured a series of the most direct personal and social commitments – to his career, to his fellow-seamen, to his adopted country. These commitments had the most far-reaching effects on Conrad's attitude to his audience, on his role as a writer, and on his understanding of human life; and their importance was not diminished by the fact that they arose from attitudes which were in perpetual opposition to the larger view of the world which Conrad the seer had absorbed from his nineteenth-century heritage.

There is no very specific statement about the conflict in Conrad's letters or essays, but its results appear very clearly in his views of his audience, and of his art, as well as in the novels. In the earliest extant letters alienation is the pervading theme, and there is very little about commitment; where the conflict of the two does occur, it is very much from the point of view of alienation, as in an early letter to Madame Poradowska. We are condemned, Conrad wrote in 1894, to go through life accompanied by

the inseparable being forever at your side – master and slaves, victim and executioner – who suffers and causes suffering. That's how it is! One must drag the ball and chain of one's self hood to the end. It is the price one pays for the devilish and divine privilege of thought; so that in this life it is only the elect who are convicts – a glorious band which comprehends and groans but which treads the earth amidst a multitude of phantoms with maniacal gestures, with idiotic grimaces. Which would you be: idiot or convict?[13]

The war within is an internal projection of the external conflict between the uncomprehending multitudes, the idiots, and the convicts whose intelligence and self-consciousness have condemned them to loneliness and alienation. The possibility of siding with the idiots, of course, is presented by Conrad only as a rhetorical question. In this, Conrad is echoing, not so much Hegel's picture of alienation, as the familiar romantic dichotomy between the sensitive artist and the crass world outside and, more particularly, its later development, the division of the reading public into highbrow and lowbrow. These divisions must have been much more familiar to Conrad than to many of his English contemporaries, since he read such French writers as Flaubert and Baudelaire very early in his career, and for them the alienation of the writer from the bourgeois public was both more conscious and more absolute than for any English writer of the Victorian period.

Unlike Flaubert and Baudelaire, however, Conrad had no private means, and so as soon as he began his career as an author the problem of finding a public became immediate. When his first literary adviser, Edward Garnett, urged Conrad to follow his own path as a writer and disregard the multitude, Conrad retorted: 'But I *won't* live in an attic! I'm past that, you understand? I *won't* live in an attic!' On the other hand, keeping out of attics unfortunately seemed feasible only for such popular writers as Rider Haggard, and when Garnett mentioned his work, Conrad commented: 'too horrible for words'.[14]

Conrad's financial dependence on public favour must often have reinforced his sense of separateness. On the one hand, he was forced by economic necessity to degrade himself – as he once put it, 'all my art has become artfulness in exploiting agents and publishers';[15] on the other hand, his inner self remained aloof and proudly refused to accept the role of authorship as society defined it. We find Conrad on one occasion declining to send his photograph to his publisher, though he added with sardonic magnanimity, 'if I were a pretty actress or a first-rate athlete, I wouldn't deprive an aching democracy of a legitimate satisfaction'.[16] When, for advertising purposes, Algernon Methuen requested a description of *The Secret Agent*, which his firm was publishing, Conrad replied disdainfully, 'I've a very definite idea of what I tried to do and a fairly correct one (I hope) of what I *have* done. But it isn't a matter for a bookseller's ear. I don't think he would understand: I don't think many readers will. But that's not my affair.'[17]

What his readers thought was not his affair. That, at least, is one of the postures of authorship which Conrad adopted. But there was another.

How a writer comes to form an idea of his audience is no doubt a complicated and highly idiosyncratic matter; but the starting point must always be the people the writer has actually talked to and heard talk. In Conrad's case, when he became an author virtually everyone he had heard talk English was a seaman; and although collectively they were part of the mass public he scorned, yet many of them were people he respected as individuals. This may be part of the reason why when Conrad speaks of the reading public, as in this letter to John Galsworthy, his sardonic mockery is qualified by the sense that, however fatuous, the reading public is, after all, composed of human beings:

A public is not to be found in a class, caste, clique or type. The public is (or are?) individuals. . . . And no artist can give it what it wants because humanity doesn't know what it wants. But it will swallow everything. It will swallow Hall Caine and John Galsworthy, Victor Hugo and Martin Tupper. It is an ostrich, a clown, a giant, a bottomless sack. It is sublime. It has apparently no eyes and no entrails, like a slug, and yet it can weep and suffer.[18]

There is no sense here, such as one finds in many other modern authors, that the writer must make a conscious choice of a public, and set his sights either at the literary élite or at the masses who have to be written down to. Conrad the seer viewed both with the same jaded scepticism, and he chose neither. Still, the humbler side of his double vision reminded him that the target of his scorn could also weep and suffer; and so he retained sufficient faith in a 'direct appeal to mankind' to write for a public comprising readers as different as his later literary friends and his former shipmates. After nearly twenty years of discouraging struggle, Conrad's residual commitment to mankind considered as an audience bore fruit when *Chance* (1913) became a best-seller: this response, Conrad wrote in his 'Author's Note', gave me a considerable amount of pleasure, because what I had always feared most was drifting unconsciously into the position of a writer for a limited coterie; a position which would have been odious to me as throwing a doubt on the soundness of my belief in the solidarity of all mankind in simple ideas and sincere emotions. . . . I had managed to please a number of minds busy attending to their own very real affairs. (pp. viii–ix)

The checks which the committed seaman imposed on the alienated writer in his attitude to his audience also affected Conrad's general literary outlook; and this despite his awareness, as he put it in the 'Familiar Preface' to *A Personal Record* (1912), that 'as in political so in literary action a man wins friends for himself mostly by the passion of his prejudices and by the consistent narrowness of his outlook'. Most obviously, Conrad's training at sea ran counter to any intransigent expression of his inner alienation. '. . . to be a great magician', he wrote in the same preface, 'one must surrender to occult and irresponsible powers, either outside or within one's breast.' But this direction, he continued, was not for him, because his sea training had strengthened his resolve to 'keep good hold on the one thing really mine . . . that full possession of myself which is the first condition of good service'; and Conrad concluded that the conscience must sometimes 'say nay to the temptations' of the author: 'the danger lies in the writer becoming the victim of his own exaggeration, losing the exact notion of sincerity, and in the end coming to despise truth itself as something too cold, too blunt for his purpose – as, in fact, not good enough for his insistent emotion'.

As for literary doctrine, Conrad's disenchantment with the accepted literary modes was with him from the beginning of his career as a writer. He expressed it most fully and most eloquently in the famous preface to *The Nigger of the 'Narcissus'*. None of the 'temporary formulas of [the artist's] craft' is reliable, Conrad begins: 'they all: Realism, Romanticism, Naturalism, even the unofficial sentimentalism (which, like the poor, is exceedingly difficult to get rid of), all these gods must, after a short period of fellowship, abandon him' (pp. x–xi).

All the conceptual formulae, whether of literature or of science or of philosophy, are much too unreliable a basis for the writer: he must depend on those primary facts of the experience which he shares with mankind at large. So the positives of the nearer vision, of ultimate commitment, somehow enabled Conrad to bypass the findings of the alienated intellect, and to convert the most esoteric of literary doctrines – Art for Art's sake – into the most universal:

The changing wisdom of successive generations discards ideas, questions facts, demolishes theories. But the artist appeals to that part of our being which is not dependent on wisdom; to that in us which is a gift and not an acquisition – and therefore, more permanently enduring. He speaks to our capacity for delight and wonder, to the sense of mystery surrounding our lives; to our sense of pity, and beauty, and pain; to the latent feeling of fellowship with all creation – and to the subtle but invincible conviction of solidarity that knits together the loneliness of innumerable hearts, to the solidarity in dreams, in joy, in sorrow, in aspirations, in illusions, in hope, in fear, which binds men to each other, which binds together all humanity – the dead to the living and the living to the unborn. (p. viii)

At this point I can begin to answer the first question: the breadth of Conrad's appeal was made possible by the fact that, almost alone among his great contemporaries, he thought a broad appeal worth making; he was glad, he wrote in the 'Author's Note' to *Chance*, that 'apparently I have never sinned against the basic feelings and elementary convictions which make life possible to the mass of mankind' (p. x). This alone surely does much to account both for Conrad's decline in critical esteem during the twenties, and for the way he acquired a wider and more miscellaneous audience than his literary peers. If alienation had been the sum of his subjects and literary attitudes, Conrad might have captured the highbrow vote more quickly; but the wide variety of people whom he respected and admired, and their very various ways of looking at life, were always there as a constant check to the extremes of the vision of the isolated writer. Conrad's writings do not proclaim their author's radical separateness from the rest of mankind; their style does not flaunt his alienation like a banner announcing a certified Dark Knight of the Soul. It was characteristic of Conrad that he should praise the work of his friend Ford Madox Ford on the grounds that 'he does not stand on his head for the purpose of getting a new and striking view of his subject. Such a method of procedure may be in favour nowadays but I prefer the old way, with the feet on the ground.'[19]

On the other hand, of course, the alienation is still there; there is nothing promiscuous about Conrad's commitment; he is very far from what D. H. Lawrence called 'the vast evil of acquiescence'; and even in his most affirmative works the heroic, romantic or popular elements are always qualified by the general atmosphere – an atmosphere, to use Conrad's own phrase, of 'cold moral dusk'.[20] The tone of desperate alienation which one finds in Conrad's early letters is not directly expressed in the novels; but one can often recognize its muffled presence, whether in the defeated cadences of his rhetoric, or in the tendency of the narrative progress to seem under the constant threat of enveloping torpor. Nevertheless, it seems broadly true that, in Conrad's most characteristic work, the negative voices of alienation are confronted and largely overcome by the possibilities of commitment, or, in Conrad's term, of solidarity.

What Conrad meant by solidarity is sufficiently evident from the preface to *The Nigger of the 'Narcissus'*. In the terms of our argument we can see it as an intangible and undemonstrable but existent and widespread acceptance of common human obligations which somehow transcend the infinite individual differences of belief and purpose and taste. It is not a conscious motive, and it rarely becomes the dominating factor in human affairs; its existence seems to depend very largely upon the mere fact that, in the course of their different lives, most individuals find themselves faced with very similar circumstances; nevertheless, it is solidarity which gives both the individual and the collective life what little pattern of meaning can be discovered in it. Conrad's own experience, of course, tended to confirm this view of solidarity; and his most typical writing is concerned to present its achievements, to enact its discovery, or to assay its powers.

The theme of solidarity is most obvious in what are surely Conrad's most perfect, if not his most important works, in *The Nigger of the 'Narcissus'*, *Typhoon*, *The Shadow-Line*. But in some form it also controls most of the other novels, which characteristically present the movement of the protagonist towards another person or persons; the movement is often incomplete, or too late to succeed; but, from Marlow's involvement in the fate of Kurtz and Lord Jim, to the sexual relationships of *Chance* and *Victory*, the reader's attention is usually engaged in following the fortunes of an isolated and alienated character towards others; and this quest eventually assumes both for the character and for the reader a much larger moral importance than that of the personal relationship as such.

In *Lord Jim*, for example, Marlow is presented with an apparent breakdown of his unquestioned belief in the values of solidarity when an unknown first mate, a young man, 'one of us', deserts his post and leaves the 800 passengers on the *Patna* to their fate; for no apparent cause Marlow discovers that his deepest being demands that he know:

Why I longed to go grubbing into the deplorable details of an occurrence which, after all, concerned me no more than as a member of an obscure body of men held together by a community of inglorious toil and by fidelity to a certain standard of conduct, I can't explain. You may call it an unhealthy curiosity if you like; but I have a distinct notion I wished to find something.

Perhaps, unconsciously, I hoped I would find that something, some profound and redeeming cause, some merciful explanation, some convincing shadow of an excuse. I see well enough now that I hoped for the impossible – for the laying of what is the most obstinate ghost of man's creation, of the uneasy doubt uprising like a mist, secret and gnawing like a worm, and more chilling than the certitude of death – the doubt of the sovereign power enthroned in a fixed standard of conduct. (p. 50)

The doubt can never be set at rest; but the concern remains, not only in *Lord Jim*, but in most of Conrad's novels. Of course, it takes different forms. In Conrad's later works, for example, the protagonist is often closer to our sense of the younger, the more sceptical, Conrad, as with Decoud, for example, or Heyst. There the concern for solidarity tends to an opposite pattern: the protagonist's moral crisis is not that the fixed standard of conduct is challenged, but that, to his surprise, the alienated protagonist encounters its overwhelming imperatives.

This movement from alienation towards commitment is rather rare in the other great modern writers. They tend, indeed, to equate the achievement of individuality with the process of alienation; the poetry of Eliot and Pound, for example, typically leads us away in revulsion from contemporary actuality; while the novels of Joyce and Lawrence tend to focus on the breaking of ties with family, class and country: both poets and the novelists leave us, not with a realization of man's crucial though problematic dependence on others, but with a sharpened awareness of individual separateness.

It is here, of course, that we may find one reason for the renewed interest in Conrad. For since the Second World War, the experience of a whole generation has brought it close to Conrad's personal position; partly because world history has played over so many of his themes in deafening tones; and partly because our habituation to alienation, reinforced by the vision of the other great modern writers, has inevitably brought us back to the dominating question in Conrad: alienation, yes, but how do we get out of it?

One can observe the recent convergence on this typical Conradian preoccupation in many different intellectual areas. Most directly, it can be seen in recent Conrad criticism, which, since Morton Dauwen Zabel's article 'Chance and Recognition' in 1945,[21] has concentrated on Conrad as the master of the process of moral self-discovery leading to human commitment; most widely, we can turn to the extremely close parallel between this aspect of Conrad and the main philosophical and literary movement of the last two decades, Existentialism.

Existentialism, like Conrad, rejects all traditional philosophy as too theoretical, too concerned with cognitive problems treated in isolation from the actual personal existence. It attempts instead a full understanding of the individual confronting life; and this, as in Conrad, involves much attention to such themes as death, suicide, isolation, despair, courage and choosing to be. In each case the starting point is the alienated man who, believing, in Sartre's words, that 'there can no longer be any *a priori* good',[22] or in Conrad's that there is 'no sovereign power enthroned in a fixed standard of conduct', concludes that the whole external world and man's attempt to establish a valid relationship to it are equally absurd. The way out of the dilemma, apparently, is that, at a certain point, the existential hero, realizing that 'he is free *for nothing*',[23] comes out on the other side of despair to discover a more realistic kind of provisional commitment.

There are, of course, vital differences. Conrad does not see commitment as a single willed reversal occurring with dramatic clarity and violence in the individual consciousness; for him it is, rather, an endless process throughout history in which individuals are driven by circumstances into the traditional forms of human solidarity: are driven to accept the position that fidelity must govern the individual's relation to the outside world, while his inner self must be controlled by restraint and honour. This conservative and social ethic is certainly very different from the existentialist position, and embodies the main emphases of the most widely shared secular codes of behaviour over the ages. It is also rather closer to the philosophical materialism of Marx than to the basically subjective metaphysic of Existentialism, since Conrad sees solidarity as an eventual consequence of corporate activity. Thus Conrad begins his essay on 'Tradition' by quoting Leonardo da Vinci's 'Work is the law', and comments:

From the hard work of men are born the sympathetic consciousness of a common destiny, the fidelity to right practice which makes great craftsmen, the sense of right conduct which we may call honour, the devotion to our calling and the idealism which is not a misty, winged angel without eyes, but a divine figure of terrestrial aspect with a clear glance and with its feet resting firmly on the earth on which it was born.[24]

The origins of solidarity, then, are derived from the economic necessities to which men find themselves involuntarily but inexorably exposed: as Conrad writes elsewhere:

Who can tell how a tradition comes into the world? We are children of the earth. It may be that the noblest tradition is but the offspring of material conditions, of the hard necessities besetting men's precarious lives. But once it has been born it becomes a spirit.[25]

It is surely remarkable that Conrad's way of looking at the conditions of positive individual commitment would have such strong affinities with three such contradictory ideologies – the conservative, the existentialist and the Marxist. It helps, of course, to explain the present width of his appeal, but we are bound to return to Forster's view of the discrepancies between Conrad's nearer and his further vision, and to wonder if there is not some radical confusion in a position which leads in three such different directions; whether, in fact, Conrad's obscurity may not be an unavoidable result of his failure to establish any real connexion between the alienation he felt and the commitment he sought.

Conrad would probably have answered that his outlook was based on common elements of experience which were more enduring than any particular social or economic or intellectual system. He thought of his own age, he wrote in *Victory*, as one 'in which we are camped like bewildered travellers in a garish, unrestful hotel' (p. 3); and the best we could do at any time was to assume that in any given circumstance the direction of individual commitment would be sufficiently clear to anyone who, like Axel Heyst in *Victory*, finds that he cannot scorn 'any decent feeling' (p. 18). This, indeed, was close to the teaching of his uncle and guardian, Thaddeus Bobrowski, who once wrote to him: 'I have taken as my motto "*usque ad finem*", as my guide, the love of duty which circumstances define.'[26]

The way people actually react to the circumstances of their lives – such seems to be Conrad's only justification for his view of solidarity. We would no doubt like more; but it is only fair to observe that the logical difficulties of demonstrating the validity of any ethical system are just as great either in traditional philosophy or in Existentialism; so that we must be careful not to condemn Conrad because his working assumptions echo the greatest of English empiricists, who in *Twelfth Night* gave Sir Andrew Aguecheek the immortal words: 'I have no exquisite reason for 't, but I have reason good enough.'

The reason good enough, we might now be tempted to add, is that the way things are with our poor old planet, the time has come for bifocals. Such, it appears, was Conrad's view, and he once justified the patent irrationality of this dual perspective on the simple grounds that it reflected the facts of common human experience:

Many a man has heard or read and believes that the earth goes round the sun; one small blob of mud among several others, spinning ridiculously with a waggling motion like a top about to fall. This is the Copernican system, and the man believes in the system without often knowing as much about it as its name. But while watching a sunset he sheds his belief; he sees the sun as a small and useful object, the servant of his needs . . . sinking slowly behind a range of mountains, and then he holds the system of Ptolemy.[27]

In the perspective of the history of ideas, the wheel has indeed come full circle: Conrad seems to accept an impasse to which his great contemporaries, more ambitious, and perhaps less deeply alienated from the possibilities of belief, tried to find solutions. Most of twentieth-century literature, for example, may, broadly speaking, be said to have an implicit programme; it urges a direction which, to put it simply, is based on an adherence to the ideology either of the future, or of the past, or of the supernatural world. But Conrad, as we have seen, had no belief in liberal reform, in the politics of the future to which Shaw, Wells and Galsworthy devoted so many of their writings; and he had equally little interest in the backward look, in the utopianism of the past which, in various forms, can be found in the thought of Yeats, Joyce, Pound and Eliot: Conrad speaks, for example, of 'the mustiness of the Middle Ages, that epoch when mankind tried to stand still in a monstrous illusion of final certitude attained in morals, intellect and conscience'.[28] Nor, finally, did Conrad find any appeal in supernatural transcendence: his objection to Christianity combined a Voltairean rejection of myth, superstition and hypocrisy, with a primary emphasis on the impracticality of Christian ideals; as he once wrote to Garnett:

I am not blind to [Christianity's] services, but the absurd oriental fable from which it starts irritates me. Great, improving, softening, compassionate it may be, but it has lent itself with amazing facility to cruel distortion and is the only religion which, with its impossible standards, has brought an infinity of anguish to innumerable souls – on this earth.[29]

Conrad the seaman, then, could not allow the seer to make that leap out of the chaos of immediate reality which must precede the construction of any system. More willingly than most of his contemporaries, he followed Heyst in *Victory* and entered 'the broad, human path of inconsistencies' (p. 176). We, surely, can join Thomas Mann in admiring the 'refusal of a very much engaged intelligence to hang miserably in the air between contraries',[30] and to concentrate not on the illogicality, but on the achievements, of men who live their lives according to Ptolemy's erroneous notion that man is the centre of the universe. To do this, Conrad seems to argue, we must not be too demanding about the intellectual foundations of human needs; Marlow, for instance, probably speaks for Conrad when he says of Jim's need for a truth, or an illusion of it, to live by: 'I don't care how you call it, there is so little difference, and the difference means so little' (p. 222). In *Heart of Darkness* Marlow's final act is even more explicit: when he preserves the 'great and saving illusion' about the dead Kurtz which is enshrined in the Intended's 'mature capacity for fidelity' (pp. 159, 157), he enacts the notion that, once we have experienced the heart of darkness, we may be driven to the position that, in cases where fidelity is in conflict with truth, it is truth which should be sacrificed.

Commitment to human solidarity, of course, also implies that whatever disgust and doubt we experience at the spectacle of history, we must nevertheless feel that in some sense the past and the future of mankind are a part of ourselves; not as nostalgia, and not as programme, but as experienced reality, the kind of reality expressed by Emilia Gould in *Nostromo*, who thought that 'for life to be large and full, it must contain the care of the past and of the future in every passing moment of the present' (pp. 520–1). Conrad's pessimism about the direction of contemporary history, shown in *Heart of Darkness*, for example, or in *Nostromo*, was logically incompatible with any optimism about the future of man; and yet even here the gloom was pierced by a moment of Ptolemaic affirmation.

In 1950 Conrad's greatest literary descendant, William Faulkner, seems to have had a passage of Conrad obscurely in mind when he declared in his Nobel Prize Address:

It is easy enough to say man is immortal simply because he will endure; that when the last ding-dong of doom has clanged and faded from the last worthless rock hanging tideless in the last red and dying evening, that even then there will still be one more sound: that of his puny inexhaustible voice, still talking. I refuse to accept this. I believe that man will not merely endure: he will prevail.

The Conrad passage this seems to recall comes from a 1905 essay on Henry James; in it Conrad's further vision cannot but foresee disaster, and though the nearer vision appeals against the verdict, it does so in terms so qualified by the ironic distance of the seer that they underline how Faulkner, yielding to his own insistent emotion, finally protests too much:

When the last aqueduct shall have crumbled to pieces [wrote Conrad], the last airship fallen to the ground, the last blade of grass have died upon a dying earth, man, indomitable by his training in resistance to misery and pain, shall set this undiminished light of his eyes against the feeble glow of the sun. The artistic faculty, of which each of us has a minute grain, may find its voice in some individual of that last group, gifted with a power of expression and

courageous enough to interpret the ultimate experience of mankind in terms
of his temperament, in terms of art . . . whether in austere exhortation or in a
phrase of sardonic comment, who can guess?

For my own part, from a short and cursory acquaintance with my kind, I
am inclined to think that the last utterance will formulate, strange as it may
appear, some hope now to us utterly inconceivable. For mankind is delightful
in its pride, its assurance, and its indomitable tenacity. It will sleep on the
battlefield among its own dead, in the manner of an army having won a
barren victory. It will not know when it is beaten.[31]

NOTES

1 'Joseph Conrad: a Note', *Abinger Harvest* (London, 1946), pp. 136–7.
2 G. Jean-Aubry, *Joseph Conrad: Life and Letters* (London, 1927), vol. 1, p. 216.
3 *Ibid.* 1, 222.
4 *Ibid.* 1, 226.
5 Cf. Florence Clemens, 'Conrad's Favourite Bedside Book', *South Atlantic Quarterly*, 38 (1939), 305–15.
6 Dent Collected Edition (London, 1948), p. 208. Future references from Conrad are to this collection, unless otherwise stated.
7 *Life and Letters*, 1, 214–15.
8 *Ibid.* 1, 269.
9 Cf. Herbert Marcuse, *Reason and Revolution: Hegel and the Rise of Social Revolution* (New York, 1941), pp. 34–9, 246–7; Lewis Feuer, 'What is Alienation? the Career of a Concept', *New Politics*, 1 (1962), pp. 1–19; Melvin Seeman, 'On the Meaning of Alienation', *American Sociological Review*, 24 (1959), 783–91; and, more generally, Robert A. Nisbet, *The Quest for Community* (New York, 1953).
10 Marcuse, *Reason and Revolution*, pp. 272–95.
11 *Letters from Conrad, 1895–1924*, ed. Edward Garnett (London, 1928), pp. 152–3.
12 *Ibid.* p. 216.
13 *Letters of Joseph Conrad to Marguerite Poradowska, 1890–1920*, trans. and ed. J. A. Gee and P. J. Sturm (New Haven, 1940), p. 72.
14 *Letters from Conrad, 1895–1924*, p. xiii.
15 *Ibid.* p. 183.
16 *Joseph Conrad: Letters to William Blackwood and David S. Meldrum*, ed. William Blackburn (Durham, N.C., 1958), p. 171.
17 *Life and Letters*, II, 38.
18 *Ibid.* II, 121.
19 *Letters to Blackwood*, p. 114.
20 'A Glance at Two Books', *Last Essays*, p. 135.
21 *Sewanee Review*, 53 (1945), 1–23.
22 *L'existentialisme est un humanisme* (Paris, 1946), p. 35.
23 *Le sursis* (Paris, 1945), p. 286: 'Je suis libre pour rien.'
24 *Notes on Life and Letters*, p. 194.

25 'Well Done', *Notes on Life and Letters*, p. 183.
26 *Life and Letters*, I, 148.
27 'The Ascending Effort', *Notes on Life and Letters*, pp. 73–4.
28 'The Censor of Plays: an Appreciation', *Notes on Life and Letters*, pp. 76–7.
29 *Letters from Conrad, 1895–1924*, p. 265.
30 'Joseph Conrad's *The Secret Agent*', in *Past Masters and Other Papers*, trans. Lowe-Porter (New York, 1933), p. 247.
31 'Henry James: an Appreciation', *Notes on Life and Letters*, pp. 13–14.

CHAPTER 2

Almayer's Folly: *introduction*

THE BEGINNINGS: BORNEO, 1887 AND LONDON, 1889

It was in London and in 1889 that a thirty-one-year-old ship's officer whom the world was to know as Joseph Conrad began to write his first novel. One fine autumnal morning he did not, as usual, dawdle after his breakfast but instead summoned the landlady's daughter to clear the table. Conrad told the story some twenty years later, in *A Personal Record*; that book's 'immediate aim', he explains, was to present 'the feelings and sensations connected with the writing of my first book and with my first contact with the sea'.[1] As regards writing his 'first book' Conrad insists on the obscurity of his sudden impulse: 'I was not at all certain that I wanted to write, or that I meant to write, or that I had anything to write about' (p. 70); nevertheless, Conrad concludes, 'What I am certain of is, that I was very far from thinking of writing a story, though it is possible and even likely that I was thinking of the man Almayer' (p. 74).

Conrad had met 'Almayer' some two years earlier. A back injury had forced Conrad into a hospital at Singapore in the summer of 1887; and when he was better he shipped as first mate on the *Vidar*, an 800-ton steamship which traded in local products in various islands of the Malay Archipelago. On one of its routine stops at an isolated settlement of Eastern Borneo Conrad had dealings with a Dutch trader called Charles William (or William Charles) Olmeijer.[2] *A Personal Record* gives a memorable account of their first meeting: alongside the little wharf on the edge of the jungle Almayer emerges through the mist clad 'in flapping pyjamas of cretonne pattern (enormous flowers with yellow petals on a disagreeable blue ground) and a thin cotton singlet with short sleeves' (p. 74). He is to take delivery, oddly enough, of a riding pony; but as soon as it touches ground the pony knocks Almayer down and takes off into the jungle. After relating some memories of their subsequent encounters – extending at most to four visits of a day or two each (Najder, pp. 97–98) – Conrad makes the singular assertion that 'if I had not got to know Almayer pretty well it is almost certain there would never have been a line of mine in print' (p. 87).

The casually preposterous hyperbole is characteristic of how, whereas he presented his career as a British mariner as much more purposeful and successful than was in fact the case, Conrad liked to maintain that he had become an author by pure accident. Actually, it seems probable that some years before, in 1886, Conrad had already written a short story, 'The Black Mate'; he thought later that it was 'for a prize competition, started, I think, by *Tit-Bits*'.[3] This story, which now exists only in the presumably much-rewritten form of its publication in 1908, is amusing but trivial; it only faintly qualifies Conrad's assertion that '*Almayer's Folly* may keep its place as my first serious work.'

We need not, however, wholly believe Conrad's statement that 'the ambition of being an author had never turned up amongst these gracious imaginary existences one creates fondly for oneself at times in the stillness and immobility of a day-dream' (*A Personal Record*, p. 68). Conrad may well have found 'the coming into existence' of his first book 'quite an inexplicable event' (p. 90); but it was a good deal less inexplicable than it would have been for most sailors. Few of them elect to spend their shore leaves in rooms where there are books 'lying about' and where pen and paper are also at hand; even fewer of them are, like Conrad, the son of a distinguished writer, as his father, Apollo Korzeniowski, had been.

Still, why it should have been a few chance encounters with 'Almayer' that precipitated Conrad into authorship is not easy to explain. To begin with, what little we know about the actual Olmeijer makes it clear that *Almayer's Folly* is in no sense the story of his life. Unlike Almayer, the original Olmeijer was not of pure Dutch parentage, but an Eurasian of mixed Dutch and Malay ancestry; and so was his wife. It is true that he was a trader on the Berau River (then, as in the novel, usually called the Pantai); but unlike Almayer, Olmeijer was apparently a fairly successful and respected one, at least in 1893, when he was reported to be 'the head of the area', whose counsel was sought by various local sultans; and he apparently died back home at Surabaya in 1900[4] – that is, five years after publication of *Almayer's Folly*.

There is no first-hand testimony about Olmeijer's character; and virtually all we have to go on to explain his appeal to Conrad is Conrad's account in *A Personal Record*. There he is an extraordinary combination of ambitious dreamer and habitual defeatist. Thus Conrad comments that 'What he wanted with a pony goodness only knows, since I am perfectly certain he could not ride it; but here you have the man, ambitious, aiming at the grandiose' (p. 76). At the same time, when Almayer asked, 'I suppose you haven't got such a thing as a pony on board?', he was 'hardly audible: and spoke in the accents of a man accustomed to the buffets of evil fortune'. Behind this lack of conviction, however, Conrad became aware of Almayer's abiding sense of his own importance: 'the worst of this country', Almayer later mumbles, ' "is that one is not able to realise . . . very important interests . . ." he finished faintly . . . "up the river" ' (p. 86).

Conrad tells us that his 'pathetic mistrust in the favourable issue of any sort of affair touched me deeply' (p. 77), but he adds that he found 'nothing amusing whatever' in Almayer (p. 84). What he did find was probably the vast disparity between the extravagant hopes of Almayer's inner life and the petty actualities of his achievement, a disparity which Conrad was familiar with, no doubt, in himself. This kind of identification would at least be consistent with a passage in *A Personal Record* where Conrad imagines himself placating Almayer's aggrieved shade for the 'very small larceny' of his name, and for having given him a fictional incarnation which was 'not worthy of your merits' (pp. 87–88). At first, Conrad's defense is jocular and ironical, but he goes on to disclaim any intention of mocking Almayer's aspirations: 'What made you so real to me was that you held this lofty theory with some force of conviction and with an admirable consistency.'

For the novel Conrad invented an action which remorselessly broke down the 'admirable consistency' of Olmeijer's megalomania; but part of that action was based on two kinds of historical reality.

One of them begins in the fact that, in so abandoned a spot as Tanjung Redeb, three other whites were present, and one of them was called Jim Lingard. He was apparently the nephew of William Lingard, a very famous trader and adventurer. This William Lingard had special interests on the Eastern coast, the least developed part of Borneo; in particular he had long ago discovered a channel for navigating the labyrinthine estuary of the Berau River; and, at Tanjung Redeb (the novel's Sambir) had set up its first permanent trading post.[5] Lingard had apparently helped the Sultan of Gunung Tabor, just across the river, either in a sea battle with a neighboring sultan or by forgiving him his debts or supplying rice (at a fairly high price) during a famine. As a reward the Sultan ceremonially named him Pangeram ('Prince') and Rajah Laut ('King of the Sea'); and he also, probably at Lingard's request, ceded him a piece of land on which he built a store and living quarters. The Dutch authorities were annoyed that one of their sultans should receive a foreigner without their permission, and in February 1863 sent a gunboat up the Berau River to investigate. Its commander made a report which showed that the Sultan apparently had more or less cleared himself; but thereafter Lingard learned that it was wiser to keep on good terms with the Dutch.

Olmeijer had been William Lingard's representative in Tanjung Redeb for some seventeen years; and the two men had apparently both prospected for gold further upriver and dealt in contraband arms and gunpowder with the Dyaks, the more primitive inhabitants who had preceded the Moslem Malays and Arabs in the occupation of Borneo. But Lingard's fortunes had declined; his monopoly of trade in Berau had been broken and his last ship, the *Rajah Laut*, was put up for sale in 1884.[6] There are few records of him between his return to England in 1883 and his death in 1888.[7]

In the novel Conrad invents a picturesque plot from these materials. Charles Olmeijer becomes Kaspar Almayer, the son of a minor Dutch official in Java; he leaves home to work as a clerk at the port of Macassar in the Celebes, and there he meets a famous English trader called Tom, not William, Lingard. Tom Lingard proposes that Almayer marry his ward, a native girl who is to inherit his fortune. Though he has no feeling for the girl, and is ashamed to be marrying a Malay, Almayer agrees because he believes that he will then be able to realize the 'earthly paradise of his dreams' – make a huge fortune and live in a 'big mansion in Amsterdam'.[8] The main action of *Almayer's Folly* occurs some twenty years after the marriage. Lingard has disappeared, apparently trying to raise further capital somewhere in Europe; the trading post is derelict because Lingard's secret channel for navigating the Pantai River has been betrayed to rival Arab traders; and the splendid new house on which Almayer has wasted his last resources in the vain – and momentary – hope that his trade would flourish again, and that the British Borneo Company, not the Dutch, would take over Sambir,[9] has now been mockingly dubbed 'Almayer's Folly' by his trading rivals.[10] It now stands unfinished, untenanted, and already much decayed; while its universally despised master is suffered to live on by the Malay and Arab leaders merely because they believe that only Almayer can tell them the secret of Lingard's rumored mountain of gold inland.

There may, then, be some faint historical basis for the character and actions of Tom Lingard in the novel; but a second and much more general historical process pervades the moral world of *Almayer's Folly*, and it supplies another possible reason why Conrad found 'nothing amusing whatever' in Olmeijer.

What has really foreclosed the dreams of Almayer is that he has pinned all his hopes on Lingard's monopoly of trade at Berau; but that monopoly has in fact been condemned by the coming of steam, which has made river navigation much easier and fostered the development of regular coastal trade routes.[11] The Malay Archipelago had seen two generations of heroic individual achievement: that of Sir Stamford Raffles (1781–1826), founder of Singapore, and then that of Sir James Brooke (1803–68), who became the rajah of Sarawak, in north-eastern Borneo. Later, some of their merchant-adventurer successors in the 1850s and 60s, such as William Lingard, had at least become figures of legend. One man who met Lingard in 1887, W. G. St Clair, describes him as 'a personage of almost mythical renown, a sort of ubiquitous sea-hero, perhaps at times a sort of terror to evildoers, all over the Eastern waters from Singapore to Torres Straits, and from Timor to Mindanao' (*CEW*, pp. 315–16). But this 'type of the adventurer-skipper' was now 'quite extinct'. As the Western powers set up coaling stations for the new steamships, and their men-of-war put down piracy, opportunities for individual enterprise declined; and so on the whole the merchants and sailors of the seventies and eighties were a much more humdrum lot.[12] Even Borneo, one of the last areas to be taken over by the Western colonial powers, had been largely settled by the 1880s.

That Olmeijer was, in the simplest sense, the victim of history, no doubt gave him his appeal to Conrad, who was another. The effective partition of Borneo and the coming of steam had sealed Olmeijer's fate exactly as the partition of Poland and the coming of steam had Conrad's. Conrad went up the Berau in 1887 on a steamship which was owned by the very Arab traders who had supplanted Olmeijer and Lingard – the Singapore firm of Syed Mohsin Bin Salleh Al Jooffree; while the whole period of the writing of the manuscript of *Almayer's Folly* (from 1889 to 1894) was when Conrad was discovering that, in the world of the steamship, he himself no longer had a dependable future as a sailor.

During his first voyage to the East in 1879, Conrad had written from Australia to his uncle and guardian, Tadeusz Bobrowski, 'with the greatest enthusiasm' about the 'beauty and wealth' of the area, and had even talked of taking up a position there, which he said he had been offered by a famous captain and shipowner whom he had met at Sydney.[13] Nothing came of the project, and when, in 1883, 1885, and especially in 1887, Conrad actually went to Southeast Asia (which he had not done when he wrote to Bobrowski), he must have seen that he had come East too late; too late to share the dreams of William Lingard or even those of his foolish protégé Olmeijer; and yet the disappointment continued to rankle.

THE WRITING: 1889–95

Almayer's Folly, then, reflects both large historical processes and Conrad's personal experience of them; but although we have more physical evidence to document its writing than we have for most first novels, these records reveal very little about Conrad's unique experiences. Nonetheless, the records have their own intrinsic, and very considerable, interest and importance.

The Manuscript: 1889–94

The first of the documents is the manuscript, complete except for Chapter 9. It is extant only through a series of lucky chances, many of which Conrad describes in *A Personal Record*. For instance, the manuscript survived the misfortunes and perils of Conrad's 'canoe' journey on the Congo; and between its beginning in the autumn of 1889 and its completion four and a half years later, also in London, it shared Conrad's various other travels – to Australia (twice), to the Ukraine (twice), and to Belgium, Switzerland, and France (pp. 3–26, 68–69). Later, the survival of the manuscript depended on a further and rather commoner vicissitude. Like many writers, Conrad sometimes destroyed his first drafts after a new revised or typed version was completed, but the manuscript of *Almayer's Folly* was apparently kept hidden away by Conrad's wife, Jessie. As a result it survived to be sold, some eighteen years later, along with many of his other manuscripts, to John Quinn, a wealthy New York lawyer who was an enlightened patron of the arts with modern tastes. Quinn's collection, which contained the manuscripts of many writers who were later to become celebrated, including those of Ezra Pound, T. S. Eliot, and James Joyce,[14] was sold at auction by the Anderson Galleries in 1923. Conrad's fame was then at its peak, and the manuscript of *Almayer's Folly* fetched $5,300, compared to only $1,975 for *Ulysses*. The buyer was a colorful magnate of bookdealing,

Dr A. S. W. Rosenbach; and he ensured that the manuscript of *Almayer's Folly*, together with many others, can now be seen in one of his houses, which has become the Philip H. and A. S. W. Rosenbach Museum and Library in Philadelphia.

Two incidental features of the manuscript bring us fairly close to Conrad's life during the time of the writing. First, the back of the fourth leaf of Chapter 3 records the familiar nervous distractions of the writer unable to write: there are a number of 'K's and 'Konrad's; sketches of four ships, of a hansom cab, and – in a premonitory adumbration of what was to be a continuing obsession of Conrad's poverty-threatened career as a writer – pictures of English coins from a penny to a half-crown. Second, some of the other occasional notes fill in a few details of the chronology of the novel's composition. Conrad wrote that *Almayer's Folly* was written 'line by line, rather than page by page' (*A Personal Record*, p. 19); but despite this, Conrad's early progress was rather rapid. There is a letter written in Polish on the back of the first leaf of Chapter 4 which suggests that Conrad had progressed that far early during the winter of 1889–90, when he was largely unemployed. There presumably followed a pause during his voyage to the Congo in the last half of 1890, but work was resumed on his return. Conrad went to convalesce in Switzerland, at Champel, near Geneva, between 21 May and 14 June 1891; and on the back of the fourth leaf of Chapter 6 (originally folio 6 of Chapter 7) there is 'a computation of 536 francs for five weeks' board', and a word which John Gordan interpreted as 'Genéve' (though it may be 'Guineas'), followed by the words 'Receive from London 375 fr.'[15]

Conrad probably finished Chapter 7 while at Champel and 8 after his return to London, but then progress again slowed down for the next two years. This period was mainly occupied by Conrad's two voyages as first mate of the sailing ship *Torrens*, beginning mid-November 1891. He recounts how, on his second voyage, which began on 25 October 1892, he showed the manuscript to its first reader, a passenger named W. H. Jacques. 'Would it bore you very much reading a MS. in a handwriting like mine?' Conrad asked him, and was told, 'Not at all' (*A Personal Record*, pp. 15–16). Next day Jacques returned the MS, silently. Finally Conrad asked him: 'Well, what do you say? . . . Is it worth finishing?' 'Distinctly.' 'Were you interested?' 'Very much!' But a westerly blow was coming on, and Conrad had time only for one more question: 'Now let me ask you one more thing: Is the story quite clear to you as it stands?' Jacques, Conrad tells, 'raised his dark, gentle eyes to my face and seemed surprised', but he answered: 'Yes! Perfectly.'

They never mentioned the tale again, and Jacques soon died, either in Australia, or on the homeward journey; but, from the way Conrad refers to this episode as 'these quiet rites of Almayer's and Nina's resurrection', we can probably take it that there had earlier been some hesitation in Conrad's mind as to whether he should go on with the novel. Even during that voyage, 'not one line was added to the careless scrawl of the many pages which poor Jacques had had the patience to read'; but although, as Conrad writes, 'the purpose instilled into me by his simple and final "Distinctly" remained dormant', it was 'alive to await its opportunity'.

The opportunity was nearly lost forever. Conrad recounts that, after leaving the *Torrens* late in July of 1893 to pay his last visit to Tadeusz Bobrowski that autumn, 'on an early, sleepy morning, changing trains in a hurry', he left his Gladstone bag in the refreshment room of the Friedrichstrasse railway station in Berlin (*A Personal Record*, p. 19). Luckily it was retrieved by a porter; and at that time the manuscript had only 'advanced . . . to the first words of the ninth chapter'. However, in the period of enforced leisure which followed Conrad's return from the Ukraine, the last four chapters were finished in a relatively sustained burst of energy. Chapter 9 was written in the autumn of 1893; and the next chapter was begun in the inactivity of Conrad's berth on the steamship *Adowa*. He had accepted the position of second mate, and sailed with the *Adowa* from London to Rouen, arriving on 6 December 1893. Conrad wrote that 'the shade of old Flaubert . . . might have hovered with amused interest over the decks' as he penned the opening lines of the new chapter (*A Personal Record*, p. 3). Conrad also remembered that, as he wrote the tenth chapter's first sentence on 'the grey paper of a pad which rested on the blanket of my bed-place', he was interrupted by the 'cheerful and casual' young third mate, who asked, 'What are you always scribbling there, if it's fair to ask?' Conrad 'did not answer him, and simply turned the pad over with a movement of instinctive secrecy'; the story was then 'put away under the pillow for that day'.[16] The *Adowa* never made its voyage, and Conrad returned to London, not knowing that he had experienced his 'last association with a ship' (*A Personal Record*, p. 7).

Before leaving Rouen, however, Conrad had mentioned *Almayer's Folly* in his correspondence with the main confidante of his early years. Marguerite Poradowska was then the beautiful 46-year-old widow of the refugee first cousin of Conrad's maternal grandmother. She came from a distinguished Belgian family, and had already published three novels. Their friendship had begun early in 1890, and she was the first author that Conrad knew personally. Conrad's extant letters contain frequent praise of her works, but the first mention of his own novel is not until 7 January 1894. On that day he ends a letter (written as usual in French): 'If you are a well-behaved little girl, I shall let you read my story of Almayer when I have finished it'.[17] Conrad's reference is so brief, and without any other explanation, that we can assume that Marguerite Poradowska had already learned of the project at one of their meetings, although she had not yet seen the manuscript.

The tenth chapter seems to have taken Conrad about three months to complete. One cause for the delay was his depression at the death of his guardian, Tadeusz Bobrowski, on 10 February; another was that he was still looking for a job at sea. Conrad seems to have finished Chapter 10 only by late March 1894. He wrote to Marguerite Poradowska, either on 29 March or 5 April:

Forgive me for not having written sooner, but I am in the midst of struggling with Chapter XI; a struggle to the death, you know! If I let go, I am lost! I am writing to you just as I go out. I must indeed go out sometimes, alas! I begrudge each minute I spend away from the page. I do not say from the pen, for I have written very little, but inspiration comes to me while gazing at the paper. Then there are vistas that extend out of sight; my mind goes wandering through great spaces filled with vague forms. Everything is still chaos, but, slowly, ghosts are transformed into living flesh, floating vapours turn solid, and – who knows? – perhaps something will be born from the collision of indistinct ideas. (*Letters*, 1, 151)

The letter is characteristic of many later ones in its preoccupation with the extreme difficulties he found in composition; it also shows Conrad was obviously putting great pressure on himself to finish. On 16 April he wrote to Marguerite Poradowska that 'Chapter XI is completed (9000 words) – longer but much worse than the others. I am beginning Chapter XII in a quarter of an hour' (*Letters*, 1, 152). Conrad wrote this last chapter at a furious pace, in nine days. This appears from a letter to Marguerite Poradowska where Conrad describes writing the end of the novel and his feelings about it:

24 April 1894
11 a.m.

My dear Aunt,

I regret to inform you of the death of Mr Kaspar Almayer, which occurred this morning at 3 o'clock.

It's finished! A scratch of the pen writing the final word, and suddenly this entire company of people who have spoken into my ear, gesticulated before my eyes, lived with me for so many years, becomes a band of phantoms who retreat, fade, and dissolve – are made pallid and indistinct by the sunlight of this brilliant and sombre day.

Since I woke this morning, it seems to me I have buried a part of myself in the pages which lie here before my eyes. And yet I am – just a little – happy. (*Letters*, 1, 153–54)

The Typescript, Acceptance, and Publication: 1894–95

The manuscript of *Almayer's Folly* is a remarkably finished production for a beginner's draft; still, it is only a working copy, and the extant typescript, which is obviously later, stands as vital evidence of Conrad's creative intentions in the crucial period between the completion of the manuscript and the novel's publication.

Little is known about the early history of the typescript. The first mention of typing comes in Conrad's letter to Marguerite Poradowska of 24 April 1894, announcing that he had finished the manuscript. Conrad added: 'I shall send you the two chapters as soon as typed' (*Letters*, 1, 154). These were 11 and 12; and in the next few weeks Conrad repeated the promise regarding Chapter 12 in three other letters (*Letters*, 1, 156, 158, 159). But as late as his 4 October letter to his publisher, T. Fisher Unwin, Conrad says that although 'last June' Marguerite Poradowska had seen the manuscript and 'proposed to me to translate it into French' for the *Revue des Deux Mondes*, he also says that she had 'not even seen the last 2 chapters which were not written at the time' (*Letters*, 1, 176). Conrad, then, had not sent her the chapters even by the time *Almayer's Folly* was about to be submitted to Unwin for publication.[18] A letter probably written on 17 or 24 May, which gave as his excuse for the delay that the 'manuscript' was 'in the hands of a rather distinguished critic, Edmund Gosse' (*Letters*, 1, 158), may supply some indirect evidence. The excuse itself is unconvincing, as Conrad would surely not have left himself without any copy, especially since he was probably still completing his revisions;[19] on the other hand, it suggests that at least one typed copy of each of the chapters existed by late May or shortly before.

One confusing element in the testimony concerning the history of the typescript may be due to the fact that, as here, when Conrad said 'manuscript', he may have meant what we should now call a 'typescript'; the latter term did not come into common use until a decade later.[20] We can surmise that Conrad may have had the first ten chapters typed by the time he visited Marguerite Poradowska in March of 1894 (*Letters*,

1, 150) and showed her the novel. That so much was in typed form is further implied when Conrad, in a letter of 29 March or 5 April, says that he is sending her 'the first page (which I have copied)' of Chapter 11 'to give you an idea of the appearance of my manuscript', and that this is only fair 'since I have seen yours'. This only makes sense if one assumes that what she had seen previously was typewritten.

The whole had almost certainly been typed in some form by the time Conrad wrote that the novel was in the hands of Gosse, and thus probably by late May. Only the typing of 'the twelfth and last chapter', according to a later letter to Marguerite Poradowska, seems to have been delayed (*Letters*, 1, 159), but this probably involved the second typing of that chapter. The wrapper on the manuscript says that the 'T.S.' was 'finished on the 22 May 1894', though Conrad may have got the date wrong.

The transition from the manuscript to the typescript continues the verbal and stylistic improvements found in the revisions in the manuscript. Some of these were probably suggested by friends, and particularly by Edward Lancelot Sanderson – another friend from the *Torrens* – with whom Conrad spent about ten days in the middle of April 1894. The Sandersons presumably played a significant role in one important aspect of the process of revision. John Galsworthy's sister recalled: 'I remember that both Ted [Sanderson] and his mother . . . took a hand, and considerable trouble, in editing the already amazingly excellent English of their Polish friend's "Almayer" manuscript, and in generally screwing up Conrad's courage to the sticking-point of publication.'[21] One effect of their discussions may have been the reduction of gallicisms – as when 'rapprochement' became 'reconciliation' (p. 45) and 'entremise' was replaced with 'agency' (p. 31).

The history of the extant revised typescript after May 1894 is relatively simple. It was sent to Fisher Unwin on 4 July 1894 (*Letters*, 1, 172). Next, it served as printer's copy for setting up the novel. It was later returned to Conrad, who in 1912 sold it to John Quinn for £5.[22]

Compared to most writers Conrad was very lucky in getting his first work published so quickly; but if we can judge by his letters during those ten months everything between sending in the 'manuscript' and the book's eventual publication involved agonizing delays and self-doubts.

In the latter part of May, it will be recalled, Conrad had sent the 'whole manuscript' to Edmund Gosse (*Letters*, 1, 158). Conrad had presumably approached Gosse because he was then the editor of Heinemann's 'International Library'. Conrad may have thought that a novel by a Pole about Borneo would have fitted that bill, but unfortunately the series consisted of foreign novels in English translation. Nothing more is known about this relationship.[23] Conrad's friend and first biographer, Jean-Aubry, suggested later that Conrad had two possible publishers in view. He wrote that 'It was actually from the offices of the Shipmasters' Society, where he used to go in the hopes of finding some employment, that, one day in the beginning of June, he decided to send his MS. to a publisher just on the chance. He had hesitated for a moment between two of them, but that morning he made up his mind, and he called a messenger boy to take his MS. to T. Fisher Unwin' (*LL*, 1, 158–9). Jean-Aubry's mention of June is contradicted by Conrad's letter to Fisher Unwin which gives 4 July as the date (*Letters*, 1, 172), but his account is otherwise plausible.

Conrad probably chose Unwin partly because they ran a collection of short novels known as the 'Pseudonym Library' (see *Letters*, 1, 161); one of them was *John Sherman and Dhoya* by William Butler Yeats, using the pseudonym Ganconagh (Karl, p. 331). Many years later, in 1918, Conrad wrote this account of his choice to W. H. Chesson: 'At that period of his existence T. F. Unwin had published some paperbound books by various authors and I bought one or two of them, *Mademoiselle Ive* and *The Pope's Daughter*, I believe. My ignorance was so great and my judgment so poor that I imagined *Almayer's Folly* would be just suitable for that series. As a matter of fact it was much too long, but that was my motive in the choice of a publisher' (*LL*, 1, 159).

Once he had sent the typescript, there was nothing more to do, and Conrad began to profess an attitude of indifference. In a letter to Marguerite Poradowska Conrad wrote on 12 July 1894: 'To be completely frank, I don't feel any interest in the fate of *Almayer's Folly*. It is finished. Besides, it could in any case be only an inconsequential episode in my life' (*Letters*, 1, 161). Conrad's casual disclaimer of any intention of turning author for good probably cannot be taken very seriously, except perhaps as an attempt to conceal his anxieties. In a letter of 25 July he expressed to her the 'depression of complete discouragement' – more than he had ever confessed to anyone; and shortly after, on 30 July, he reports having had ten days in bed with a fever, and comments: 'I have had no response from Fisher Unwin. That could go on for months, and then I do not think they will accept it' (*Letters*, 1, 165).

A few days later, as had happened before in 1891, Conrad went to take the cure at Champel. He wrote from there to Marguerite Poradowska: 'Since you have been kind enough to take an interest in the matter, let us speak of that imbecile Almayer. I have requested the return of the manuscript' (*Letters*, 1, 170). Conrad presumably expected a rejection, and went on to suggest a desperate and humiliating expedient – that Marguerite Poradowska translate *Almayer's Folly* into French and publish it either as a collaboration (*Letters*, 1, 165), or even entirely under her own name: 'The name "Kamoudi" [sic] somewhere in small print will be adequate. Let your name appear on the title-page – with merely an explanatory note to say that K. collaborated in the book.'

Conrad was somewhat preoccupied at this time with a new tale called 'Two Vagabonds', which he described as 'very short – let us say twenty to twenty-five pages' (*Letters*, 1, 171). This was to become his second – and considerably longer – novel, *An Outcast of the Islands*. Conrad returned to London at the end of August, and on 8 September he wrote to Unwin:

I venture now upon the liberty of asking You whether there is the slightest likelihood of the MS. (Malay life, about 64.000 words) being read at some future time? If not, it would be – probably – not worse fate than it deserves, yet, in that case, I am sure You will not take it amiss if I remind you that, however worthless for the purpose of publication, it is very dear to me. A ridiculous feeling – no doubt – but not unprecedented I believe. In this instance it is intensified by the accident that I do not possess another copy, either written or typed. (*Letters*, 1, 173)

One need not accept the improbable assertion that Conrad had honored Unwin by depriving himself of the unique copy of his work; nor need we take Conrad's elaborately apologetic strategy too seriously. Letters to publishers are often characterized by a special rhetoric of ostentatious, but false, unconcern; it is part of the conventional dispensation of authors from disclosing the humiliating truth of their anxiety. The apologies and indirections, like the underlying despairs, are also, no doubt, greater in the case of a first work. No Unwin reply is recorded; but Conrad's novel was in fact getting the best attention he could possibly have hoped for.

One of the house readers for Unwin was Wilfrid Hugh Chesson; he was favorably impressed, and called it to the attention of another. This was Edward Garnett, who wrote much later:

My wife recollects that I showed her the manuscript, told her it was the work of a foreigner and asked her opinion of his style. What particularly captivated me in the novel was the figure of Babalatchi, the aged one-eyed statesman, and the night scene at the river's edge between Mrs. Almayer and her daughter. The strangeness of the tropical atmosphere, and the poetic 'realism' of this romantic narrative excited my curiosity about the author, who I fancied might have eastern blood in his veins. I was told however that he was a Pole, and this increased my interest since my Nihilist friends, Stepniak and Volkhovsky, had always subtly decried the Poles when one sympathized with their position as 'under dog'.[24]

Both his readers, then, were enthusiastic, and on 4 October Conrad reported to Marguerite Poradowska that on the previous day Unwin had accepted *Almayer's Folly* for publication in what he later wrote was 'the first typewritten letter I ever received in my life' (*LL*, 1, 159). If Conrad felt either joy or pride his letter to Marguerite Poradowska makes no mention of it; instead, he is severely business-like: 'I wrote accepting the terms. . . . I have taken what they offered me because, really, the mere fact of publication is of great importance. . . . Now, I need only a ship in order to be almost happy' (*Letters*, 1, 177–78).

Still, publishing business had to be attended to, and on 10 October Conrad wrote to Marguerite Poradowska about his meeting with the two readers and Unwin:

At first the firm's two 'readers' received me, complimenting me effusively (were they, by chance, mocking me?). Then they led me into the presence of the great man in order to talk business. He told me frankly that if I wished to share in the risk of publication, I could participate in the profits. Otherwise, I receive £20 and the French rights. I chose this latter alternative. 'We are paying you very little,' he told me, 'but, remember, dear Sir, that you are unknown and your book will appeal to a very limited public. Then there is the question of taste. Will the public like it? We are risking something also. We are publishing you in a handsome volume at six shillings, and . . . planning not to publish you until next year, in April, during the season. We shall print immediately, so that you can make corrections, and shall send the proof-sheets to Mme Marguerite Poradowska before Christmas. Write something shorter – same type of thing – for our Pseudonym Library, and if it suits us, we shall be very happy to be able to give you a much better cheque.' (*Letters*, 1, 180)

Conrad's account of this interview raises two minor issues. First, the question of 'French rights'. The idea that Marguerite Poradowska should translate *Almayer's Folly* belongs to the period before Unwin had accepted it; but Conrad kept the idea open in the early negotiations with Unwin because of the advantages of his novel appearing in the well-known *Revue des Deux Mondes*. But in late October or early November of 1894, Conrad wrote to tell Marguerite Poradowska that she was doing herself an injustice in considering doing the translation, and recommended that she concentrate on her own novels (*Letters*, 1, 184). Later, on 12 March 1895, he wrote to Unwin saying that his aunt was 'too unwell to undertake the work now' but that he had another person in mind who might write a critical notice of *Almayer's Folly* for the *Revue des Deux*

Mondes (*Letters*, 1, 203–4). This attempt was unsuccessful, and it was only in 1919 that *Almayer's Folly* was finally translated into French, by Geneviève Seligmann-Lui.

Second, Edward Garnett's recollection of the meeting shows that from the beginning Conrad was far from subservient in his dealings with his publisher. Garnett described how, in this or perhaps a later meeting, 'in answer to Unwin's casual but significant reference to "your recent book," Conrad threw himself back on the broad leather lounge and in a tone that put a clear cold space between himself and his hearers, said "I don't expect to write again. It is likely that I shall soon be going to sea." A silence fell' (Garnett, pp. vii–viii). In fact, as we have seen, Conrad had, since August, been engaged on a long novel which was to become *An Outcast of the Islands*.

Conrad's letters make it clear that his corrections on the proofs were on a much larger scale than he himself had anticipated. He had written Marguerite Poradowska on 14 or 21 November:

I've had a long interview with Mr T. Fisher Unwin. They will definitely not set the work in type before next year, in February. It's all absolutely the same to me. I have nothing to revise in the way of style or composition, and, as for misprints, the firm's readers will see to them. But I hope with all my heart and soul that I shall no longer be in London at that time. (*Letters*, 1, 187–88)

But Conrad was in London when the first sixteen pages of proofs arrived on Christmas Eve. They plunged him into the deepest gloom: as he wrote to Marguerite Poradowska, 'I was horrified: absolutely horrified by the thing in print, looking so stupid – worse – senseless' (*Letters*, 1, 193). Conrad, then, had the common, but not the less painful, experience of finding that, faced with the fateful prospect of this being the final chance of improving what the public would at last see, there was much more to change 'in the way of style or composition' in his revised typescript than he had previously imagined.

Conrad eagerly anticipated the novel's appearance; but when, even in early March, there was no news of its publication, he wrote to Unwin with an anxiety masked by an elaborately facetious irony:

I return to town next week – for the *18th*. Isn't the 18th the date for the appearance of a certain Immortal work?!

I warn you that if I am disappointed I shall – surely – have some kind of a fit; and if I die on your office-carpet the Conservative papers will have big headlines. "Horrible cruelty of a well-known Publisher" . . . [Unwin was a Liberal].

The above frivolity of expression disguises very deep feeling. In common mercy to a suffering fellow creature let it be the 18th without fail. (*Letters*, 1, 204)

The proposed March publication was nevertheless pushed forward to early April, and, writing in much the same playful spirit to disguise 'very deep feeling', Conrad, who was staying with the Sandersons at Elstree, tried again at the end of March:

I do not want to make myself a nuisance – at least not very much, but since I have been staying with my friends here I became aware that the expectation of Almayer's Folly is unsettling this glorious and free country. All the people that have been told to look out for the book in March are writing letters full of anxiety and tears to know when – Oh! When! they will be able to get the immortal work. Letters by every post. They come from North and west and south and east – they are as numerous as the raindrops – as persistent and loud as the wild west wind. . . . You will ruin my career at its very outset by a too prolonged delay. Can You? Will you? give me a date so that I can appease the universal thirst for information – and be called blessed by [an] anxious and enthusiastic crowd of respectable and intelligent people. (*Letters*, 1, 206)

By 12 April Conrad had received his advance copies but no publication date had been set. He wrote to Marguerite Poradowska, giving the reason for the delay: 'I have not yet been published but shall be this month, for certain. They cannot give me a definite date yet. The Macmillan Company of New York is undertaking the American publication, and, because of the copyright law, we must wait until they are ready over there.'[25]

Conrad was referring to the Chace Act of 1891, which stipulated that a foreign work could be copyrighted in the United States – and thus be protected from appearing in pirated editions – only if it were set and printed there, and if its publication was simultaneous with that in Britain. After a further delay *Almayer's Folly* was finally published on 29 April in London, and on 3 May in New York. The English edition Conrad estimated as of 1,100 copies; the American edition was probably of 650 copies.[26]

Conrad had submitted *Almayer's Folly* under the pen name of 'Kamudi'; it was doubly symbolic, since it was a Malay word, and it meant 'rudder'. But when his novel did not appear in Unwin's Pseudonym Library, this was dropped, and *Almayer's Folly* eventually appeared under what was really another pseudonym. Conrad's real surname, of course, was Korzeniowski, and to his death he regarded it as such; for official matters, such as passports, he was still using Konrad Korzeniowski (Najder, p. 183). But years of exasperation at the way his name was mispronounced and misspelled had gradually led him to use his two easiest given names, Józef Konrad, for most purposes; and on 17 January 1894 he had, for the first time, signed an official document – his discharge papers from the *Adowa* – J. Conrad (Najder, p. 161). When he became an English author, therefore, it was natural that he should use these two names, in their anglicized forms, and eventually became known, even in his native Poland, as Joseph Conrad.

Almayer's Folly was dedicated 'To the memory of T. B.' We do not doubt Conrad's deep feeling for his beloved uncle, Tadeusz Bobrowski; but we must also observe that, like his chosen pen name, the initials avoided raising the issue of Polish nationality.

Meanwhile, Conrad was so exhausted by the process of getting published that, the day after the London appearance of *Almayer's Folly*, he wrote to Marguerite Poradowska: 'I am not at all well. To set myself up again, I am quitting my bed and going to Champel for hydrotherapy' (*Letters*, 1, 210–11).

The Author's Note: 1895

Although Conrad had written a preface for *Almayer's Folly* soon after receiving the first proofs of the first English edition, it did not appear in print until 1921, when the collected editions were published in America and Britain. Because its publication was delayed until then, the 'Author's Note' has been lumped in popular memory with the other retrospective notes written in his last decade when 'Conrad was looking back and defining himself to his newly-acquired reading public'.[27] Actually, however, this 'Author's Note' had been written by 4 January 1895, for on that date Conrad mentioned in a letter to Garnett that he would 'send on the preface tomorrow' (*Letters*, 1, 197). Before 9 January 1895, Chesson had read the 'preface' and suggested at least one change, for on that date Conrad responded to a now lost letter: 'As to that preface (which I have shown you) I trust it may be dispensed with, but if it must appear you are quite right – "*aversion from*" not "aversion for" as I wrote – and stuck to like a lunatic. You will correct?' (*Letters*, 1, 199).[28]

Why did Conrad write the preface? Traditionally, novelists have written prefaces to state an artistic creed, to define, explain or justify a subject, to engage in a literary quarrel, or, from the vantage of several years, to reminisce about the creation of their work. Henry James, for example, would probably not have written 'The Art of Fiction' had it not been for the provocation of Walter Besant's earlier essay; and the 'Author's Note' to *Almayer's Folly* partly belongs to this category, since in it Conrad quarrels directly with one of his noted contemporaries.

The opening paragraph of the 'Author's Note' (p. 3) clearly identifies both the target and the grounds of the quarrel:

I am informed that in criticising that literature which preys on strange people and prowls in far off countries, under the shade of palms, in the unsheltered glare of sun beaten beaches, amongst honest cannibals and the more sophisticated pioneers of our glorious virtues, a lady – distinguished in the world of letters – summed up her aversion from it by saying that the tales it produced were "de-civilized." And in that sentence not only the tales but, I apprehend, the strange people and the far-off countries also, are finally condemned in a verdict of contemptuous dislike.

Who was this lady – 'distinguished in the world of letters' – of intuitive, clear, felicitous, and infallible judgment? Conrad identified her, in the brief paragraph added to the 'Author's Note' in the 1921 Heinemann edition: 'I wrote the above in 1895 by way of preface for my first novel. An essay by Mrs. Meynell furnished the impulse for this artless outpouring. I let it now be printed for the first time, unaltered and uncorrected, as my first attempt at writing a preface and an early record of exaggerated but genuine feeling.'[29] Today Alice Meynell (1847–1922) is almost forgotten, but in 1895 she was a prominent literary figure. Ruskin, Dante Gabriel Rossetti, and George Eliot had praised her first collection of poems, *Preludes I*, published in 1875, and in the 1890s she was frequently mentioned as a possible successor to the poet-laureateship. She continued to write poetry, essays, and reviews, and also assisted her husband in editing various magazines – *The Pen*, *The Weekly Register*, and *Merry England*.

'Decivilised', the essay which provoked Conrad's preface, appeared in the 24 January 1891 issue of the *National Observer* and was reprinted as the second essay in Meynell's *The Rhythm of Life* in 1893.[30] In it she uses the term 'decivilised', which seems to have enjoyed some popularity in reviews and journals at the time, possibly because of its use by Herbert Spencer in *Principles of Sociology*;[31] but it is difficult to tell whether she is attacking colonial literature or reacting to the primitivism which was then surfacing in European painting, sculpture, music, and literature. Basically, she objects to colonial literature because it ignores the value of continuity, and argues that, though we cannot select our posterity, 'we may give our thoughts noble forefathers' and 'follow their ways to the best well-heads of the arts'. Decivilized art, on the other hand, presents the 'mentally inexpensive', and is 'designed to . . . reveal the good that lurks in the lawless ways of a young society'.

Conrad's attitude toward this view is succinctly indicated in his suggestions concerning literary notices for his novel. 'I am quite content', he wrote Chesson, 'to be in your hands but it struck me that perhaps a suggestion from me would meet with your approval. Could you not say something about it being a "civilized story in savage surroundings?" Something in that sense if not in those words' (*Letters*, 1, 199). His 'Author's Note' focuses almost exclusively on the idea that the 'savage surroundings' serve only to throw the basic similarities of man in sharp relief, and, in line with this idea, argues that the Borneo of *Almayer's Folly* essentially mirrors man's metaphysical, not his physical, condition. Conrad juxtaposes Borneo and London in the third paragraph of the 'Author's Note' and asserts that man is everywhere the same:

The picture of life there as here is drawn with the same elaboration of detail, coloured with the same tints. But in the cruel serenity of the sky, under the merciless brilliance of the sun the dazzled eye misses the delicate detail, sees only the strong outlines, while the colours, in the steady light, seem crude and without shadow. Nevertheless it is the same picture. (p. 3)

The fourth passage restates this assumption, and Conrad returns to it again in the final paragraph. In 1920, he dismissed his preface as an 'artless outpouring'; but the recurrence of its ideas in *A Personal Record* (p. 9) suggests that he stood by it.

Why this first critical essay written by Conrad was not published until 1921 remains something of a mystery. Conrad's 9 January 1895 letter to Chesson hints that he wished to see it published, and in 1913 he spoke of it as being 'suppressed'; but Conrad does not indicate who suppressed it or why.[32] The most probable hypothesis is that prefatory writings were rarely included in novels, at least until the author was famous, and even then – as in the case of Henry James, as well as Conrad – were retrospective assessments which helped the publisher to justify and sell a new collected edition. In the present case, we can say that the loss of Conrad's brief preface was not particularly significant at the time; and it makes no contribution to general literary theory. Yet the 'Author's Note' at least establishes some of the critical assumptions with which Conrad began writing, and it surely reveals a novelist who, from the very beginning of his career, was deeply concerned with the relationship between subject-matter, authorial vision, and the general role of the artist. In that sense it strikingly anticipates Conrad's later and more famous critical pronouncements.

THE RECEPTION OF *ALMAYER'S FOLLY*

When Unwin was explaining his terms to Conrad he gave as one advantage that 'you know that whatever we bring out always receives serious critical attention in the literary journals. You are certain of a long notice in the *Saturday Review* and the *Athenæum*, not to mention the press in general. That is why we are planning not to publish you until next year, in April, during the season' (*Letters*, 1, 180). Unwin was something of an innovator[33] as regards pushing his books, and we must remember that in any case, the novel, before the days of movies, radio, or television, played a relatively larger part in the entertainment of the public. The chances of a first novel by an unknown author being widely reviewed were therefore rather better then than they are now, even though, as Conrad wrote, 'every week some dozens of novels appear' (*Letters*, 1, 178); and in the event *Almayer's Folly* was very widely, remarkably promptly, and on the whole quite favorably, reviewed.

There were, first of all, a number of short notices before the date of publication – in the *Sunday Times* (21 April), the *Westminster Gazette* (23 April), and the *Daily News* (25 April). The first review was a fairly detailed notice in a Scottish daily, the *Scotsman*. Its unsigned review began by calling it 'a remarkable book, which will probably attract all the more attention because its author's name is new to readers of novels'; and concluded that 'every one who reads it will look with hopeful anticipations for the future productions of its author's pen'.[34] Conrad apparently followed the reviews assiduously, and occasionally commented on them. He wrote to Marguerite Poradowska from Champel on 2 May about how 'the *Scotsman*, the major Edinburgh paper, is almost enthusiastic', and added that the *Glasgow Herald* 'speaks with a more restrained benevolence' (*Letters*, 1, 214). Conrad concluded: 'Now we are waiting for the London dailies and, *especially*, the non-political weeklies.' The first of the London dailies, the *Daily Chronicle*, said all that Conrad could have hoped: it wrote that 'we have been struck with the book, and know nothing quite like it of recent years', and ended with the encouraging words that 'Mr. Conrad may go on, and with confidence; he will find his public, and he deserves his place' (*CH*, pp. 49–50). Conrad must have been very satisfied at the number of people who welcomed *Almayer's Folly* as, to quote a retrospective comment in the *London Mercury* of 1920, 'an immense and exhilarating surprise to those who cared for good letters' (*CH*, p. 342).

The American reception, though favorable, was in general briefer and less enthusiastic than the English. The *Atlantic Monthly* (September 1895) began: 'In spite of plainly evident marks of inexperience on the writer's part, there is undeniable power in this tale, as well as a somewhat unusual measure of freshness and originality.' Its final comment stressed Conrad's descriptive power: 'The scene, a new one in fiction, of this wretched tragedy is depicted with a vividness which must make it visible even to an unimaginative reader.' In *The Dial* (16 August 1895) William Morton Payne stressed the racial conflict, writing of Nina that 'the strain of Malay savagery struggles with the European, and finally asserts its mastery'; and he concluded that the novel 'enforces once more the lesson that "East is East, and West is West, and never the twain shall meet."'

The themes (and the clichés) which the critics selected were very varied on both sides of the Atlantic. The most obvious was place. The English *Daily News* congratulated Conrad for annexing 'the island of Borneo – in itself almost a continent' (*CH*, p. 47); while the *Daily Chronicle* reviewer allowed himself a pun in the middle of his praise – Conrad was 'a man who can write of Borneo and never bore, if so frivolous a phrase, used in honest and deserved compliment, do not offend him' (*CH*, p. 49). Arthur Waugh, in the *Critic*, the first 'non-political weekly' to consider *Almayer's Folly*, commented that Borneo was 'a tract hitherto untouched by the novelist, but now annexed by Mr. Joseph Conrad, a new writer' (*CH*, p. 50), while the *Spectator* ended a perceptive review by announcing that Conrad 'might become the Kipling of the Malay Archipelago' (*CH*, p. 61). Not that this area of the world won universal approval; the reviewer in the American weekly journal the *Nation*, who reported his general impression of the novel as 'a mob of raging heathen engaged in battles for rum and wives', wrote that 'Borneo is a fine field for the study of monkeys, not men', and ended with a jocular insult: 'The only interesting native of Borneo', he commented, in allusion to a popular song, 'got away and was long ago introduced to an astonished civilisation as "The old man from Borneo / Who's just come to town"' (*CH*, p. 60).

In general, however, the reviewers admired Conrad's mastery of his chosen scene, and that included its way of life. As the reviewer of the *Daily Chronicle* perceptively wrote, the novel showed 'the emasculating and despair-breeding effect of the tired but scheming East upon a weak neurotic Western organisation', and Conrad tells 'as only one who has seen it can, of the creeping decay of house and boat, stage, balcony, and building; he makes one know the warm moisture that slowly rots, as readily as he makes one feel the inertia that fails ever to repair or reconstruct' (*CH*, pp. 49–50). Another reviewer, James McArthur, in the *Literary News*, focused on the clash of races: Nina 'is a fine illustration of what may happen to the Malay in the transition which Mr. Swettenham[35] sees is imminent. The phase of character is a revelation to us, and in this whole story of an Eastern river we are impressed with the fact that a new vein has been struck in fiction' (*CH*, p. 59).

Among the many other general issues raised by the reviews, three figure in much of Conrad's later critical career: first, that what Conrad offered was real literature; second, that his work continued important elements of romance; and third, that both the nature of his subject and his treatment of it raised doubt as to whether he would find many readers.

The exceptional and original literary quality of *Almayer's Folly* was recognized by many reviewers. 'Breaks fresh ground in fiction', and 'stands far apart from the common run of novels' wrote another (*CH*, pp. 61, 58). H. G. Wells said of the three ' "local colour" stories' in his unsigned review for the *Saturday Review* that 'only one of them is to be regarded seriously as a work of art'; he meant *Almayer's Folly*, and wrote that it was 'exceedingly well imagined and well written, and it will certainly secure Mr. Conrad a high place among contemporary storytellers' (*CH*, p. 53). Another of the weeklies, the *Speaker*, said that the novel was 'written with manifest knowledge of the life which it portrays – the life of a solitary European in one of the remoter possessions of the Dutch in the East. . . . His marriage with a native woman may have degraded him, but it has never turned him into a brute'. The reviewer concluded that 'If Mr. Conrad can give another story as striking and life-like as this, his place in our literature ought to be an assured one' (*CH*, pp. 55–56). The longest and most impressive review was that in the *Weekly Sun*, where a very well-known journalist and member of Parliament, T. P. O'Connor, made it his 'Book of the Week', and hailed this 'startling, unique, splendid book'. His enthusiasm is evident from the beginning of a review which takes the first two sides of a full-sized newspaper page: 'This is a book a few people have already read with rapture; by-and-bye everybody will have read it, and then the world will know that a great new writer and a new and splendid region of romance have entered into our literature.'[36]

Conrad mentions O'Connor's review in several letters. In particular, he wrote on 11 June 1895 that he has 'gone back to writing, strongly encouraged by *seven and a half* columns in the *Weekly Sun*, where T. P. O'Connor has buried me under an avalanche of compliments, admiration, analysis, and quotations, all of it with an enthusiasm which certainly makes him say some quite ridiculously stupid things' (*Letters*, 1, 229). One of the 'stupid things' O'Connor wrote may have been that, 'Almayer is the Lear of the Malay Archipelago'; another, more plausibly, may be his conclusion: 'It is only a writer of genius who could write that and many another passage in this startling, unique, splendid book.'

In general the reviewers were not much concerned with literary influences, but some of them touched on the popular writers of the period, notably Louis Becke, with his pictures of the 'Pacific Islands', and there were also more celebrated authors, most notably the French naturalist, Emile Zola. In the *Athenæum* Zola was seen as Conrad's inspiration (*CH*, p. 52), where the reviewer wrote: 'Mr. Conrad has, we imagine, studied Zola to some purpose', and quoted as an example 'the following overloaded, but powerful description of a Bornean forest'.[37] In America the *New York Times*, whose general judgment was exceptionally favorable, ended with the comment: 'The reader may have been carried away by the cleverness of a Pierre Loti or a Lafcadio Hearn through their high literary art in the description of far distant countries, but Mr. Joseph Conrad is quite their equal, and for dramatic effectiveness, their superior' (12 May 1895).

The heading of the *Times* review was 'An Oriental Romance', and this term was used by a good many reviewers, including that of the *Guardian*, who wrote that 'It is a romance in all senses of the word; the scene laid in the strange, weird world lying within the Malay Archipelago, and the actors, Dutch, Arab, Malay, and half-caste, essentially romantic personalities' (*CH*, p. 57). The *Academy* saw it as a 'romance' and then congratulated Conrad for possessing 'the art of laying on just sufficient local colour', but not going so far as to make his work 'unintelligible to the "general"' (*CH*, p. 54). The *Daily Chronicle* liked the way that the story made 'one feel that the old notion of hero and heroine may still have some excuse, that there are still novelists who can breathe life into the old ideals of love and bravery'. It also congratulated Conrad on his powers in 'the art of creating an atmosphere, poetic, romantic' (*CH*, pp. 49–50).

Conrad, who was himself aware that some elements in his novels made it unlikely that he would find much popular appeal, must have paid particular attention to the reviewers who pointed in that direction. He commented, for instance, that 'the poor old "World" kicks at me (in

15 lines) like a vicious donkey' (*Letters*, 1, 219). What the *World* said may be indicated by quoting its first sentence and its last two: '*Almayer's Folly* . . . is a dreary record of the still more dreary existence of a solitary Dutchman doomed to vegetate in a small village in Borneo . . . The life is monotonous and sordid, and the recital thereof is almost as wearisome, unrelieved by one touch of pathos or gleam of humour. Altogether the book is as dull as it well could be' (*CH*, p. 51). There were several reviewers who objected to the conduct of the action. The *Sketch*, for example, found that Conrad committed the 'terrible offence' of forcing 'his readers too often to turn back and re-read something of import-ance to the narrative'; while the *National Observer* complained of Conrad's 'laboured and muddle-headed involution' which made 'the sequence of events . . . very hard to follow'.[38] Few reviewers were so completely negative; but even some sympathetic critics noted weaknesses in Conrad which might well have discouraged readers. H. G. Wells wrote that 'It is a gloomy tale', and the *Bookman*, though in general laudatory, found several faults: 'human nature has not in Mr. Conrad so powerful a painter as have the wood, the river, the Eastern sky by night and day'; the reviewer also wrote that 'as a whole it is a little wearisome', and 'hard to follow', that 'the action drags', and that 'the style has beauty, but it lacks swiftness' (*CH*, p. 58).

There were, then, lots of lessons which Conrad could, if he chose, learn from the reviewers; but, at the same time, he must have felt that Fisher Unwin had been as good as his word, and that he had been better launched on his literary career than he, or anybody else, could reasonably have expected.

To this account of the reception of *Almayer's Folly*, we can add three notes. First, that its sales proved somewhat disappointing. Conrad wrote triumphantly on 2 May 1895 to Marguerite Poradowska that 'the first edition of 1100 copies has been sold' (*Letters*, 1, 214). So quick a sale would have been a remarkable success for a first publication; but Conrad had been deceived by the unintended effects of Garnett's enthusiasm. Garnett wrote later:

The fact that the critics' handsome praise of *Almayer's Folly* failed to sell the novel is attested by my old friend, Mr. David Rice, then Mr. Fisher Unwin's town traveller, who at my instigation had prevailed on the booksellers to subscribe practically the whole edition. Mr. Rice tells me that the majority of the copies rested for years on the booksellers' shelves, and that the title *Almayer's Folly* long remained a jest in 'the trade' at his own expense. Conrad's first book took seven years to get into the third impression. (Garnett, p. xx)[39]

Second, even though the general public did not find Conrad's work to their taste, he had not only won golden opinions from most of the critics, but from old friends and new admirers. One of the latter was Justin McCarthy, a celebrated writer and politician (*Letters*, 1, 224); another was Harriet Capes, who was to remain a friend, and whose appreciation Conrad found to be 'very rare' (*Letters*, 1, 233).

The third point, which Conrad did not know for over a year after the appearance of *Almayer's Folly*, was that it had received the attention of reviewers in far-away Singapore with unexpected speed.[40] The first (anonymous) review came out in the *Straits Times* on 16 January 1896. Under the title of 'A Romance of the Indian Archipelago' it contains a fairly long account of the novel, and ends by conceding that although 'our author is weak in his Malay . . . in error in representing Bali as one kingdom, and in describing a prince of Bali as a Brahmin', 'these blemishes' did not 'detract from the general truthfulness of the book'. The reviewer commented on how the natives are forced to judge white civilization 'by the ethics of the trader and the manners of the beach-comber', and concluded with an emphatic judgment on the racial conflict: 'The power of the European has substituted a sullen peace for the open war of the past. It has done so in the interest of trade, not of civilisation, however much we may disguise the fact. Civilisation makes no proselytes; it indeed rejects them with its barrier of racial prejudice. . . . The result is deplorable but it has nonetheless to be faced.'

This racial interpretation of *Almayer's Folly* produced another and fairly lengthy comment which was published in the *Straits Times* on the next day. It is signed only by 'G', and is largely concerned, 'as one who knew well the late Captain Lingard, the "Rajah Laut" of Bornean waters, to refute a few of the pernicious libels on his memory'. The writer has no difficulty in showing that Lingard held 'the respect and esteem of all who knew him', and was never, as the reviewer wrote, 'a penniless adventurer' who disappeared 'in the labyrinth of London life'. More surprising, 'G' believes that 'the author and his reviewer must know very little of Dutch Indian Society when they dwell so deeply on the social disabilities of the results of mixed marriages'. He believes that it is 'ludicrous' to suppose that Almayer's society, which is that of 'a mercantile clerk in Macassar', would be similar to that of Kipling's 'British India'. There is no time here to give the full argument, but we can note that the letter writer was probably correct in believing that Conrad exaggerated the racial 'disability' which Almayer felt in his marriage. We must also observe that 'G' found *Almayer's Folly* to be 'undoubtedly, a powerful and interesting work'.

Language

The narrative begins with Almayer, having been called to dinner, still irresolutely lingering on the verandah of his private domain, the Folly.[41] He is

looking fixedly at the great river that flowed – indifferent and hurried – before his eyes. He liked to look at it about the time of sunset; perhaps because at that time the sinking sun would spread a glowing gold tinge on the waters of the Pantai, and Almayer's thoughts were often busy with gold . . . There was no tinge of gold on it this evening for it had been swollen by the rains and rolled an angry and muddy flood under his inattentive eyes, carrying small drift-wood and big dead logs, and whole uprooted trees with branches and foliage, amongst which the water swirled and roared angrily.

One of those drifting trees grounded on the shelving shore, just by the house, and Almayer, neglecting his dream, watched it with languid interest. The tree swung slowly round, amid the hiss and foam of the water, and soon getting free of the obstruction began to move down stream again, rolling slowly over, raising upwards a long, denuded branch, like a hand lifted in mute appeal to heaven against the river's brutal and unnecessary violence. Almayer's interest in the fate of that tree increased rapidly. He leaned over to see if it would clear the low point below. It did; then he drew back, thinking that now its course was free down to the sea, and he envied the lot of that inanimate thing now growing small and indistinct in the deepening darkness. (pp. 5–6)

As narrative writing this is more than competent. The traditional opening description of the place and time of day has been skillfully combined with an initial prefiguring of character, situation, and theme; and these are given considerable visual and psychological effectiveness by being presented through combining concrete images of the external world with the internal reverie of the protagonist. The visual imagery is not particularly arresting in itself – Conrad still tells rather more than he shows: nevertheless, by making us identify with the developing sequence of Almayer's observations, the passage makes us both par-ticipate in his consciousness and yet anticipate the fate to which he is still blind, but which is presaged in the imagery.

Almayer's fate began in the past, with his dreams of gold; but now the sun is setting on a stormy present, with the angry flood suggesting the capsizing of Dain's boat, and hence the final wreck of Almayer's hopes; while the future is prefigured when our attention is captured by the mute appeal of the denuded branch. It is a strong dramatic irony that Almayer should have 'envied the lot' of the uprooted tree because 'its course was free down to the sea'; only two days later he will go down the river to the sea with Nina and Dain, but from there he is bound not for a voyage to Europe and his dream, but for a return to Sambir and his death.

That we look for general implications in the passage is largely because it is so full of verbal emphasis. The most obvious manifestation of this emphasis is repetition – for instance, in the three uses of the word 'gold' in the first paragraph, and in the duplication of 'angry' and 'angrily' at its end. Tautology and anaphora are the easiest of rhetorical devices for demanding attention; and Conrad uses them a good deal throughout *Almayer's Folly*.

In the present passage the repetition is too heavily done. Some of this may be the inadvertent residue of difficulties with the English language. For instance, Conrad could easily have avoided one of the verbal repetitions, that of 'tree', by writing 'Almayer's interest in *its* fate', which would also have been less cumbrous than 'interest in the fate of that tree'. Even 'the tree' would have sufficed, but Conrad often had trouble with articles, probably because there are none in Polish; and here the difficulty may have been compounded by the fact that Conrad had learned French long before he knew English – French often uses the demonstrative ('*cet arbre*') where the indefinite article would be normal in English. Another and more general result of not being a native user of the language may also underlie Conrad's tendency to repetition: it is the anxious overexplicitness of any foreigner; he says it twice to make sure.

Ford Madox Ford much later diagnosed the 'slightly stilted nature of Conrad's earliest prose' as being the result of his knowing only two of the three English languages. Conrad had mastered the official 'literary' tongue – 'that of the *Edinburgh Review* which has no relation to life', as Ford put it;[42] and he was also fairly familiar with the slang of the streets and the forecastle; but of the third language, which Ford called the 'dialect of the drawing room or the study', Conrad had had relatively little experience; and it is, of course, precisely that middle style which lays the basis for rapidity and ease in written prose.

The stiltedness to which Ford refers is partly a matter of vocabulary. Very few of Conrad's lapses are of the kind which would have been avoided by consulting a dictionary; they mainly seem the result of

Conrad's late exposure to educated colloquial English, together with the contamination of his previous exposure to Polish and French. Thus when Conrad wrote 'they had dwelt together in cordial neighbourhood' (p. 36), his dictionary would probably not have explained that, whereas *voisinage* in French is very currently used for 'neighbourly intercourse', this particular sense of 'neighbourhood' is so rare in English as to sound anomalous and awkward.

Many of Conrad's difficulties with grammar and syntax are of a similar nature. He once unidiomatically joked: 'I know nothing of grammar myself as he who runs may see' (*Letters*, II, 216); and most writers, one imagines, have been much less influenced by their formal knowledge than by their intuitive linguistic sense, absorbed through a lifetime's experience; so it is not surprising that Conrad had particular difficulty in the more indeterminate areas of English grammatical practice. One obvious example, that of tense sequences, is found in a passage about a woman's look of surrender: 'Men that had felt in their breasts the awful exultation such a look awakens become mere things of to-day' (p. 129). Sequence demands that it be either 'have' for 'had' at the beginning or 'became' for 'become' at the end, while the sentence as a whole requires the present – 'men who feel . . .'. Behind Conrad's difficulties here one could no doubt trace the equally complicated but much more definite rules for tense agreements in French, and the quite different but equally categorical rules in Polish.[43]

Another major difficulty about Conrad's English concerns the order of the words. The inflected nature both of French, and even more of Polish, syntax makes the reference of modifiers, whether adjectives, adverbs, phrases, or clauses, much less dependent on word order than is the case in English. For instance, Conrad was probably influenced by the French and Polish practice of more regularly putting adverbs and adverbial phrases after the verb; in English position is often a matter of judgment, and Conrad often gets it wrong, sometimes to the point of extreme gaucheness; as when, for instance, he writes: 'Mahmat had to produce the bangle and saw with rage and mortification the lieutenant put it in his pocket' (p. 109).

Conrad's difficulties with prepositions, his awkwardness in the placing of modifiers, and his uncertainty with levels of diction combine to provide the ludicrous climax to an already tangled sentence describing Nina's first glimpse of Dain: she espies him with half her face shyly hidden behind a curtain, thus 'leaving only half a rounded cheek, a stray tress and one eye exposed, wherewith to contemplate the gorgeous and bold being so unlike in appearance to the rare specimens of traders she had seen before' (p. 43). It sounds awful, but awful in exactly the way that any literal translation from an inflected language can sound in English.

The passage also illustrates the heavy use of qualifiers in Conrad's early style, where almost every noun has its adjective, and often two or three. In the opening passage about the Pantai, for instance, Conrad's phrase about the 'river's brutal and unnecessary violence' has an artificial and strained quality which is quite absent in the French translation: 'la violence brutale et inutile de la rivière'.[44] The device of paired or tripled qualifiers is most obtrusive when they are placed after the noun or verb, as in the earlier 'the great river that flowed – indifferent and hurried – before his eyes'. There Conrad's measured cadence perhaps suits the content and thus justifies the departure from common English usage; but more often the use of paired and post-positioned qualifiers, usually adjectives, suggests a flat-footed striving for elegance which is a rather wearisome hallmark of Conrad's early writing.

Repetition and over-qualification in their various forms are the commonest defects in the prose style of *Almayer's Folly*; and they tend to become most prominent when Conrad is least sure of himself or is trying to force a climax. The two sometimes coincide, as in the sentence describing Dain's emotions on first seeing Nina: 'Dain . . . forgot . . . the object of his visit and all things else, in his overpowering desire to prolong the contemplation of so much loveliness met so suddenly, in such an unlikely place – as he thought' (p. 43). The elaborate balance of three phrases of similar form and cadence – 'so much loveliness', 'met so suddenly', and 'in such an unlikely place' – seem inappropriate to the subject; and the very attempt at stylistic elegance draws attention to such lapses from it as the rather vague archaism of 'all things else', and the awkwardly otiose explanatory parenthesis of 'as he thought'.

These various weaknesses, however, are not the dominant features of the prose of *Almayer's Folly*. They have been given considerable attention here for three reasons: partly because critics have often raised the matter in over-general terms, or passed over it too easily; partly because an examination of the style of his first novel enables one to see more clearly how, although Conrad never wholly lost some of the awkwardness of idiom and syntax illustrated here, his writing became much more fluent, colloquial, and effective with each succeeding work; and partly because we can infer that the pervading unconscious presence in Conrad's mind of other languages and rhetorical traditions probably provided counter-models which helped him to achieve the very eloquent and original prose style of his mature work.

Literary influences

In a sense, Conrad is the least derivative of major writers; he wrote very little that could possibly be mistaken for the work of anyone else. Still, he did read very widely; and as is usual in an author's first significant work, the main residues of his reading are perhaps more clearly present in *Almayer's Folly* than elsewhere.

In 1895 the days of the great Victorian novelists had long been over; and among their successors, Robert Louis Stevenson had died the previous year, while Thomas Hardy was about to close his career as a novelist with *Jude the Obscure* in 1896. As the reviews of *Almayer's Folly* make clear, Conrad was in part following current market formulae. *Almayer's Folly* could, after all, be regarded as a romance in the most popular sense, since it contained a love story with a happy ending; and it also fitted in with contemporary interest in exotic adventure. Following the fashion set earlier by Chateaubriand and Byron, the exotic had become a major mode of nineteenth-century literature. In the 1880s the novel about foreign lands had become an established and popular genre in France with the immensely successful Pierre Loti, and in England with Stevenson and Rudyard Kipling; at a lower literary level the exotic had attracted many best-selling novelists, notably Rider Haggard and such prolific but now almost forgotten writers as the Australians Louis Becke (1855–1913) and Carlton Dawes (1865–1935). Conrad was early compared with most of these, and he certainly knew their work: he found Rider Haggard 'too horrible for words' (Garnett, p. xiii), but seems to have had some admiration for Becke, Stevenson, and Kipling.[45] There is, however, little reason to suppose that Conrad was particularly indebted to any of these, beyond their part in creating an audience for narratives about foreign lands.

In any case, the exotic novel could hardly have provided a permanent direction for Conrad, if only because he had been ashore much too briefly to have anything but the most superficial understanding of Malay life. But in *Almayer's Folly* the genre at least afforded Conrad an opportunity of developing one of his characteristic strengths as a writer, his power to describe the outside world. The power is of a special kind: Conrad looks at the visible universe with the eye of one who believes that only by deciphering its features can the individual hope to find clues to life's meaning or lack of it. For instance, in the scene where the lovers, Dain and Nina, are parting after a secret tryst, the passage begins like an Oriental travelogue, but soon modulates into something quite different:

the two little nutshells with their occupants floated quietly side by side, re-flected by the black water in the dim light struggling through a high canopy of dense foliage; while above, away up in the broad day, flamed immense red blossoms sending down on their heads a shower of great dew-sparkling petals that descended rotating slowly in a continuous and perfumed stream; and over them, under them in the sleeping water; all around them in a ring of luxuriant vegetation bathed in the warm air charged with strong and harsh perfumes, the intense work of tropical nature went on; plants shooting upward, entwined, interlaced in inextricable confusion, climbing madly and brutally over each other in the terrible silence of a desperate struggle towards the life-giving sunshine above – as if struck with sudden horror at the seething mass of corruption below; at the death and decay from which they sprang. (p. 55)

The passage is typical of Conrad in presenting a picture, not of a static landscape but of nature in motion: within a single sentence the lush tropical aubade, with the jungle showering the happy lovers with nuptial petals, is soon disclosed as an ephemeral moment in a larger and grimmer process; nature's cycle begins in death and decay, and though some spectacular flowers may manage to thrust themselves up into the sunshine, they soon fade, die, and sink back into the corruption where they began.

This kind of writing – exhibiting what Cedric Watts calls the anti-pathetic fallacy[46] – is rather common in *Almayer's Folly*. It emphasizes, contrary to the pathetic fallacy (which suggests a conscious harmony between man and nature), that for Conrad the opposite is the case: the Darwinian struggle for survival affords man no consolation, and all human aspirations can plainly be deciphered among its fated victims. The reviewer for the *Athenæum* had cited the passage as an example of Zola's influence; and, more generally, we must see that the determinist perspectives which dominated the Naturalist novel are in direct contra-diction to the basic assumptions of the popular romance: its heroes and heroines require a world offering that unconditional freedom which is the essence of individual wish-fulfilment. In themselves Nina and Dain are perfect romantic lovers – they have ideal beauty, grace, courage, mutual devotion; and their destiny (the wandering son of a great rajah arrives from beyond the sea and bears away the granddaughter of another) is equally romantic. Yet, as we have seen, the environment denies the primary absolute of romantic love – that it is eternal; while as regards plot, Conrad though seeming to follow, actually undermines the prescriptions of popular romance.

Almayer's Folly, like much of Conrad's later fiction, embodies many standard adventure-story motifs: Lingard's secret channel up the river; his notebook with its vague clues to the treasure; pirates and gunrunning and mysterious political intrigues; and, above all, the hunted hero, Dain. At different times Dain's life is threatened by the Dutch, the Arabs, the Malay chief Lakamba, even Almayer, and he is saved by two of the most implausible but time-hallowed devices of fiction: first, that of mistaken identity – the false clue of Dain's ring on the drowned corpse; and second, that of the heroine's dauntless self-sacrifice – Nina interposing herself between her lover and her irate father's drawn revolver. Despite these standard melodramatic elements, however, the novel never reads like a romance or an adventure story for very long: by the accepted convention such intrigues and dangers are clever, exciting, larger than life; but in *Almayer's Folly* they come to seem foolish and irrelevant because they are overpowered by the dominant presences of the novel – the changeless torpor of Sambir and its symbolic representative, Almayer.

Almayer is an example of what we have come to call an anti-hero; and he belongs to a variant of that tradition which is typical of the later nineteenth century. Conrad was characteristically unhelpful about what literary models may have influenced *Almayer's Folly*, and wrote only that it was 'very likely' that 'on the evening before I began to write myself' he had read 'one of Anthony Trollope's novels' (*A Personal Record*, p. 71). But it was surely not Trollope, any more than Scott, Marryat, Dickens, or Thackeray, who had provided Conrad with the antecedents for the character of Almayer, or shaped his idea of the novel. For Conrad at this time the exemplary novelists were French, and, in particular, Flaubert and Maupassant.

It was probably Guy de Maupassant who influenced Conrad most directly and powerfully at the outset of his career. He would feel personal affinities with another aristocrat, skeptic, orphan, depressive, even would-be suicide; and as a writer no one had a clearer conception of his craft than Maupassant, or worked at it more assiduously. When Conrad took up writing, he studied both Maupassant's theory and practice intensively. 'I fear I may be too much under the influence of Maupassant', he wrote to Marguerite Poradowska in 1894; 'I have studied *Pierre et Jean* – thought, method, and all – with the profoundest despair. It seems nothing, but it has a technical complexity which makes me tear my hair' (*Letters*, 1, 184–85). There is no doubt that Conrad's works show a considerable indebtedness to Maupassant: there is imitation and even much detailed borrowing, of which a good many convincing, and even disturbing, examples have been pointed out;[47] the grave charge of plagiarism, however, must be somewhat qualified when we consider that Arthur Symons wrote that Conrad always had a volume of Maupassant open on his worktable,[48] and that Ford recalled that Conrad could recite a great deal of Maupassant by heart.[49] Most of the borrowings look like unconscious residues of Conrad's remarkable but erratic memory: he probably forgot that he was remembering. In any case, although Conrad was perhaps too proud to own up to what he owed, he was also too proud to owe very much to anyone; and as regards influence in the wider sense, Conrad is never very much like Maupassant. The economy of Maupassant's style, the rapidity of the narrative development, and the cool distant clarity of his moral analysis were not Conrad's way; and in a 1904 essay on Maupassant he made it clear that he found the determinism of the Naturalist perspective too narrow as a view of life. It was primarily the 'conscientious art' of Maupassant[50] which won and retained his enthusiasm.

In the last half of the nineteenth century the supreme figure of the novelist as artist was unquestionably Maupassant's master, Gustave Flaubert. Hugh Walpole wrote in 1915 of the 'unmistakable' influence of the style of 'the author of *Madame Bovary*' on Conrad's.[51] Conrad at once wrote Walpole a letter strongly denying that he had 'been under the formative influence of *Madame Bovary*', and claiming that he had 'read it only after finishing *Almayer's Folly*' (*LL*, II, 206). The chronological argument is certainly wrong, for a letter of 1892 survives in which Conrad writes that he has 'just reread' *Madame Bovary* 'with respectful admiration' (*Letters*, 1, III). Admittedly Conrad mentions him less often than Maupassant; but there is no question of his early and detailed familiarity with Flaubert,[52] and it is likely that *Madame Bovary* had some influence on *Almayer's Folly*.

Almayer is a Borneo Bovary. Like Emma, he devotes his entire life to one obsessive fantasy – though not of great love, but of great wealth. Both Almayer and Emma begin by making a loveless marriage merely as a step towards realizing their fantasies; and then, refusing to abandon their early dreams and come to terms with the ordinariness of their own selves and of the lives offered by Sambir or Yonville, they are steadily driven into a deepening tangle of circumstances from which death is the only way out.

Albert Béguin said of *Madame Bovary* that it is the book 'of the impossible escape, the heavy-hearted poem of eternal ennui'.[53] *Almayer's Folly* represents a different and later variant of Emma Bovary's attempt to escape the boredom of ordinary life. Since the brave days of the Romantics, the idea of existence as essentially an attempt by the individual to realize his private dream had been widely diffused and progressively debased both in literature and in life. In the decades after *Madame Bovary* the diffusion and internationalization of Romantic individualism had proceeded in highbrow as well as in popular literature; and Almayer's ennui can be seen as a distant demotic variant of that flaunted by the decadent heroes of J. K. Huysmans's novel *A Rebours* (1884) and Villiers de l'Isle Adam's play *Axël* (1890). The world-weary isolation of Des Esseintes and Axël is obtained and solaced through great wealth; and these two might perhaps have recognized, as Emma certainly would not, a remote kinship to their contemporary Almayer, whose sense of selfhood is expressed by his unique pony and flock of geese, his flowered pajamas, his pet monkey, and even his final recourse to opium in the architectural extravagance of his folly.

If Almayer in some measure belongs both to the petty bourgeois and the Decadent stages in the history of *Bovarysme*, the narrative methods by which he is presented are much more direct developments from Flaubert. Conrad's obtrusive detachment as narrator, for instance, follows from Flaubert's conception of the novelist as God, felt everywhere but never seen.[54] In *Almayer's Folly* we are at least continually aware, as in Conrad's work generally, that every compositional unit, from the basic structure to the cadence of each phrase, has been carefully and consciously fashioned; while the main action is highly unified, and, as in *Madame Bovary*, everything works remorselessly to foreclose the hopes of the protagonist and bring on the ordained catastrophe.

Conrad also decisively departed from the Victorian tradition of the intrusive author in favor of Flaubert's attitude of narrative impersonality and emotional *impassibilité* towards his creation; and he seems to have adopted Flaubert's idea of artistic completeness in the rendering of a single unified theme. The most specific aspect of his likeness to Flaubert can be seen in the way that, both in *Almayer's Folly* and his later fiction, Conrad proceeds through an exhaustive and primarily visual presentation of each aspect of the central subject. Conrad's letter to Walpole had singled out Flaubert's skill 'only from the point of view of the rendering of concrete things and visual impressions. I thought him marvellous in that respect' (*LL*, II, 206). This admiration is implicit from the first pages of *Almayer's Folly*, where we are introduced to Almayer through the impressions evoked in him by the river; and the method dominates the whole narrative, where every important aspect of the action has patently been conceived so that it can be rendered in concrete and predominantly visual terms. Such is the passage which T. P. O'Connor singled out for praise – when Nina's prau finally drops from his sight, and the mortal wound to Almayer's hopes is enacted visually:

Now she was gone his business was to forget, and he had a strange notion that it should be done systematically and in order. To Ali's great dismay he fell on his hands and knees and creeping along the sand erased carefully with his hand all traces of Nina's footsteps. He piled up small heaps of sand leaving behind him a line of miniature graves right down to the water. (p. 147)

Here Conrad no doubt obtrudes himself considerably more than Flaubert would have done when he supplies the explanatory metonymy of 'graves' for Almayer's piles of sand; and the symbolic action itself is rather more inherently unlikely than anything in *Madame Bovary*; but it is difficult not to see the scene as a recollection, though not necessarily conscious, of several in Flaubert's novels.

Point of view, theme, and meaning

Conrad undoubtedly worried rather consciously about his method of narration, and he knew that *Almayer's Folly* contained 'a good deal of retrospective writing' (*A Personal Record*, p. 17). Thus Chapters 2 to 4 are a continuous flashback; and a great deal of anterior information is also conveyed not only in the first chapter, where it is given through Almayer's reverie about his past, but in the last seven chapters of the novel – Conrad's account of Taminah's love for Dain in Chapter 8, for instance, or of Nina's relation to her father in Chapter 11. So if we take full account of these, the novel probably contains almost as much narrative of past events as of present ones. This is a formal reflection of the fact that the three days into which the present-tense action of the novel is compressed are really only the final stage in the working out of an already predetermined fate.

In general Conrad handles the retrospective method with consider-able skill. For the most part the time setting of past events is clearly conveyed; and the story of Almayer, who made a choice in the past to live only for the future, is kept going by making frequent shifts in chronological sequence and point of view. For instance, we first see the mutilated corpse through Almayer's eyes, and like him assume it to be Dain's; Conrad then keeps up the mystery either by not recounting the scenes where other characters – Nina, Mrs Almayer, Babalatchi, and the slave-girl, Taminah – learn the truth, or by postponing these scenes and recounting them later, out of their temporal order. For instance, just to maintain suspense about the identity of the corpse, Conrad makes two changes of narrative point of view, both of them involving switches in time. Thus we get the full disclosure that the corpse is not really Dain's only in the eighth chapter, when we are given Taminah's doings on the previous night in the form of a retrospective flashback told from her point of view. Then in the next chapter we go forward in time to see the Dutch officers hold their enquiry, and Almayer produce the dead body. The reader already knows that it is not Dain's, and so he can appreciate the irony that Almayer still thinks it is; while Almayer's ignorance makes possible the climactic scene later that night when Taminah awakens him from his drunken stupor to announce that Dain is alive, and has taken Nina away from him.

The manipulation of chronology and point of view to achieve suspense helps the romantic and adventurous side of the novel; but it also has the effect of keeping us from any continuous closeness to the minds of the characters. With most of them this involves no particular difficulty. Lakamba, Babalatchi, and the rest are undoubted successes as characters, but only because they are flat and the plot does not require them to have a real or developing inner life. Romance, adventure, and melodrama are alike in requiring only that the individual performers be easily recognizable; the most successful characterization in these genres usually comes with people like Babalatchi, or the eccentrics in Dickens or Stevenson, who are picturesquely different, not only from all the rest of the cast, but from any actual human being; and this, of course, means that their moral and psychological life does not carry over to that of the reader, and that they are essentially separate from the other characters in the novel.

Conrad's protagonist, Almayer, on the other hand, must have a wider truth to life if he is to represent the novel's central subject, which is individual and subjective; and this purpose also requires that the relationship between him and Nina be much more inward than those we expect between fathers and daughters in romance. At the same time suspense demands that the reader be kept guessing as to Nina's real feelings towards Almayer, and so Conrad is forced to avoid going inside Nina's mind. This is most obvious when, after Nina has avowed her love, Conrad shifts into the role of intrusive and yet secretive commentator to say that: 'a faint smile seemed to be playing about her firm lips. – Who can tell in the fitful light of a camp fire? It might have been a smile of triumph, or of conscious power, or of tender pity or – perhaps – of love' (p. 129). The teasing evasion does not particularly matter here; but our ignorance of Nina's actual feelings towards her father has the ultimate effect of feeding our curiosity about the plot at the cost of starving our understanding of its protagonists. In *Almayer's Folly* the reader can hardly help asking the question: does Conrad keep us guessing to maintain our interest, or because he does not know the answer?

As regards Almayer, there are moments when Conrad takes us into his mind with convincing power, but even there a note of cold detachment inhibits our response. In general Conrad seems least effective when he is dealing with Almayer in his more conscious and social roles, as in his last scene with Nina. The main exception is significant: Almayer is most convincing when he echoes Conrad's own sardonic accents. For instance, when Almayer finally uncovers the drowned corpse to the Dutch officers, he comments: '"Cold, perfectly cold . . . Sorry can do no better. And you can't hang him either. As you observe gentlemen" – he added gravely – "there is no head and hardly any neck"' (p. 108). Nothing we have heard Almayer say before has prepared us for this composed and laconic graveyard humor; but it is recognizably a variant of Conrad's own mordant voice.

Both here and later, Conrad either deliberately preferred, or unconsciously required, a way of distancing himself from the inner lives of his main characters; and he was at his best when he found modes of writing which gave free play to the movements of the remembering mind. This freedom could most easily be achieved by the use of intermediate narrators. Thus Almayer's sufferings seem most real when they are reported at secondhand, as in one passage from the brief coda of the novel which is allotted to Almayer's final efforts to forget Nina and all his former dreams. It occurs after Almayer has told his solicitous visitor, Captain Ford, 'I am – a firm man'; Conrad then adds: 'Ford looked at his face – and fled. The skipper was a tolerably firm man himself – as those who had sailed with him could testify – but Almayer's firmness was altogether too much for his fortitude' (p. 153).

This tightly ironic indirection is only one of Conrad's many ways of avoiding the more inward narrative methods which would have been needed to enable the personality of Almayer to bear the psychological and moral weight which his central role in the novel requires. One reason for this indirection probably had its origins in the contradictions of Conrad's own attitude toward Almayer, contradictions which can be discerned both in his title and in his epigraph.

The primary reference of 'folly' is, of course, to the lavish house Almayer builds when he briefly imagines that his fortunes will rise again. But this literal reference is largely peripheral to the action of the novel itself, since the possible British takeover of Sambir is raised at the end of one retrospective paragraph only to be dashed early in the next. The decaying house remains, of course, as an appropriate material symbol for Almayer's folly in the other main sense – it is a monument to his foolishness. But folly in the sense of mere foolishness seems to have too little moral weight to bear the main burden of the novel's theme. Here a matter of linguistic connotation may be involved. In French, quite apart from its special meaning for an absurdly costly building or enterprise, the primary sense of *folie* is not foolishness but madness. This much stronger usage was lost when the word was naturalized in English; but Conrad's prior knowledge of French may have led him to assume that his title would cover a wider range of meanings than it does, including that of actual insanity.[55] After Nina's departure, Almayer's mental state can justly be described as madness; but that final collapse is merely the culmination of Almayer's lifelong schizophrenic division between his inner picture of himself and what he actually is and does; his whole existence has been a continuously accelerating process of protecting his ego ideal by insulating it from reality.

In any case Conrad does not go very deeply or consistently into Almayer's consciousness, perhaps because it would have meant a full exploration of the hidden identification between himself and his first hero. One aspect of this unresolved identification is suggested in the novel's epigraph, drawn from Henri Frédéric Amiel: 'Qui de nous n'a eu sa terre promise, son jour d'extase et sa fin en exil?' (Who of us has not had his promised land, his day of ecstasy, and his end in exile?).[56] The opening verbal gesture of the novel, then, invites us to an act of universal spiritual recognition; who has not dreamed of the Promised Land and failed to attain it? But in the novel this imputed universality of theme hardly stands up to examination. We can accept the inevitability of disillusionment and still feel disinclined to pay much heed to the particular case of Almayer; after all, he dies, not in heroic exhaustion and on the brink of his people's victory like Moses, but in petulant disappointment at the failure of the future to behave as he thinks it ought, and make him very rich.

His hero's leaden sense of posthumous survival was no doubt deeply familiar to Conrad, but the unexamined residues of his own past were still too problematic to enable him to view Almayer either with consistent sympathy or resolute detachment. When he had finished *Almayer's*

Folly, Conrad felt he had 'buried a part of myself in the pages' (*Letters*, I, 153–54), but although the memory of Olmeijer was vivid, and apparently urgent, his personal meaning for Conrad seems to have remained obscure. The models of detachment offered by Maupassant and Flaubert not only worked against the close identification required for popular fiction, but also against the deeper probing of the buried motives which might explain why the man who had impelled him into authorship should then have become the object of his disdain. Conrad used much of his already formidable technical skill not to confront, but to avoid confronting this basic irresolution; and the reader may well feel inclined to shrink from committing too much of his sympathy to a hero who comes out of the past only to tell us that the present is merely epilogue.

Why should Joseph Conrad, at the age of less than forty, have felt this way about the present? In *A Personal Record* he writes that once he had begun *Almayer's Folly*, he would 'hold animated receptions of Malays, Arabs and half-castes' in his imagination (pp. 9–10). 'They came', he continues, 'with silent and irresistible appeal', which in retrospect 'seems now to have had a moral character, for why should the memory of these beings . . . demand to express itself in the shape of a novel, except on the ground of that mysterious fellowship which unites in a community of hopes and fears all the dwellers on this earth?' Conrad goes on to affirm that this sense of mysterious fellowship lay behind all his output. 'After all these years . . . I can honestly say that it is a sentiment akin to piety which prompted me to render in words assembled with conscientious care the memory of things far distant and of men who had lived.'

No other novelist talks like that about his work; it seems closer to more archaic notions of art as a ceremonial invocation of the tribal gods and heroes; and the attitude of sacred homage to the people of his past life is dominant in much else that Conrad said about his approach to fiction. For instance, he once wrote that 'a man who puts forth the secret of his imagination to the world accomplishes, as it were, a religious rite' (*LL*, II, 89). This seems puzzling if we consider how often Conrad's attitude to his characters is ironic and irreverent, as it is with Almayer; but there is no question that Conrad's recorded statements about writing novels persistently affirm the spirit of retrospective piety. Why that abiding reverence for people in his past merely because they had left traces in his memory?

David Hume had long before located the 'source of personal identity' in the individual memory; it 'alone acquaints us with the continuance' of the images of our past perceptions,[57] and Conrad's attitude seems particularly close to that of his contemporary, the Spanish writer, Unamuno. Unamuno writes: 'We live in memory and by memory, and our spiritual life is at bottom simply the effort of our memory to persist'; and he concludes that memory is really 'the effort of our past to transform itself into our future'.[58] For Conrad it was through memory that the past of the sailor was to become the future of the writer; the names enshrined in Conrad's memory were the most objective bridge between his past and his present; they were the symbolic tokens of the unknown but continuing identity of the man who had carried them in his mind.

Proper names, Jean Starobinski has written, are the 'common denominators' between the inner (*être profond*) and the social being.[59] This may help to explain why it was in Conrad's first novel that there should have occurred the most extreme correspondence between the name of a fictional and a real character. If it was indeed the memory of Olmeijer which set off the unconscious process by which Conrad interlocked both the outer and the inner world of his past self with his present existence, and projected them into future life through his novel, it becomes somewhat easier to understand why Conrad, while failing to come to terms with his central character, should nevertheless have asserted that if he had not 'got to know Almayer . . . there would never have been a line of mine in print'.

The present account of *Almayer's Folly* obviously does not follow the extravagant praise which the novel has received from some critics – most notably from H. L. Mencken: 'I challenge the nobility and gentry of Christendom to point to another Opus 1 as magnificently planned and turned out. . . . If it is not a work of absolute genius then no work of absolute genius exists on this earth.'[60] Nor does this critical analysis take up by any means all of the points which other critics have focused on most heavily or recently. For instance, it has not given very full consideration to the views of Albert Guerard, who finds that the best elements in the novel are the presentation of Bornean life, together with the novel's technical side which made it 'an important first experiment in the impressionist method.'[61] Nor has it considered Thomas Moser's argument that the romance between Nina and Dain lacks 'moral and psychological interest', and thus anticipates 'certain fundamental weaknesses in Conrad's imagination' whenever he dealt with the 'uncongenial subject' of love.[62] Nor have we considered the various defenses that have been made against this reasonable charge. John Hicks, for instance, argues that, even though Conrad's erotic dialogue may often be 'turgid', love functions in *Almayer's Folly* as a general test of the great Conradian conflict between 'fidelity and illusion'.[63] A similar defense has been made by Royal Roussel, who finds that Dain and Nina 'discover a more authentic world by returning to the primitive source of life', the 'dark' side, which Almayer and the white side of Nina's 'dual nature' habitually despise and betray.[64] This question is also taken up by Juliet McLauchlan in her general defense of Conrad's first two novels, 'Almayer and Willems – "How not to be"'; she studies, for example, the parallelism between Almayer's longing for 'the lost glories of Amsterdam', and Nina's dreams of 'savage glories'.[65]

There is another issue, which we have approached only from one point of view: what, finally, were the psychological motives which led Conrad to find himself in that foredoomed loser Almayer? In his 1930 study of *The Polish Heritage of Joseph Conrad*, Gustav Morf argues that Conrad, the exile, had 'recognized himself' (p. 86), or at least recognized what he might become, in Almayer and his fate. In the later study, *The Polish Shades and Ghosts of Joseph Conrad* (1976), Morf complements Conrad's personal identification of Almayer with a national one; he writes that 'the formula of *Almayer's Folly* obviously stems from Conrad's Polish background and heritage' (p. 117). Almayer's dreams of glory, we may say, were like Poland's glorious past; they were real, of course, but they could never be made real in the present; and it was idle to imagine otherwise.

On this, and on many other topics, then, the case of *Almayer's Folly* is by no means closed.

NOTES

1 P. xxi. References to Conrad's works are usually given in the text, preceded when necessary by a shortened title. Citations are taken from volumes of the Cambridge Edition already published, or else from the Doubleday collected edition in its Sun-Dial printing (1921) or in the Dent printings (1923 and subsequently). Where there are several quotations from the same or immediately contiguous pages, only the first is given a reference.

2 On Conrad's life, see Jocelyn Baines, *Joseph Conrad: A Critical Biography* (1960), Frederick R. Karl, *Joseph Conrad: The Three Lives* (1979), Zozislaw Najder, *Joseph Conrad: A Chronicle* (1983), and Jeffrey Meyers, *Joseph Conrad* (1991); these and other authorities disagree about the order of Olmeijer's Christian names.

3 *Joseph Conrad: Life and Letters*, ed. G. Jean-Aubry (1927) II, 264 (hereafter *LL*). For a discussion of the facts and myths of this episode, see Keith Carabine, '"The Black Mate": June–July 1886; January 1908', *Conradian*, 13 (1988), 128–48.

4 See John Gordan, *Joseph Conrad: The Making of a Novelist* (1940), p. 38; Norman Sherry, *Conrad's Eastern World* (1966) (hereafter *CEW*), p. 113.

5 A. B. Lapian, 'The Sealords of Berau and Mindanao: Two Responses to the Colonial Challenge', *Masyarakat Indonesia*, 1 (1974), 143–54.

6 See *CEW*, pp. 107, 110, which gives by far the fullest account of William Lingard (pp. 89–135).

7 Hans van Marle, 'Jumble of Facts and Fiction: The First Singapore Reaction to *Almayer's Folly*', *Conradiana*, 10 (1978), 165, nn. 10, 12.

8 See Joseph Conrad, *Almayer's Folly* (Cambridge: Cambridge University Press, 1994), p. 10; subsequent references to the text of this edition appear in round brackets.

9 In 1844–5, officers of both the Dutch and British navies had almost simultaneously negotiated agreements with the Sultan of Berau; but both governments soon lost interest (Graham Irwin, *Nineteenth-Century Borneo: A Study in Diplomatic Rivalry* [1955], pp. 154–5). However, there is no evidence that by the time of Lingard Britain was ever seriously interested in annexing parts of Eastern Borneo as far south as Tanjung Redeb; its main differences were with the Spanish claim to the Sulu Archipelago, which had been accepted by Britain and Germany in 1895 on the condition of free trade there, and the acceptance of the British Protectorate over Sarawak, Brunei, and North Borneo. The Dutch had accepted this settlement mainly because they were forced to acknowledge that they were unable to colonize all of Borneo themselves. See L. R. Wright, *The Origins of British Borneo* (1970), pp. 13, 133–4, 140–1, 159–60, 201.

10 There is a photograph of Olmeijer's house, taken in 1903, in Najder.

11 For the revolution in far-eastern trade created by steamships, especially after the opening of the Suez Canal in 1869, see Francis Hyde, *Far Eastern Trade, 1860–1914* (1973), pp. 16–26.

12 For further information see, Hans van Marle, 'De rol van de buitenlandse avonturier' (The Role of the Foreign Adventurer [in nineteenth-century Indonesia]), *Bijdragen en Mededelingen betreffende de Geschiedenis der Nederlanden*, 86 (1971), 32–9; G. J. Resink, 'The Eastern Archipelago under Joseph Conrad's Western Eyes', in his *Indonesia's History between the Myths* (1968), pp. 305–23.

13 *Conrad's Polish Background: Letters to and from Polish Friends*, ed. Zdzislaw Najder (1964), p. 180.

14 B. L. Reid, *The Man From New York* (1968), pp. 73, 124–7, 169, 602.

15 See Gordan, p. 179. Chapter numbers given here are the final ones of the manuscript (and of all subsequent documents), not the ones Conrad originally used for the first seven chapters. It is unclear whether Conrad was thinking of the original or final sequence in his comments in *A Personal Record*, p. 14. Gordan cites the original numbering.

16 *A Personal Record*, pp. 3–5. The absence of this grey paper from the manuscript leaves now extant shows that Conrad was revising his text even at this stage.

17 *The Collected Letters of Joseph Conrad* ed. Frederick R. Karl (1983–   ), I, 144 (hereafter *Letters*).

18 Conrad's 8 September letter (*Letters*, i, 174) provides further confirmation, at least for Chapter 12.

19 For further information on this and other aspects of the script, see *Almayer's Folly* (1994), 'The Texts', p. 171.

20 *OED*, under 'type'; the first English citation is dated 1906.

21 Quoted in Baines, *Joseph Conrad: A Critical Biography*, p. 134.

22 At the 1923 sale of Quinn's collection the typescript, Lot 1,781, was purchased for the then remarkably large sum of $650. Finally, in the early 1970s the typescript, together with that of *Chance*, was offered for sale by the House of El Dieff, New York City, on behalf of W. B. Leeds, and bought for approximately $25,000 by the Harry Ransom Humanities Research Center of the University of Texas at Austin. See *Complete Catalogue of the Library of John Quinn* (1924), p. 166; Gordon Lindstrand, 'An Unknown Conrad Manuscript and a Record Price Set for Conrad Typescripts', *Conradiana*, 2 (1969–70), 152.

23 Gosse is silent on this matter; perhaps he preferred to forget his rejection of the first novel of an eventually eminent author, though identified only as 'Kamudi' at this point.

24 *Letters from Joseph Conrad, 1895–1924* ed. Edward Garnett (1928), p. vi.

25 *Letters*, i, 209. The advance copies had arrived no later than the 2nd (*Letters*, i, 208).

26 *Letters*, i, 214. *A Conrad Memorial Library: The Collection of George T. Keating* (1929), p. 13.

27 Frederick R. Karl, 'Joseph Conrad's Literary Theory', *Criticism*, 2 (1960), 333.

28 This change is made in the extant manuscript, perhaps in a hand different from Conrad's.

29 Conrad sent this paragraph to Heinemann on 3 September 1920 (see *LL*, ii, 248).

30 Pp. 25–52; pp. 7–11.

31 'De-civilized', 3rd edn, i (1897), p. 161.

32 Ugo Mursia, 'The True "Discoverer" of Joseph Conrad's Literary Talent and Other Notes on Conrad Biography', *Conradiana* 4 (1972), pp. 9–10.

33 Frank Arthur Mumby, *Publishing and Bookselling* (1949), pp. 290–91.

34 29 April 1895, quoted from Norman Sherry, *Conrad: The Critical Heritage* (1973) (hereafter *CH*), p. 48.

35 Frank Swettenham (1850–1946) wrote a number of books about the Malays.

36 *The Weekly Sun*, 9 June 1895, pp. 1–2.

37 'In a moment . . . from which they sprang' (p. 55). On Louis Becke, see p. 49 below.

38 Gordan, pp. 273–74.

39 The complex printing history of the first English edition suggests Garnett's last statement is virtually, if not literally, faithful to the facts.

40 See, for example, van Marle, 'Jumble of Facts and Fiction', pp. 161–66.

41 This critical treatment draws considerably on earlier writings of Ian Watt, notably '*Almayer's Folly*: Memories and Models', *Mosaic*, 8 (1974), 165–82, and *Conrad in the Nineteenth Century* (1979), pp. 34–67.

42 'Introduction', *The Sisters* (1968), pp. 22–24.

43 On the general influence of the Polish language and literary style on Conrad, see I. P. Pulc, 'The Imprint of Polish on Conrad's Prose', in *Joseph Conrad: Theory and World Fiction*, ed. Wolodymyr T. Zyla and Wendell M. Aycock (1974), pp. 117–39, and Najder, pp. 116–17.

44 *La Folie-Almayer*, trans. Geneviève Seligmann-Lui (1947), p. 8.

45 A. Grove Day, *Louis Becke* (1966), p. 146; *LL*, II, 223; Cedric Watts, *A Preface to Joseph Conrad* (1982), pp. 47–51; Lawrence Graver, *Conrad's Short Fiction* (1969), pp. 10–15; Albert J. Guerard, *Conrad the Novelist* (1958), p. 43n.

46 *Conrad's 'Heart of Darkness': A Critical and Contextual Discussion* (1977), pp. 18–21.

47 Especially by Paul Kirschner, *Conrad: The Psychologist as Artist* (1968), pp. 191–229.

48 Keating, p. 180.

49 At least by 1898: Ford Madox Ford, *Joseph Conrad: A Personal Remembrance* (1924), p. 36.

50 *Notes on Life and Letters*, p. 26.

51 *Joseph Conrad* (1915), p. 77.

52 Richard Curle, *Joseph Conrad: A Study* (1914), p. 188.

53 In 'En relisant *Madame Bovary*' (1950), quoted from *Madame Bovary*, ed. Paul de Man (1965), p. 297.

54 'L'artiste doit être dans son oeuvre comme Dieu dans la création, invisible et toutpuissant; qu'on le sente partout, mais qu'on ne le voie pas' (*Correspondance* [1926–33], IV, 164).

55 Conrad discussed the issue briefly but inconclusively in two letters about the Polish version, commenting that *Almayer's Folly* 'can't exactly be translated into any other language' (Najder, *Letters*, pp. 262, 271).

56 The original is from Amiel's little known collection of poems and prose meditations *Grains de Mil [Grains of Millet]* (1854), p. 196, or his *Fragments d'un journal intime* (1882). Conrad's somewhat less idiomatic version of Amiel's original French suggests he was quoting from memory (see 1:4–5n in the 'Notes'). The context in Amiel obviously establishes the epigraph as decidedly more appropriate to Conrad's youthful romantic reveries than to Almayer's more material aspirations.

57 *A Treatise of Human Nature* (Book I, Part IV, section 6), ed. L. A. Selby-Bigge (1958), p. 261.

58 Miguel de Unamuno, *The Tragic Sense of Life*, trans. J. E. Crawford Flitch (1921), p. 9.

59 'Stendhal Pseudonyme', *L'Oeil vivant* (1961), p. 198.

60 Quoted from 'The Monthly Feuilleton', *Smart Set*, 69 (1922), 144.

61 *Conrad the Novelist*, pp. 72, 81.

62 *Joseph Conrad: Achievement and Decline* (1957), pp. 50–54.

63 'Conrad's *Almayer's Folly*: Structure, Theme, and Critics', *Nineteenth-Century Fiction*, 19 (1964), 29.

64 *The Metaphysics of Darkness* (1971), pp. 37–43.

65 *Conradiana*, 11 (1979), 113.

CHAPTER 3

Conrad criticism and
The Nigger of the 'Narcissus'

So our virtues
Lie in the interpretation of the time
Coriolanus, IV, vii, 49–50

The increasing critical attention of [the 1950s] brought forth in the centenary year of Conrad's birth a tolerably heated literary controversy: Marvin Mudrick's attack on the views of – among others – Robert W. Stallman, in his 'Conrad and the Terms of Modern Criticism' (*Hudson Review*, Autumn, 1954), was answered in the Spring, 1957, issue of the *Kenyon Review* ('Fiction and Its Critics . . .'), an answer which provoked a pretty note of injured innocence from Mudrick in the subsequent issue. Their mutual acerbities may, I think, be welcomed, if only as a reminder that Billingsgate has an ancient title to not the least attractive among the foothills of Helicon; my present concern, however, is with the ultimate grounds of their disagreement and this because it involves several problems of some importance both for Conrad and for our literary criticism in general. It also happens that Mudrick amplified his case against Conrad in the March, 1957, issue of *Nineteenth-Century Fiction* with an essay on *The Nigger of the 'Narcissus'*, a book which was at the same time the subject of a full-scale essay in the *Kenyon Review* by another of the writers attacked by Mudrick, Albert J. Guerard; and since *The Nigger of the 'Narcissus'* has also received considerable attention in the last few years from a representative variety of modern critics, it would seem that our discussion can conveniently be centered on the criticism of Conrad's first masterpiece.

I

In 'The Artist's Conscience and *The Nigger of the "Narcissus"*' Mudrick grants Conrad's mastery of 'sustained passages of description unsurpassed in English fiction'; the storm, for example, and the early presentation of

Wait, are wholly successful, for there Conrad gives us 'an extraordinarily close and convincing observation of the outside of things'. But – alas! – our verbal photographer does not always 'keep his introspection to a respectful minimum'; he has the gall to tell us 'what to think about life, death, and the rest'; and there results 'gross violation of the point of view' and 'unctuous thrilling rhetoric . . . about man's work and the indifferent universe and of course the ubiquitous sea'.

The sardonic irony of that last phrase may give one pause; on an ocean voyage the sea is rather ubiquitous – if you can't bear it *The Nigger of the 'Narcissus'* and, indeed, a good deal of Conrad, is best left alone. True, Stallman can show how impatient Conrad was with being considered a writer of 'sea stories', but this methodological strategy seems suspect – minimizing the importance of overt subject matter so as to ensure for the critic that amplitude of sea-room to which his proud craft has of late become accustomed. One may, indeed, find Mudrick's contrary assertion in his earlier essay that the sea is 'Conrad's only element' less than final and yet salutary in emphasis; in any case his present jaded impatience seems ominously revelatory.

Mudrick's main charges, however, are not easily dismissed. A number of previous critics have drawn attention to the inconsistencies in the point of view of the narration in *The Nigger of the 'Narcissus'*, and to the marked strain of somewhat portentous magniloquence in Conrad's work generally. Mudrick has only given old objections new force, partly by his enviable gift for the memorably damaging phrase, and partly by allotting them a much more decisive significance in his final critical assessment. In some form, I take it, the charges are incontrovertible; but a brief analysis of Conrad's practice and of its historical perspective (the book appeared in 1897) may lead both to a more lenient judgment on the technique of *The Nigger of the 'Narcissus'* and to a clearer realization of some of the problematic implications of our current critical outlook.

Among the 'gross violations of point of view' specified is that whereby the reader directly witnesses the final confrontation of Wait and Donkin, although no one else, of course, was present. Mudrick argues:

though the violation in itself compels no distressing conclusions, it is a more important fact . . . than it would be in other, more loosely organized fiction. From the outset, and through more than half of the novel, Conrad has made us almost nervously sensitive to the point of view as product and evidence of the stereoscopic accuracy of the account: I, a member of the crew, restricted in my opportunities but thoughtful and observant, tell you all that I see.

A brief historical reflection forces us to recognize that it is not really Conrad who has made us 'almost nervously sensitive to the point of view', or, at least, not directly; it is a generation of critics who have developed, partly from Conrad's technique, partly from the theory and practice of Henry James, and even more from its formulation in Percy Lubbock's *The Craft of Fiction* (1921), a theory of point of view in narrative which has been tremendously influential in providing both the critic and novelist with an until-then largely unsuspected key to the technique of fiction. But there is a vast difference between welcoming a valuable refinement of formal awareness and accepting as a matter of prescription the rule that all works of fiction should be told from a single and clearly defined point of view. Yet in the last few years something like this seems to have happened, and one of Mudrick's phrases seems even to bestow on the dogma a quasi-ethical sanction: when he speaks of 'illicit glimpses of the "inside"', doesn't that 'illicit' attempt to convict Conrad of some kind of moral turpitude? To be fair we must at least admit that the charge only became criminal a generation after the fact. And, waiving the chronological defense, hasn't the time come to ask whether Dr. Johnson's point about an earlier formal prescription – the unities of time and place – isn't relevant here? 'Delusion, if delusion be admitted, has no certain limitation': the reader knows that *The Nigger of the 'Narcissus'* is just a story; and Conrad is surely at liberty to turn his pretended narrator into a veritable Pooh-Bah of perscrutation if it will serve his turn.

If it will serve his turn. Interestingly enough, Albert J. Guerard in his fine essay on *The Nigger of the 'Narcissus'* can show very convincingly that the changes in point of view serve a number of turns, and yet there are signs of a lingering embarrassment. He writes, unexceptionably, that, in general, 'the best narrative technique is the one which, however imperfect logically, enlists the author's creative energies and fully explores his subject'; in the present case he finds 'the changes in point-of-view done unobtrusively and with pleasing insouciance', and shows how they mirror the story's 'general movement from isolation to solidarity to poignant separation'. However, when Guerard comes to another kind of change in Conrad's method of reporting – the shift from objective reporting to lofty generalization – he comments that it is one of the 'incorrigible necessities of the early Conrad', and in that 'incorrigible' concedes that such variations in narrative strategy are indisputably literary offenses, although he is prepared to be good-tempered about it.

But Guerard's earlier position is surely equally applicable here; for both kinds of change in Conrad's point of view, not only those concerning the identity of the presumed narrator but also those concerning his varying tone and attitude toward what he is narrating, are closely related responses to the rather complicated imperatives of Conrad's subject as it develops. If Conrad had wholly restricted himself to the mind of one individual narrator, he would have had to expend a great deal of mechanical artifice – the kind of dexterous literary engineering later exhibited in *Chance* – in arranging for them to be plausibly visible: but this particularization of the point of view could only have been achieved at the expense of what is probably Conrad's supreme objective in *The Nigger of the 'Narcissus'*; the continual and immediate presence of an individualized narrator, sleeping in a certain bunk, member of a certain watch, caught up in a particular set of past and present circumstances, could not but deflect our attention from the book's real protagonist – the ship and its crew. So protean a protagonist could be fully observed only from a shifting point of view: sometimes hovering above the deck, seeing the ship as a whole; sometimes infinitely distant, setting one brief human effort against the widest vistas of time and space, of sea and history; occasionally engaging us in a supreme act of immediate participation, as when the narrator becomes identified with one of the five 'wes' who rescue Wait; and finally involving us in the pathos of separation, when the narrator becomes an 'I' to pronounce the book's closing valediction to the crew as they disperse.

The terms of this valediction, indeed, seem to emphasize how well advised Conrad was not to make his narrator too immediate a person to the reader. In general, as soon as we feel that the author's reflections are issuing from an individual character we naturally expect them to be expressed in an appropriate personal vernacular; and this either sets severe limits on the range of reflection, or creates an almost insoluble stylistic problem. Both difficulties, and especially the second, obtrude in the last paragraph of *The Nigger of the 'Narcissus'*; for example when Conrad writes: 'Haven't we, together and upon the immortal sea, wrung out a meaning from our sinful lives?' The particularized individual cannot – in prose, at least, and since the rise of realism – be both microcosm and macrocosm without some kind of apparent inflation; such was the problem which the Irish dramatists, trying to escape from the 'joyless and pallid words' of Ibsen and Zola, had to face; and in this moment-ary anticipation of the very note of Synge, Conrad surely reveals how inappropriate such quasi-colloquial elevation was for his purposes.

The intrusiveness of the 'I' narrator, who only becomes evident in the last two paragraphs of *The Nigger of the 'Narcissus'*, thus underlines the book's need for a variable narrative angle easily adjustable to different kinds of vision and comment. Until then, I think, we can find many logical contradictions in Conrad's manipulations of point of view, but not, unless our critical preconceptions are allowed to dominate our literary perceptions, any consequent failure in narrative command; and we should perhaps conclude that E. M. Forster was in the main right, when he insisted, in *Aspects of the Novel*, that 'the whole intricate question . . . resolves itself . . . into the power of the writer to bounce the reader into accepting what he says'.

The shifting point of view in *The Nigger of the 'Narcissus'*, then, enacts the varying aspects of its subject; in a wider sense, it may be said to enact the reasons for Conrad's greatness: the fact that he was a seaman but not only a seaman, that he was able to convey, not only the immediacies of his subject, but their perspective in the whole tradition of civilization. The actual prose in which some of the loftier elements of this perspective are conveyed, however, is a good deal more grandiloquent than we can today happily stomach. As an example, we may take a well-known passage which Mudrick quotes as his clinching specimen of Conrad's 'unctuous thrilling rhetoric', the opening of the fourth chapter:

On men reprieved by its disdainful mercy, the immortal sea confers in its justice the full privilege of desired unrest. Through the perfect wisdom of its grace they are not permitted to meditate at ease upon the complicated and acrid savour of existence [, lest they should remember and, perchance, regret the reward of a cup of inspiring bitterness, tasted so often, and so often withdrawn from before their stiffening but reluctant lips]. They must without pause justify their life to the eternal pity that commands toil to be hard and unceasing, from sunrise to sunset, from sunset to sunrise: till the weary succession of nights and days tainted by the obstinate clamor of sages, demanding bliss and an empty heaven, is redeemed at last by the vast silence of pain and labour, by the dumb fear and the dumb courage of men obscure, forgetful, and enduring.

Conrad himself, apparently, was uneasy about some of this, and deleted the passage in brackets when revising for the collected edition some twenty years after. He had no doubt become more aware, and more critical, of the influence of the stylistic aims of French romanticism, the only specific literary influence on his work which he admitted. The passage is, in part, an attempt to write 'la belle page' – to achieve the grandiose richness of verbal and rhythmic suggestion found, for example, in Victor Hugo's *Les Travailleurs de la Mer*; and it can, therefore, if we wish, be explained away in terms of a literary indebtedness which Conrad later outgrew.

But there are other, perhaps more interesting, certainly more contemporary, issues raised by the historical perspective of the passage.

We have today an unprecedented distrust of the purple passage; the color has been banned from the literary spectrum, and 'poetic prose' has become a term of abuse in the general critical vocabulary, including Mudrick's. Since T. E. Hulme, at least, we have demanded in poetry – and, *a fortiori*, in prose – tautness of rhythm, hardness of outline, exactness of diction; we have insisted that every word, every rhythmical inflection, every rhetorical device, shall contribute to the organic unity of the whole work, shall not exist for its local effect. Mudrick takes comment on the passage to be superfluous, but the grounds of his objection are, I take it, somewhat along these lines. So, indeed are mine, I suppose. At least I can hardly read the passage, or others in Conrad like it, without momentary qualms ('Should I let myself go and enjoy it? No, in real life relaxing's fine, but in literature? . . . Think of Leavis. . . .'); and yet, if we consider the Hulmean principle seriously, isn't the cost more than we are prepared to pay?

To begin with, a rather large series of literary rejections may be involved; not only Hugo and Pater and much of Flaubert but also a good deal of Proust and Joyce – not only the *Portrait* but much of *Ulysses* – Molly Bloom's reverie, for example. There are countless passages in the greatest literature which, though no doubt related by subject and theme to the rest of the narrative, are essentially set-pieces, developed largely as autonomous rhetorical units; and in a good many of them every device of sound and sense is, as in Conrad, being used mainly to induce feelings of rather vague exaltation. Nor is it only a matter of the illustriousness of the precedents; they may have valid literary justification. For, although we are no doubt right to reject de Musset's romantic certitude that our most beautiful feelings are our saddest, is there any more justification for the antiromantic prescription that our deepest or most complicated feelings – so often vague and penumbral – can and should be expressed through clear images? And why in images at all? How can we reconcile the symbolist rejection of logic and conceptualization with the fact that our minds often work by partial and groping movements toward conceptualization and logical ordering? More specifically, isn't it carrying the demand for imagistic particularity too far to assert that in literature every part of the picture must be in clear focus? Can we not, on the contrary, assert that Conrad, a preeminently pictorial writer, requires, on occasion, a chiaroscuro effect between one series of concretely detailed presentations and another? Such certainly is the way this passage – and many others of a similar kind – are disposed in *The Nigger of the 'Narcissus'*: we get a relief from the immediate image, from the particularities of time and space, and this, by contrast, both brings out these particularities more clearly and at the same time reminds us that there are other less definite and yet equally real dimensions of existence.

It is probably because these less definite dimensions cannot be made real visually that Conrad's style changes abruptly and at once evokes analogies that are musical rather than pictorial. In the Preface to *The Nigger of the 'Narcissus'* he wrote that one of his aims was to approach 'the magic suggestiveness of music'; and though nowadays we are very suspicious of 'word music', there may in this case at least be something in Coleridge's apparently outrageous assertion that 'a sentence which sounds pleasing always has a meaning which is deep and good'. Conrad's particular sentences here certainly suggested a meaning not lacking in depth or goodness to one of the greatest practitioners of the prose poem; for this is one of the passages by which Virginia Woolf, in 'Mr. Conrad: A Conversation' (*The Captain's Death Bed*), exemplifies her assertion that in Conrad's prose 'the beauty of surface has always a fibre of morality within'. She goes on, 'I seem to see each of the sentences . . . advancing with resolute bearing and a calm which they have won in strenuous conflict, against the forces of falsehood, sentimentality, and slovenliness'; and so brings us, at long last, away from this rather inconclusive review of some of the theoretical issues raised by the passage by forcing us to ask whether the relation of form and content in the passage is as she suggests.

To make full sense of its content we must, of course, grant Conrad the benefit of the kind of flexible and cooperative interpretation we are accustomed to give poetry, allow him his steady reliance on ironic, elliptical, and paradoxical, personification. We must accept, for example, the dependence of the paradox of 'desired unrest' upon an implicit assertion by the narrator that 'life', which is what men literally 'desire', is in fact always 'unrest'; we must also accept the personifications of the sea's 'mercy' and 'grace' as necessary to prepare for the final modulation of 'the eternal pity', where the sea's order is equated with God's; and we must excuse the somewhat obscure quality of the irony at God's supposedly merciful attributes and at the 'empty heaven' because it is evident that Conrad wants to achieve his juxtaposition of religious illusions against the only redemptive power which he acknowledges, 'the vast silence of pain and labour', without undermining the traditional sort of literary theism on which the passage's elevation of tone in part depends.

The gnomic compression, the largeness of reference, the latent irony, all suggest a familiar literary analogue, the Greek chorus: and the formal qualities of the passage offer striking confirmation. The Greek chorus's lofty and impersonal assertion of the general dramatic theme depends for its distinctive effect on the impact, at a point of rest in the action, of a plurality of voices and an intensified musicality: a plurality of voices, not an individualized narrator, because the function of a chorus in general, as of Conrad's in particular, is to achieve what Yeats called 'emotion of multitude', which is difficult to achieve through a wholly naturalist technique for the presentation of reality; an intensified musicality because it emphasizes the requisite impersonal urgency, as in the present case Conrad's tired and yet hieratic emphasis on repetition and balance of sound and rhythm is itself the formal expression of his controlled exaltation at the prospect of the laborious but triumphant monotony offered by the endless tradition of human effort. The placing and the assertion of the passage are equally choric in nature, for Conrad seizes a moment of rest between two contrasted phases of the crew's exertion to remind us that, contrary to their longings and to what any sentimental view of existence would lead us to hope, man's greatness, such as it is, has no reward in this life or the next, and is a product only of the unending confrontation of their environment by the successive human generations, a confrontation that is unsought and yet obligatory, although 'the forces of falsehood, sentimentality, and slovenliness' seek perpetually to confuse, defer, or evade its claims.

II

Mudrick's denigration of *The Nigger of the 'Narcissus'* on the grounds of Conrad's rhetorical attitudinizing and of his use of point of view follows two of the major emphases of our modern criticism of fiction; and as we shall see his operative premises are typical in much else. But we must not overlook the fact that Mudrick, who has cast himself as the spectral Mr Jones interrupting the feast celebrating Conrad's victory over the critics, is also possessed of a marked cannibalistic trait: he cannot abide the enthusiasm of his confreres for the 'modish clues of myth, metaphor, symbol, etc.' In his earlier essay on Conrad, Stallman's reading of 'The

Secret Sharer' was his main target; but he now finds *The Nigger of the 'Narcissus'* subject to the same general charge: a heavy overemphasis on 'catch-all' and 'claptrap' symbolism which only a naive predisposition for that sort of thing could possibly render acceptable.

That many critics have found a clue to *The Nigger of the 'Narcissus'* in a unifying symbolic structure is certainly true. James E. Miller, for example, in his '*The Nigger of the "Narcissus"*: A Reexamination' (*PLMA*, December, 1951), sees 'James Wait and the sea as symbols of death and life; Singleton and Donkin as symbols of opposed attitudes toward death and life'; the other members of the crew hesitate whether to follow the true knowledge of Singleton or the deceptions offered by Donkin; and the conflict is only concluded when they unanimously reject Donkin's offer of a drink after being paid-off – 'the crew has passed from a diversity based on ignorance through a false unity based on a lie perpetrated by Donkin, to, finally, the true "knot" of solidarity based on genuine insight into the meaning of life and death'.

Miller's analysis is, of course, presented as a confessedly simplified paradigm and I have had to simplify it further; his scheme certainly has the merit of drawing our attention to a certain number of important interrelationships which we might not have noticed: but the whole conception of a neat allegorical drama surely does violence to the patent diversity of Conrad's narrative; this may be the figure in one of the carpets but what of the many other richly furnished floors? Surely no one would have seized upon this particular pattern if he had not, in the first place, felt sure that there must be some such neat symbolic plot waiting to be discovered, and in the second, felt justified in giving decisive interpretative priority to a few selected details of character and incident which could be made to support it?

Essentially the same method – *reductio ad symbolum* – appears in Robert F. Haugh's 'Death and Consequences: Joseph Conrad's Attitude Toward Fate' (*University of Kansas City Review*, Spring, 1952). Briefly, from the muster, in which they each challenge the order of the ship, both Donkin and Wait are seen as 'emissaries of darkness and disorder, Conrad's synonyms for evil'. Donkin's level is the overt, the social, while Wait's is the religious; the book as a whole dramatizes 'all of the elements in the human solidarity of Conrad's world, arrayed against those forces which would destroy them', with Wait the deeper menace since he 'somehow' comes to stand for the crew's 'own darker natures'. This analysis seems a good deal closer to our sense of the book's chief concerns, and in the main Haugh applies it convincingly; but as soon as the stress shifts from interpretative analytic summary to the attribution of specifically symbolic meanings to characters and incidents doubts begin to arise. Wait may be 'a moral catalyst . . . who brings death aboard ship in many ways', but is he himself evil? And isn't it forcing the facts to say that when, after rescuing Wait, the crew return to the deck and find that 'never before had the gale seemed to us more furious', this is somehow related to Wait's influence which has 'undone . . . their courage', rather than to the material fact that, being on deck again, they are more exposed to the weather?

Vernon Young's 'Trial by Water: Joseph Conrad's *The Nigger of the "Narcissus"*' (*Accent*, Spring, 1952) reveals a very Galahad of the symbol. If the ship plunges 'on to her *port* side', a parenthetic gloss at once nautical and symbolic reminds us that this is 'the left, or sinister, side'; and if Conrad compares the *Narcissus* and her tug to a white pyramid and an aquatic beetle, 'the antithesis . . . is unquestionably a sidelong glance at the Egyptian figure of the pyramid, prime-symbol of direction and sun-worship, and of the scarab, symbol of creative energy'. It will serve us nothing to protest, for example, that this last image is patently visual, for we are in the presence of a Faith. In Young – as in many other of the more symbolically inclined critics – that faith is of the Jungian persuasion; and if I mention that I believe Jung to be a latter-day example of the same arrogant credulity which has given us astrology, the British Israelites, and the Baconian fringe, it is only because it seems to me that the kind of thinking exhibited there is exactly analogous to that in some kinds of literary symbol hunting: everything 'proves x' because 'proves' and 'x' are defined with such accommodating tolerance – the terms of argument do not of their nature admit either of proof or of disproof.

Most of Young's essay, I must in fairness add, is concerned with elucidating a symbolic structure of a much less sectarian tendency. In its general view it is fairly similar to that of Haugh, though somewhat more schematically presented: Wait, for example, is defined as 'serv[ing] a purpose comparable to that of El Negro in Melville's *Benito Cereno*: he is the spirit of blackness, archetype of unknown forces from the depths', and the mysterious adjuration of his presence 'all but deprives the crew of their will to live'. Allistoun and Singleton, on the other hand, stand for the superego, and they, together with Podmore, 'discover, behind the mask of a dying shirker, the infrahuman visage of the Satanic'.

Wait's portentous first appearance, and the way he later becomes the chief protagonist round whom the actions and the attitudes of the crew revolve, these certainly justify our impulse to look for some hidden significance in him. Some early readers no doubt thought the same, for in the 1914 note 'To My Readers in America' Conrad wrote the very explicit denial: 'But in the book [Wait] is nothing; he is merely the centre of the ship's collective psychology and the pivot of the action.' If we set aside this disclaimer, as Young specifically (and scornfully) does, it should surely be only for the most imperative reasons; and those offered seem to be based upon the loosest kind of metaphorical extension.

Both Vernon Young and Albert Guerard make Wait's blackness their starting point, and this leads them to parallels in *Benito Cereno* and *Heart of Darkness*. Yet it is hardly necessary to adduce Conrad's antipathy to Melville to cast doubts on the former analogy: Conrad does not, in Melville's sense, believe in any absolute or transcendental 'evil', and his Negro has not done any. As for the *Heart of Darkness* parallel, it is surely suspicious that Young should apply the color metaphor literally, and thus find his analogy in the 'barbarous and superb woman', while Guerard, more metaphorical, plumps for Kurtz: in any case the native woman, quite unlike Wait, is conspicuous for her heroic resolution, while there seems to be little in common between Wait and Kurtz except that they are tall, proud, have African associations, are rescued with difficulty, and die painfully. Nor is the general metaphorical implication – Guerard's statement that Wait 'comes in some sense to represent our human "blackness"' – particularly convincing. Wait, we know, was based on an actual Negro, and his color offered Conrad a whole series of valuable dramatic oppositions. These are made full use of in Wait's first appearance, where his color at once establishes his difference, his mystery, his threat: yet later in the book the color issue becomes relatively unimportant; the crew assimilates him to their group with the jocular nickname of 'Snowball'; only Donkin makes a serious issue of Wait's color, calling him 'a black-faced swine'; and if the narrator's own first description ends with the phrase 'the tragic, the mysterious, the repulsive mask of a nigger's soul' we must remember that he is here only the spokesman of the first general and primarily visual reaction, that the color is after all 'a mask', and that there is no suggestion later that the soul behind it is black.

Deferring the question of what James Wait's secret is – if any – we must surely ask why, in the absence of any convincing internal evidence or of any problem so intractable as to make recourse to extravagant hypothesis obligatory, critics capable of the perceptive felicities of Young and Guerard, to name only two, should try so hard (though not, as my present concern may inadvertently have led me to suggest, all or even most of the time) to discover some sort of occult purport in what is, on the face of it, a rich and complex but by no means equivocal narrative? More generally, why have the critics of the last decade or so put such emphasis on finding esoteric symbols? In the phrase which the hero of Kingsley Amis's *That Uncertain Feeling* uses in another connection, I can see why the critics like them, but why should they like them *so much*?

The superstition and obscurantism of our time, reflected, for example, in Young's indignation at Conrad's 'fear of wholesale commitment to the irrational', will no doubt explain something, as I have already suggested; but what is perhaps more decisive is the prestige with which literary criticism is now invested. It is no longer the poet, but the critic who typically functions as the romantic seer; and a seer, of course, is someone who sees what isn't there, or at least has never been seen before. This role seems to enforce a no-doubt unconscious operative strategy along the following lines: a little like the bibliophile who is too proud to deal with anything but first editions, the critic feels his status as seer jeopardized unless he can demonstrate that he saw the book first, or at least that his reading of it is the first *real* one; his version must therefore be noticeably different from any likely previous one; and since certain kinds of symbolic interpretation, unlike the emperor's clothes, are incapable of empirical proof or disproof, they are laid under contribution as offering the easiest – and safest – means toward achieving the desired novelty of insight.

This is no doubt an unfair way of putting it; and in any case such pressures would probably have insufficient force were they not complemented by the obvious fact that the novel's length makes it impossible for the critic's analysis to approach the relative completeness which that of some short poems can attain. Given the impossibility of a full account, and the somewhat pedestrian tendency of the traditional summarizing of plot and character, the discovery of some inclusive symbolic configuration appears as the readiest way to combine the imposed brevity and the solicited originality.

In the case of Conrad, it is true, such interpretations seem to find some warrant from Conrad's own statement that 'All the great creations of literature have been symbolic.' The question, obviously, is 'Symbolic in what sense?' and since the word 'symbol' can be properly used in too many ways, it may clarify the discussion to suggest a set of rather ugly neologisms for the different kinds of literary symbolism that are involved in the present discussion.

The basic problem is to determine the kind of relationship between the literary symbol and its referent, between the narrative vehicle and its imputed larger tenor; most important, perhaps, are the distances between them and the basis on which the mutual rapport is ascribed. In the kind of symbolic interpretation I have been discussing, the distance between the literary object and the symbolic meaning ascribed to it is rather great: and so I would describe making Wait a symbol of evil, darkness or Satan, an example of *heterophoric* interpretation; that is, it carries us to *another* meaning, it takes us *beyond* any demonstrable connection between the literary object and the symbolic meaning given it.

Many examples of symbolic interpretation differ from this, however, in that not only is the distance between literary object and imputed meaning relatively great, but the rapport is established, not through taking a particular quality in the literary object very far, but through referring the literary object to some other system of knowledge which it would not normally be thought to invoke. Young's interpretation of the pyramid and the scarab would be of this kind, and since it depends upon an allusion to a specific body of mythical, religious or literary knowledge, it could be called a *mythophor*: *mythophor* would be a variety of *heterophor*, since it makes the literary object stand for something very distant from it, but the correlation would depend upon a reference to a certain story or, in the Greek sense, myth; another example of this would be Guerard's drawing the parallel between Wait and the legend of Jonah.

One particular case of *mythophor* seems to require some special term because it is common and raises peculiar problems – that case in which the body of knowledge invoked is one of the depth-psychologies: this subdivision of *mythophor* could be called *cryptophor*, since it depends upon analogies which Freud and Jung agree to be hidden and unconscious; one example would be when Guerard equates the rescuing of Wait from his confinement during the storm with a 'compulsive psychic descent', or when he toys briefly with the scene's 'psychic geography', proposing that the Finn Wamibo figures as the 'savage *superego*' to Wait's *id*.

Heterophor in general tends toward allegory. Guerard, for example, although he jests at the fashion for 'analysis of "cabalistic intent"' and cautions us against reading Conrad as an allegorical writer, insisting that the overt subject is also the real subject, nevertheless argues for a series of superimposed *heterophoric* significances which are essentially of the same allegorical kind as may justly be imputed to the Negro in Melville's *Benito Cereno*. I do not think that Conrad's work is symbolic in this way; even less is it *mythophoric* or *cryptophoric*. To make it so, indeed, is surely to emphasize novelty at the expense of truth; and the literary effect of such interpretation is to reduce what Conrad actually created to a mere illustration – something both secondary and – as Mudrick would argue – second-rate. For all kinds of *heterophoric* interpretation inevitably disregard the great bulk of the concrete details of character and incident in a literary work: just as T. S. Eliot's allegorical concern in *The Family Reunion*, for example, prevents us from inspecting the psychology and the dynamics of Harry's wife's death – did she fall or was she pushed? – so a *heterophoric* interpreter of Wait will be disinclined to scrutinize the manifest developing pattern of his character and actions. The details of these latter, indeed, will seem otiose compared to the few elements which, on *a priori* grounds, have been selected as of primary importance; and so Young can write, 'Fearful of overstressing the subaqueous world of the underconsciousness, the symbol-producing level of the psyche which, in fact, was the most dependable source of his inspiration, Conrad overloaded his mundane treatment of the crew.'

To demur from Guerard's statement that, on top of the various more obvious levels of narrative statement, Conrad imposed 'an audacious symbolic pattern', is not to deny that *The Nigger of the 'Narcissus'* is in many ways symbolic. Its symbolism, however, seems to me to be of another kind. It works, characteristically, by natural extension of the implications of the narrative content, and retains a consistent closeness to it; for this the term *homeophor* seems appropriate, suggesting as it does, 'carrying *something similar*' rather than, as with *heterophor*, 'carrying *something else*'. When Guerard makes the parallel of the journey of the *Narcissus* and the age-old theme of the pilgrimage, his interpretation, if allowed, and at some level of generality it surely must be, would be *homeophoric* because ships and pilgrimages, to those who know anything of them, must suggest small human communities united for the purpose of a single journey.

The terms proposed are no doubt grotesque; the distinctions on which they are based would no doubt often prove difficult to apply; and considered against the complexity of the problem and the richness of its literature, the brevity of their exposition may appear unpardonable; but if they have made more manageable the problem of what kind of symbolic writer Conrad is, and, perhaps, suggested the need for further discriminations in this general area, they will have served their turn. It only remains now to show, very briefly, how Conrad's method in *The*

Nigger of the 'Narcissus' is symbolic in a *homeophoric* way, working through a very accessible extension of the implications of character and event. This task, however, is complicated by the need to meet the charges against Conrad's use of symbolism made by Mudrick; for, believing that, for the novelist as well as for the critic, emphasis on symbolism tends to be at the expense of character and action which, surely rightly, he takes to be the essential components of fiction, Mudrick proceeds to argue that, in *The Nigger of the 'Narcissus'*, Conrad did not 'aim at elaborating or examining character and incident beyond the static, repetitive point of illustration and symbol'. We must therefore attempt to show, not only that Conrad's symbolism is of a very exoteric kind, but that it does not have these damaging consequences for his presentation of character and incident.

III

Mudrick gives Conrad's early presentation of Wait two eloquent and appreciative paragraphs, but he finds the later treatment of him disappointing. It is true that the first commanding air of mystery slowly evaporates as we see Wait more closely: his curious pride, it appears, is merely the defense of an alien who is aboard only because, as he tells Baker, 'I must live till I die – mustn't I?'; and his climactic confrontations with Donkin, Podmore, and Allistoun give increasingly clear illumination to the ordinariness of his secret, his unacknowledged terror of approaching death. These later developments undoubtedly have a deflating effect, and if we see Wait as an emissary from some spiritual chamber of horrors, they must seem mistaken; but the cumulative anticlimax can also be seen as an essential part of the book's meaning; it reveals that the influence Wait exercises on the crew is an irrational projection of their own dangerous fears and weaknesses; to put it in our terms, it asserts, eventually, that contrary to possible earlier expectation, Wait is not a *heterophor*; order and disorder on the *Narcissus* are temporary, contingent, man-made; behind the mysterious and menacing authority of a St Kitts' Negro there is only a common human predicament; Wait is a symbol, not of death but of the fear of death, and therefore, more widely, of the universal human reluctance to face those most universal agents of anticlimax, the facts; and the facts, as always, find him out.

Mudrick, perhaps, mistook Wait for a *heterophor* and then found, as in that case I think one must, that Conrad didn't come through; but his disappointment has other grounds, notably that 'there is no development and nothing mobile or unexpected' in the novel. This charge seems, specifically, to overlook or to reject the actions which focus round Wait in the fourth chapter; for when Mudrick writes that 'Only Donkin – the gutter creature – "sees through" Wait' he is implicitly denying the picture of the case that is presented there. Donkin is no doubt the only person who most consistently sees Wait as an infuriatingly successful 'evader of responsibility'; but everyone else has some such suspicions, and the matter is obviously not so simple. No malingerer is ever wholly well, even if at times he thinks so; Wait's own agonizing divisions and contradictions about his condition seem a psychologically convincing reaction to all the elements in his situation; and his puzzling gratification at Donkin's insults is surely an expression of the desperation of his wish to believe that Donkin really has 'seen through' him.

Actually, of course, only one man – Allistoun – can be said to 'see through' Wait, as we realize in the scene when, after Podmore has told Wait that he is 'as good as dead already', and Wait, supported by the crew, has urged that he be allowed to return to duty, Allistoun mystifies and outrages everyone by his brusque refusal – 'There's nothing the matter with you, but you chose to lie-up to please yourself – and now you shall lie-up to please me.' As Allistoun explains later to the mates, it was a momentary impulse of sympathetic insight into Wait '. . . three parts dead and so scared' which urged him to enact a form of Ibsen's beneficent lie by shielding him from the deception of his own wishful illusions, and letting 'him go out in his own way'.

That it is the most total act of sympathy for Wait which precipitates the mutiny is surely a 'development' both 'mobile and unexpected', and it dramatizes one of the general themes in *The Nigger of the 'Narcissus'* which is far from commonplace: pity, emotional identification with others, as an active danger to society. Nor is the treatment of the theme by any means banal; for Conrad shows that pity, though dangerous, is also a condition of human decency, by juxtaposing the Allistoun scene between two others where Wait is subjected to the cruelty of two kinds of extreme and therefore pitiless egoism: to complete the picture, we must bear in mind the qualifications implied both in the subsequent scene where Donkin brutally satisfies his malice and cupidity by tormenting Wait to his death with fiendish cruelty, and in the earlier interview where the pious Podmore, a 'conceited saint unable to forget his glorious reward . . . prayerfully divests himself of his humanity' and terrifies Wait with visions of imminent hell-fire.

Symbolically, Conrad seems to be saying that although pitilessness is characteristic of the selfish, yet the increasing sensitiveness to the sufferings of others which civilization brings necessarily poses grave problems of control for the individual and for society; and by making Singleton not so much unsympathetic as unaware of Wait's suffering he may be thought to have reminded us that the older and less humanitarian order was not so easily deflected from its collective purpose. Such a reading can be advanced with considerable confidence, since, as is necessarily the case with *homeophoric* extension, it is arrived at merely by extracting a more generally applicable statement from the manifest implications of particular characters and actions; and the reading could easily be supported, both by showing how the juxtaposition of certain episodes implies such a meaning, and by pointing out various explicit comments on the softening, refining and corrupting effects of pity, comments which authorize the assumption that any events which raise such issues were designed to have representative significance.

This is not to say that Allistoun, Wait, and the rest are to be regarded primarily as symbols of these attitudes and values, and I do not think that Mudrick would regard them as 'elementary emblems of what they are intended to demonstrate' unless his own criteria, both of literary character in general, and of what is desirable to demonstrate, were so contrary to Conrad's.

It is undeniable that Conrad does not give us here, nor, typically, anywhere, the kind of psychological exploration focused on the individual sensibility in the manner of James or Proust: but there is surely some middle ground between this and mere 'elementary emblems'. If one assumes that Conrad's main objective is the ship – its voyage and its society – it is evident that, in what is little more than a long short story, not all its complement – twenty-six individuals – can possibly be particularized; nor, on the other hand, can any two or three of them be fully treated without disturbing the emphasis, which must be on the social group rather than the individual. It is inevitable that some characters of marginal importance should be portrayed with something approaching caricature – Belfast with his hypertonic Irish sensibility, Wamibo with his inarticulate frenzies of participation; and it would obviously be very unsettling to introduce characters who were flagrantly untypical of their setting. Mudrick takes exception to the stereotyped banality of the gentlemanly Creighton's daydreams – 'a girl in a clear dress, smiling under a sunshade . . . stepping out of the tender sky'; and one hastens to concede that Creighton would be a more interesting character if he spent all his time at sea counting the days until he could have another stab at Kierkegaard; but what would that do to the book?

Nowadays we can swallow everything except the obvious; and one of the reasons that Mudrick singles out this particular passage for reprobation is probably that he shares our terror of whatever may seem cliché. He finds cliché, for example, when Wait talks to Donkin about his 'Canton Street girl . . . cooks oysters just as I like', commenting that 'Wait provided with the white man's conventional notion of the black man's secret desires' is less convincing 'personally and symbolically' than 'Wait with no background' at all, as at the beginning. But the girl is mentioned in a context which gives Wait just the right kind of tawdry and hopeless pathos: off the Azores, with the crew talking of the joys of London, Wait naturally thinks of the London girl he will never see; the sick man's notorious dream of food (and rations are short) explains the oysters; while the fact that the remark is addressed to Donkin makes it Wait's last – and of course unavailing – effort to achieve some sort of triumph over the one man on the ship he has been unable to soften or impress.

Mudrick, both here and elsewhere, seems to me to have imported the cliché, and for two reasons: there is the already noted demand for a degree of individualization which is impossible and undesirable in many cases, including the present; and there is exactly the same fastidious rejection of the commonplace which, under the direction of other predispositions, causes the critics he attacks to coax esoteric symbols into the text. Both Mudrick's tendencies, of course, are closely related to his earlier demand for the sharpest possible definition in prose and in point of view: all his literary criteria, in fact, have total individualization as their basic premise.

His discussion of the moral and social dimensions of *The Nigger of the 'Narcissus'* is informed with the equivalent premise, expressed as ethical and political nonconformity, and it operates with the same rude vigor. Conrad's 'metaphysical and moral scheme' is based on the exaltation of the 'grim-jawed, nerveless, reticent men in charge'; they inhabit 'a hand-me-down "aristocratic" universe in which everybody in charge deserves to be and everybody else had better jump'; and if we examine them, 'all we find beneath the gritty authoritative British exterior is a collection of soft-headed Anglophilic clichés'. We have seen that Allistoun in one crucial episode, at least, is far from nerveless, and that there are some elements in the book which are neither soft-headed nor commonplace; yet to exemplify and analyze further, or to attempt to assess how severe a disablement is involved in being an Anglophile, would probably be little to the purpose. For we are in the presence of a total incompatibility: Conrad's social and political attitudes, and Mudrick's diametrically opposed convictions.

Conrad, of course, was conservative in many ways: yet surely one can be, like Donkin, Mudrick – or myself –, 'a votary of change' and still find that Conrad's picture of society commands respect. Even his presentation of the class issue, for example, has considerable objectivity: the hardships and the miserable economic rewards of the crew are not minimized, and we are given their cynical discussion of 'the characteristics of a gentleman'; among the officers, Allistoun, with his 'old red muffler' and his 'nightshirt fluttering like a flag' is not a hero but a prisoner of the class to which his command has brought him, as we see when his smart wife arrives to collect him at the dockside; and our last picture of the ship shows the first mate, Baker, reflecting that, unlike Creighton with his 'swell friends', he will never get a command. In any case, we can hardly make Conrad responsible for the fact that no ship was ever successfully sailed democratically; and we must also admit that, with all its rigidities and injustices, the *Narcissus* is a community with a genuine and in some ways egalitarian set of reciprocities: for the most part everyone on it knows and sees and wants the same things; while the class antipathy is qualified by the crew's recognition, in Allistoun or Baker, that individuals who in themselves are no way special or even particularly likeable can be wholly admirable and necessary in the performance of their roles. This dichotomy, of course, is an essential condition of Conrad's presentation of his characters: with the significant exceptions of Donkin and Wait, their function in one sense usurps their individuality but in another it endows them with heroic stature.

All these connections and contradictions, operating within a very restricted setting, gave Conrad his opportunity for a compressed drama which could, in part, be representative of society at large. The general values which emerge are on the whole traditional, if not authoritarian; but at least they are real values, and they are really there. If George Orwell could detect in Conrad 'a sort of grown-upness and political understanding which would have been almost impossible to a native English writer at that time', it is surely because, as a foreigner, Conrad could be more objective about a social order which, for all its many faults, was in some ways admirable and rewarding; while as an exile from Poland he had cause to be presciently responsive to the existence of any viable social order at all.

Mudrick's case against Conrad, then, is largely the result of the conjunction of two value systems, neither of which happens to favor *The Nigger of the 'Narcissus'*. On the one hand he takes to their logical conclusion a rather complete set of modern critical assumptions – the pieties of point of view, of prosy-prose, of authorial reticence about character and meaning, of extreme fastidiousness about permitted attitudes and endorsements; on the other he lets loose a teeming menagerie of personal *bêtes noires*, ranging from symbolism, the sea, and the stiff upper-lip to hierarchical authorities, parvenus, and Anglophiles. Mudrick had a very nice irony in 'Conrad and the Terms of Modern Criticism' about how, in our too perceptive times, 'nose to nose, critic confronts writer and, astonished, discovers himself'; one could find striking confirmation both of this thesis and of the *cryptophoric* significance of proper names by considering how vivid an image of Mudrick was reflected when he came nose to nose with Narcissus.

As for Conrad, we must conclude, I think, that Mudrick's impatient intransigence forces one to realize, both by its palpable hits and by what I have tried to chalk up as its misses, how *The Nigger of the 'Narcissus'* is, in a number of ways, not at all the answer to our modern critical prayer. No amount of symbol-juggling will or should divert us from seeing that there is an important Romantic and Victorian element in his work; and, although Conrad was, of course, in many ways a precursor of the modern movement in fiction, his deepest originality and perhaps the chief unacknowledged cause of his popularity today, derives from an attitude to his society, both as subject and as audience, which has been shared by no other great writer of our century. Many things in himself, his life and his times, gave him as deep a sense of the modern alienation as any other of our great exiled and isolated writers; and yet Conrad's most vigorous energies were turned away from the ever-increasing separateness of the individual and towards discovering values and attitudes and ways of living and writing which he could respect and yet which were, or could be, widely shared. Mudrick has more than reminded us of the occasional cost in emphasis, repetition, and cliché, but no criticism has yet adequately assessed what Conrad gave in exchange. His aim – 'to make you see' – has often been quoted: but there has been less emphasis on how Conrad specified that the objects in the 'presented vision' should be such as to 'awaken in the hearts of the beholders that feeling of unavoidable solidarity; of the solidarity in mysterious origin, in toil, in joy, in hope, in uncertain fate, which binds men to each other and all mankind to the visible world'. In the centrality of his ultimate purpose Conrad is akin to Wordsworth; and if he expresses it grandiloquently, he at least does not, in the Arnoldian phrase, give us the grand word without the grand thing.

The third chapter of *The Nigger of the 'Narcissus'*, for example, is not merely a magnificent evocation of a storm at sea; it is a sequence of unequaled enactments of the theme of solidarity. It begins as we experience gratitude for the efforts of the crew to save Wait, or of Podmore, incredibly, to produce coffee; and it achieves its final resonance in the famous ending when, after long forgetting him, our eyes are turned to Singleton at the wheel, and we are told, simply, that, after thirty hours, 'he steered with care.' It is the climactic recognition of our utter and yet often forgotten dependence, night and day, by sea and by land, on the labors of others; and by the kind of cross reference of attitudes which is Conrad's most characteristic way of achieving a symbolic dimension, this supreme image is linked with three other scenes: that where we later see how Singleton's endurance at the wheel brings him face to face with death; that where he has previously told Wait: 'Well, get on with your dying, don't raise a blamed fuss with us over that job'; and that soon after where Donkin taunts Wait with slackness on the rope – 'You don't kill yourself, old man!' – and Wait retorts 'Would YOU?'

Singleton does, and the heroic quality of his labors reminds us, not only that what has been most enduring about human society has been the mere continuity of its struggle against nature, which is, as we have seen, the tenor of the ensuing paragraph about the sea which opens the next chapter, but also that Conrad's greatest art, in *Typhoon* and *The Shadow Line* as in *The Nigger of the 'Narcissus'*, is often reserved for making us, in Auden's words, 'Give / Our gratitude to the Invisible College of the Humble, / Who through the ages have accomplished everything essential.' There is perhaps a moral for the critic here: for, in making us look up, briefly, to Singleton at the wheel, Conrad gives us a moment of vision in which, from the height of our modish attachment to ever-developing discriminations, we are compelled to affirm our endless, intricate, and not inglorious kinship with those who cannot write and who read only Bulwer-Lytton.

CHAPTER 4

Conrad's Heart of Darkness *and the critics*

You may be surprised to learn that this is a very big topic, and that I'm not going to attempt more than a sketch of one of its aspects: the question of Conrad's attitude to racism, to colonialism, and to Africa. From its first appearance in 1899, for the thousandth number of *Blackwood's Magazine, Heart of Darkness* has been considered a major attack on the horrors perpetrated in the Belgian Congo by Leopold, King of the Belgians, and his agents. When he broached the project to Blackwood, Conrad was aware of this element in the story, and said that 'the criminality of inefficiency and pure selfishness when tackling the civilizing work in Africa is a justifiable idea'.[1] In answer to a letter of praise from Cunninghame Graham for the first installment – Graham's term for Empire was 'The Stock Exchange Militant' – Conrad was again on the defensive, warning his radical friend that the latter two installments of the story might disappoint him, after the first one where 'the note struck chimes in with your convictions'.[2] So Conrad – who had been to the Congo in 1890 – knew that the first installment could be read as anti-imperialist, although not the story as a whole. In any case the general assumption that the story was, among other things, an attack on the atrocities on the Congo, was generally accepted.

At least, that is, until 1975, when the well-known Nigerian novelist Chinua Achebe made a vigorous attack. His subject was 'An Image of Africa', and his general theme was that Conrad used Africa as a historyless and barbaric opposite to European civilization, and that his treatment of the Congolese people was offensively stereotyped and unsympathetic. His general approach was political, but he also claimed that *Heart of Darkness* should no longer be regarded as a masterpiece, and even that Conrad was 'a bloody racist'.[3]

Achebe, you will note, belongs to the older generation of African writers, which was well trained in current colloquial Briticisms. In one respect he makes a case that must be answered: that is, that Conrad was influenced by the general attitudes to Africa in late nineteenth-century Europe, an attitude which had replaced the Enlightenment's sympathy for 'noble savages' brought down into slavery, with a post-Darwinian view that the African indigenes were primitive savages, but not noble.[4] The term 'racism' was not known to Conrad; the word was not mentioned in the *Oxford English Dictionary* until the 1983 *Supplement*. But we know that it means the doctrine, whether avowed or not, that finds 'racial differences in character, intelligence, etc.' and that 'asserts the superiority of one race over another or others', or in practice 'discriminates, segregates, persecutes and dominates'[5] on the basis of this theory of racial superiority. What evidence can we find in *Heart of Darkness* for racism in this rather general sense?

There is in fact more evidence than we have time to deal with. For instance, Marlow gets his job because his predecessor in command of the river steamer, a Dane called Fresleven, had been killed in a 'scuffle with the natives'.[6] The scuffle began when Fresleven decided he had been overreached in his dealings for 'two black hens', and decided to take the law into his own hands, and 'whacked the old nigger' – the village chief – 'mercilessly'; whereupon his son 'made a tentative jab with a spear' and it went through 'quite easy' (53–4). Later we observe that Marlow's aunt shared the current 'humbug', as Marlow calls it, about 'weaning those ignorant millions from their horrid ways' (59). 'Weaning', of course, implies that the Congo natives are children, and their ways are assumed to be necessarily 'horrid'. But when we come to Marlow's own experience, and his expressed views, the racial perspective changes. On his way out, the boats from the shore, he says, were 'paddled by black fellows. You could see from afar the white of their eyeballs glistening. They shouted, sang; their bodies streamed with perspiration; they had faces like grotesque masks – these chaps; but they had bone, muscle, a wild vitality, an intense energy of movement, that was as natural and true as the surf along their coast. They wanted no excuse for being there. They were a great comfort to look at' (61). We may perhaps find some racist assumption in their faces being described as like 'grotesque masks', but there is no doubt that Marlow finds them a 'comfort' compared to the white people aboard his ship. Once ashore, Marlow finds a similar contrast in favor of the blacks, though not one that is any comfort. First Marlow sees a chain gang of six blacks who 'were called criminals', but who only know that they are being punished by 'an insoluble mystery from the sea'; the whites, of course, regard their fate as 'high and just proceedings' (64–5). Conrad makes Marlow regard the whites as pitiful representatives of 'a flabby, pretending, weak-eyed devil of a rapacious and pitiless folly'; and he essentially sides with the blacks against them. When Marlow comes to the blacks in the 'grove of death', 'in all the attitudes of pain, abandonment and despair', we notice that his pity leads him to give the dying young black all that he can find, a biscuit (66–7).

Later, Marlow finds that his crew on the steamer are cannibals; and his homage to them is considerable: 'Fine fellows – cannibals – in their place. They were men one could work with, and I am grateful to them. And, after all, they did not eat each other before my face' (94). One may find the comic irony of the last sentence in bad taste, as well as wrong in its assumption that the crew would eat each other; but Marlow's admiration and gratitude are surely genuine. The blacks living on the river banks are a different matter; Marlow sees and understands them very little, and that little gives him an uncomfortable notion – 'this suspicion of their not being inhuman. It would come slowly to one. They howled and leaped, and spun, and made horrid faces; but what thrilled you was just the thought of their humanity – like yours – the thought of your remote kinship with this wild and passionate uproar' (96). Before we condemn Marlow for his surprise, we must take account of two incontrovertible facts: first, that there really was a great deal of cannibalism in this part of the Congo;[7] and second, and even more important, civilized whites had not adopted that refusal to make moral judgments which is typical of many modern anthropologists and their followers; in those days, just as such terms as 'nigger' were not regarded as offensive, so no one then would, like Stanley Diamond recently, think of glossing cannibalism as a mode of directly confronting the 'concrete humanity of the subject'.[8]

Neither Marlow nor Conrad had much personal contact with their crew: they don't speak the language. The main exceptions in Marlow's case are the fireman and the helmsman. His view of the fireman is sympathetic only if we can accept the idea that he had been 'improved', meaning educated, only to the point that he accepted the need to keep the boiler full of water lest the 'evil spirit inside the boiler would get angry' (97–8). The fireman is not up to scientifically endorsed technology; but there is surely sympathy as well as mockery in Marlow's verdict that 'He ought to have been clapping his hands and stamping his feet on the bank' instead of trying to acquire 'useful knowledge'. This passage is attacked by Chinua Achebe, especially Marlow's report that 'to look at him was as edifying as seeing a dog in a parody of

breeches and a feather hat, walking on his hind legs'. Marlow's involvement with the helmsman is rather close. He lacks 'restraint' and has
opened the pilot-house shutter; so a spear from one of the followers of
Kurtz kills him. But although Marlow's judgment is not wholly favorable, he nevertheless understands the 'intimate profundity of that look
he gave me when he received his hurt', and it 'remains to this day in
my memory – like a claim of distant kinship affirmed in a supreme
moment' (119). Achebe notes of this passage that Conrad does not go so
far as Albert Schweitzer, who remarks ironically that 'the African is
indeed my brother but my junior brother'.[9] Marlow only talks about a
claim of kinship; and it is this passage which leads to Achebe's remark
about Conrad's being a 'bloody racist'; but he does not quite play fair,
since the claim does not in fact 'frighten' Conrad, and there is no
mention of how Marlow repeats that he 'missed my late helmsman
awfully', and indeed he was 'not prepared to affirm the fellow was
exactly worth the life we lost in getting' to Kurtz (119).

The other black who makes a memorable impression on Marlow is
'the savage and superb, wild-eyed and magnificent' woman who is
contrasted with the deluded and bloodless Intended whom he later
visits back in Brussels (135–6). Again, it is a very favorable portrait. So
what are we to make of Achebe's charge of 'racism'? There is certainly
good reason to believe that Marlow, and *Heart of Darkness* as a whole,
imply that the blacks are savages who are incapable of using or understanding Western knowledge and technology. There is also relatively
little effort to show the Africans as people. Still both Marlow and Conrad
show a real readiness to see that their way of life has real meaning
and value; and if we judge comparatively, we must surely make them
superior as human beings to their white masters. This is, indeed, the
major aim of the story as a whole – Marlow's sickened disgust with the
colonizers in Africa and then with Kurtz. That is what Marlow, and
the reader, retain from the story. This point is made by many African
writers: 'However unflattering . . . this portrait of the African, that of
his "civilisers" is much less flattering and all too realistic.'[10] The African
novelist Leonard Kibera indeed says that he studies *Heart of Darkness* as
'an examination of the West itself and not as a comment on Africa'.[11]
Marlow and Conrad, then, are not fairly to be considered as 'racists',
although they are not in theory wholly opposed to the doctrine.

There is a similar difficulty in deciding what specific ideological
interpretation can be drawn from *Heart of Darkness* on the closely related
charge that it is a work in favor of colonialism. This term can be fairly

confusing. I remember my amazement when I began reading Walter Scott's *Ivanhoe*; there were those emphasized distinctions between the Saxon words for food animals when they are grown, 'ox', 'calf', and 'swine', as opposed to the Norman-French words for the meat when it is brought to the table, 'beef' from *boeuf*, 'veal' from *veau*, and pork.[12] The shock was that I had failed to realize that William the Conqueror and his successors weren't my people exactly; they were conquerors who kept the English natives in a subservient position; they were treated as colonials. There was a similar but double experience of colonial status for Conrad. He was born in the Ukraine, and therefore the master, in that the Poles there were a dominant class – most of the peasants didn't even speak Polish, but Ukrainian; on the other hand, Conrad was in the subordinate position because Russia, Prussia, and Austria had control over the whole of Poland. Colonialism, then, isn't necessarily a matter of color or race differences; the white settlers who went to Australia, or for that matter to the thirteen states of America, were colonials in that they lived in a country which was politically dependent on the motherland, England. Nor does colonialism imply conscious political power, as the term 'Imperialism' does. In the Roman empire, as in the British dominions, you were a colonial whether you were of, and identified with, the master-country, or were a native; and the term also retained a sense of its Latin original, from *colere*, to grow or farm; the issue of being dependent came later.

Marlow specifically raises the colonial issue very early when he says of the river Thames that 'this also . . . has been one of the dark places of the earth' (48). The Roman settlers, though, were, Marlow thinks, 'no colonists; their administration was merely a squeeze, and nothing more, I suspect. They were conquerors.' Marlow goes on to speak of how, in his view, 'The conquest of the earth, which mostly means the taking it away from those who have a different complexion or slightly flatter noses than ourselves, is not a pretty thing when you look into it too much' (50–1). Conrad and Marlow, then, are aware of the injustice and other faults of colonialism. But they make three important concessions. First, that modern Western man has a degree of 'efficiency' which the Roman, allegedly, lacked. Second, that the only thing which can redeem colonialism is 'the idea only', which is 'something you can set up, and bow down before, and offer a sacrifice to' (51). Third, there is the privileged position accorded to the British Empire; the map at the Trading Company's office shows 'a vast amount of red – good to see at any time, because one knows that some real work is done in there' (55).

Marlow, then, is not anticolonialist as far as his own country is concerned, although nothing is said illustrating the British worship of the 'idea'. But Marlow is going into the blank space, colored yellow on the map; it is the personal empire of Leopold, king of Belgium. There, at least, there is no question of 'efficiency'; and as for 'the idea', the only 'idea' we see is Marlow's traveling companion who, when asked why he was there, answers, 'To make money, of course, what do you think?' (71). In actual fact the Belgian Congo was the scene of the most spectacular misrule and devastation that the world had yet seen, with the black population there estimated to have lost three million in fifteen years.[13] Conrad himself had no doubt of these horrors. In his essay 'Geography and Some Explorers' he says that he picked up on the Congo 'the distasteful knowledge of the vilest scramble for loot that ever disfigured the history of human conscience and geographical exploration'.[14]

From the moment we see the French warship 'firing into a continent' because the 'French had one of their wars going on thereabouts' (61), we have no doubt that *Heart of Darkness* is resolutely opposed to the practices of French and Belgian colonists. But even so, that opposition doesn't seem to be mainly inspired by a political motive; and this is partly because it is a reminiscence of what the Congo trip had meant for Marlow personally, and largely because in that context the role allotted to Kurtz is crucial. Kurtz, of course, is himself an example of a 'heart of darkness'. Many Westerners in the post-Darwinian period believed that primitive people were morally inferior to civilized ones; and they were perhaps likely to assume that Kurtz's descent into barbarism was the result of his contact with the people he met in the Upper Congo. This was argued by an Indian critic, Frances Singh, in an article on 'The Colonialistic Bias of *Heart of Darkness*'.[15] She argues that what she calls 'Kurtz's tribalization' must 'be seen as a rejection of the materialism of the West in favor of a simpler and more honest way of life' (49). We may have strong doubts about this unduly favorable gloss on the horrors that Kurtz actually performs, his killing, violence, and accepting human sacrifices offered to him; but it is in any case not clear that such a view of native influence upon Kurtz was part of Conrad's intention. The text speaks, rather, of the 'heavy, mute spell of the wilderness – that seemed to draw him to its pitiless breast by the awakening of forgotten and brutal instincts, by the memory of gratified and monstrous passions' (144). Kurtz's fall arose from weaknesses within himself – memories – which could come to surface and flourish only in the wilderness far from the protection of the butchers and policemen of civilization (114). This is part of the atavistic element in man which Marlow invokes to show the follies of talk of progress; Kurtz had no 'innate strength', no 'capacity for faithfulness' (116); his great solitude 'echoed loudly within him because he was hollow at the core' (131). It is true that Marlow thinks that Kurtz will be 'lost, utterly lost' if he stays; but that is only because staying would mean staying with everything he has done, and continuing his appalling career.

Kurtz, then, complicates the anti-colonial theme because he 'had come out equipped with moral ideas of some sort', and Marlow is naturally 'curious to see how he would set about his work when there' (88). But Kurtz only shows that the enemy within is not such that anyone should be confident of being able to resist successfully; and so one can't make a very strong case for the story's being pro-colonial on that basis. In any case it would be wrong to assume, as Frances Singh does, that it was some failure of understanding which prevented Conrad from succeeding in writing a 'story that was meant to be a clear-cut attack on a vicious system into a partial apology for it' (53). For Conrad had no such intention. We can see this in the character of Kurtz. We are told that 'All Europe had contributed to the making of Kurtz'; his career is intended to show how the best can fall and that the most advanced ideas of political reform can be capable of infinite degradation when removed from the controlling power of the policeman and the butcher, or public opinion (114). In a sense Kurtz remains the number one exhibit in Conrad's exhibition of colonial horrors: and his story is too dreadful for Marlow to tell the truth about his life to the Intended.

There are only two blacks whom Conrad shows as in any way unsympathetic. First there is the 'one of the reclaimed' who is in charge of the chain gang; the servant of the whites who gives Marlow a 'large, white rascally grin' of collusive fellowship in the colonial enterprise (64–5). The other is the manager's boy on the boat who 'put his insolent black head in the doorway, and said in a voice of scathing contempt – "Mistah Kurtz – he dead"' (150). Both of these are clearly examples of the corruption created in the blacks by the white colonists.

In Conrad's letters and critical writings he makes clear that he had no particular ideological theory that he wished to expound, and that he did not think that this would be a desirable literary aim. His reluctance to adopt an overt political stance lasted his whole life and can be illustrated by his dealing with Roger Casement. Conrad had met him, and liked him, when he was out on the Congo. Later Casement tried to get his support for the Congo Reform movement, Conrad was a charming host to him, and wrote a very nice letter recommending Casement to Cunninghame Graham; but Conrad refused to join the movement, although he made it clear that he was still firm in his total rejection of Belgian actions in the Congo. He wrote to Casement, for example, that 'It is an extraordinary thing that the conscience of Europe which seventy years ago has put down the slave trade on humanitarian grounds tolerates the Congo State today. It is as if the moral clock had been put back many hours.'[16] Conrad also gave his view on the essence of the problem of the indigenes. The black man, Conrad wrote, 'shares with us the consciousness of the universe in which we live – no small burden. Barbarism per se is no crime . . . and the Belgians are worse than the seven plagues of Egypt insomuch that in that case it was a punishment sent for a definite transgression; but in this the . . . man is not aware of any transgression, and therefore can see no end to the infliction. It must appear to him very awful and mysterious; and I confess it appears so to me too.'

Conrad here surely shows a fine power of imaginative projection; both the blacks and Conrad share their awareness of the universe in which they live; but the violation of their usual habits and expectations of life under the cover of the colonist's pretense of progress must be 'very awful and mysterious'. Conrad's writing and his mind in general aim to advance, not political programs, but moral understanding; and this is true of *Heart of Darkness*. Anyone who puts practical political or national issues first could not be expected to like *Heart of Darkness*. Its tendency to universalize the problems raised by the Congo and Kurtz, and yet express them in a sophisticated and subjective dramatic form through Marlow's consciousness, show a temper of mind very different, and in some respects opposed to, Frantz Fanon's classic statement of the colonial problem. The only condition on which Fanon sees the possibility of the Europeans being able to help the Third World is that they should join in a common effort to 'rehabilitate mankind, and make man victorious everywhere, once and for all'.[17] Conrad would never have entertained such sanguine hopes. He had written to Cunninghame Graham: 'what would you think of an attempt to promote fraternity amongst people living in the same street. . . . Fraternity means nothing except the Cain–Abel business'.[18] Conrad would have regarded the idea of man's being victorious 'once and for all' as muddled political rhetoric. We can see this very clearly if we contrast the tone of his mind with that of William Faulkner. Faulkner was referring to Conrad's essay on

Henry James, in his Nobel Prize address, but gave it a very different direction. Faulkner spoke of his optimistic hopes for the future:

It is easy enough to say man is immortal simply because he will endure; that when the last ding-dong of doom has clanged and faded from the last worthless rock hanging tideless in the last red and dying evening, that even there will still be one more sound: that of his puny inexhaustible voice, still talking. I refuse to accept this. I believe that man will not merely endure: he will prevail.[19]

Doesn't Faulkner insist too much? we may wonder. Conrad would certainly have thought so; for him it was enough to say that voicing a hope 'to us utterly inconceivable' was the task of the artist:

When the last aqueduct shall have crumbled to pieces [wrote Conrad], the last airship fallen to the ground, the last blade of grass have died upon a dying earth, man, indomitable by his training in resistance to misery and pain, shall set this undiminished light of eyes against the feeble glow of the sun. The artistic faculty, of which each of us has a minute grain, may find its voice in some individual of that last group, gifted with a power of expression and courageous enough to interpret the ultimate experience of mankind in terms of his temperament, in terms of art . . . whether in austere exhortation or in a phrase of sardonic comment, who can guess?

For my own part, from a short and cursory acquaintance with my kind, I am inclined to think that the last utterance will formulate, strange as it may appear, some hope now to us utterly inconceivable. For mankind is delightful in its pride, its assurance, and its indomitable tenacity. It will sleep on the battlefield among its own dead, in the manner of an army having won a barren victory. It will not know when it is beaten.[20]

Conrad worries a good deal in formulating a balanced statement in exactly the terms he can accept as true. He is neither a Utopian writer nor an apocalyptic one. That, incidentally, was surely the trouble with Coppola's *Apocalypse Now*. Coppola's Viet Nam and Brando's Kurtz were the end; Conrad's story ends horribly enough, but only with the lie to the Intended; and one shouldn't assume that Kurtz or Marlow has the final word.

That sceptical balance, of course, does not clear Conrad completely from the charge of being a colonialist; but it comes close to doing so. As real evidence against Conrad we are left with a number of current clichés about the blacks, their 'rolling eyes', 'incomprehensible frenzies', 'rudimentary souls', and so on, which certainly show that Conrad had not attempted to show the natives without prejudice in his language. On the general charge of Conrad's supporting colonialism, however, we must acquit him in the main. This is largely on the basis of his treatment of the whites: There is nothing said of them which doesn't show them to be cruel, inefficient, mindless, and self-seeking. Conrad no doubt felt, or at least felt he had to say, that he was in favor of British colonization; but what we see on the Congo is a tremendous series of descriptions, episodes, and moral developments which surely amount to a denial of Achebe's view that Conrad 'chose the role of purveyor of comforting myths'.[21]

Achebe, of course, may be exaggerating in the interest of a larger cause: an attack on the ideological view of Europeans in general that sees Africa 'as a metaphysical battlefield devoid of all recognisable humanity'. Here he claims, against *Heart of Darkness*, that there is 'a preposterous and perverse kind of arrogance in this reducing Africa to the role of props for the break up of one petty European'.[22] From that viewpoint it is fairly easy to argue that 'a novel which celebrates this dehumanization, which depersonalizes a portion of the human race' cannot be called 'a great work of art'. Conrad does not, I think, lay himself open to these charges; within the limits of the story as a whole he does justice even to the land. When Marlow looks at the jungle outside the Central Station one moonlit night, he feels that 'the silence of the land went home to one's very heart – its mystery, its greatness, the amazing reality of its concealed life' (80).

Perhaps we have time for a little up-dating footnote. First, that Achebe returned to his argument in a 'Viewpoint' article in the *Times Literary Supplement*. There he says that what we need between North and South, between Europe and Africa, is dialogue, not monologue, however brilliant; and much of the current monologue is 'foolishly sensational and pretentious', including that of the alleged masterpiece, *Heart of Darkness*. Its high rating, he says, is due to the way that it 'fortifies fears and prejudices and is clever enough to protect itself, should the need arise, with the excuse that it is not really about Africa at all'.[23] He gives another example of the lack of real dialogue in V.S. Naipaul, the Trinidadian novelist now living in England.

Naipaul has known Conrad since he was a boy of ten when his father read him 'The Lagoon', and he often speaks of *Heart of Darkness*. In an essay on 'Conrad's Darkness' he mentions a page which spoke 'directly to me, and not only of Africa', the presentation of whose background, incidentally, he thought 'the most effective part of the book'. The page is about the discovery in the Russian harlequin's hut of *An Inquiry into Some Points of Seamanship*. It is a tattered and lovingly mended volume, dreary with its massive tables and diagrams; but 'its honest concern for the right way of going to work' seems 'luminous with another than a professional light'. The reason for its effect, which Naipaul carried very long in his mind, was that it seemed to speak for the whole insecurity of the post-colonial writer. 'The new politics', he wrote, 'the curious reliance of men on institutions they were yet working to undermine, the simplicity of beliefs and the hideous simplicity of actions, the corruption of causes, half-made societies that seemed doomed to remain half-made: these were things that began to preoccupy me . . . And I found that Conrad – sixty years before, in the time of a great peace – had been everywhere before me. Not as a man with a cause, but a man offering, as in *Nostromo*, a vision of the world's half-made societies as places which continually made and unmade themselves.' The vision, he commented, was 'dismal, but deeply felt'. Naipaul concludes the essay: 'Conrad died fifty years ago. In those fifty years his work has penetrated to many corners of the world which he saw as dark. It is a subject for Conradian meditation; it tells us something about our new world. Perhaps it doesn't matter what we say about Conrad; it is enough that he is discussed.'[24]

NOTES

1 *Joseph Conrad: Letters to William Blackwood and David S. Meldrum*, ed. William Blackburn (Durham, 1958), p. 37.

2 *Joseph Conrad's Letters to R. B. Cunninghame Graham*, ed. C. T. Watts (Cambridge, 1969), p. 116.

3 *Massachusetts Review*, 18 (1997), 788.

4 See, for example, Patrick Brantlinger, 'Victorians and Africans: The Genealogy of the Myth of the Dark Continent', *Critical Inquiry*, 12 (1985), 166–203.

5 *Webster's New World Dictionary*, 2nd edn (1978), s.v.

6 *Heart of Darkness*, in *Youth, Heart of Darkness, The End of the Tether* (London, 1948), p. 53. All later references to *Heart of Darkness* are from this, the Dent Collected Edition.

7 See Hunt Hawkins, 'The Issue of Racism in *Heart of Darkness*', *Conradiana*, 14 (1982), 164–6. Among the many defenses of Conrad, see the Zambian defense of C. P. Sarvan, 'Racism and *Heart of Darkness*', *International Fiction Review*, 7 (1980), 6–10, and Reinhardt Kuesgen, 'Conrad and Achebe: Aspects of the Novel', *World Literature Written in English*, 24 (1984), 27–33.

8 'The Search for the Primitive', *The Concept of the Primitive*, ed. Ashley Montagu (New York, 1980), p. 134.

9 'An Image of Africa', p. 787.

10 Ellen Mae Kitonga, 'Conrad's Image of African and Coloniser in *Heart of Darkness*', *Busara*, 3 (1970), 34.

11 Hunt Hawkins, 164.

12 *Ivanhoe: A Romance* (Boston, 1934), p. 9.
13 Neal Ascherson, *The King Incorporated: Leopold II in the Age of Trusts* (London, 1963), p. 251.
14 *Last Essays* (London, 1955), p. 17.
15 *Conradiana*, 10 (1978), 41–54.
16 Letter of 21 December 1903; Zdzislaw Najder, *Joseph Conrad: A Chronicle* (New Brunswick, 1983), p. 295.
17 *The Wretched of the Earth*, trans. Constance Farrington (New York, 1966), p. 83.
18 *Conrad's Letters to . . . Graham*, p. 117.
19 Joseph Blotner, *Faulkner: A Biography* (New York, 1974), p. 1366.
20 Henry James: An Appreciation', *Notes on Life and Letters*, pp. 13–14.
21 'An Image of Africa', p. 784.
22 'An Image of Africa', p. 788.
23 *Times Literary Supplement*, 1 February 1980, p. 113.
24 *The Return of Eva Peron* (New York, 1980), pp. 207, 216, 227.

CHAPTER 5

Comedy and humour in Typhoon

FOR some readers *Typhoon* is one of Conrad's great books. It was, for instance, the work which Ugo Mursia chose to translate into Italian, and thus initiate his publishing career as a Conradian in 1959;[1] it was also, for F. R. Leavis, one of 'Conrad's masterpieces'.[2] Leavis doubted, however, that there was much general 'recognition of just where the strength of *Typhoon* lies'; in Leavis's view, that strength 'lies not so much in the demented fury' of the typhoon itself, as in 'the presentment of Captain MacWhirr, the chief mate Jukes and the chief engineer Solomon Rout'. Conrad's 'particular effect of heroic sublimity', Leavis went on, depends on the ordinariness of the characters, and it is this which gives a 'supremely effective' irony to the treatment of the storm, which remains, in his view, 'the main theme of the tale'. I do not believe that typhoon is the 'main theme', or that 'heroic sublimity' is the particular effect, of *Typhoon*; while the 'ordinariness' of the characters, and of most of the narrative, seems to me to have a very different function: its primary aim is to achieve not the sublime but the comic and the humorous.

Here, I should perhaps explain that – without going into the issue fully – I do not intend any very specific distinction between comedy and humour. Comedy is an established literary genre, and I believe that *Typhoon* is structured in a way which is in some respects typical of stage comedy. Humour is one of the effects which comedy uses, but which is also found in real life, perhaps because the main subject of both humour and comedy is the idiosyncrasies of individuals and of their interplay, especially those that make us laugh or smile.

The passage which Leavis takes as his first example comes from the second paragraph of the tale, and continues the description of MacWhirr with which the novel opens:

He was rather below the medium height, a bit round-shouldered, and so sturdy of limb that his clothes always looked a shade too tight for his arms and legs. As if unable to grasp what is due to the difference of latitudes, he wore a brown bowler hat, a complete suit of brownish hue, and clumsy black boots. These harbour togs gave to his thick figure an air of stiff and uncouth smartness. A thin silver watch-chain looped his waist-coat, and he never left his ship for the shore without clutching in his powerful, hairy fist an elegant umbrella of the very best quality, but generally unrolled. Young Jukes, the chief mate, attending his commander to the gangway, would sometimes venture to say, with the greatest gentleness, 'Allow me, sir' – and possessing himself of the umbrella deferentially, would elevate the ferule, shake the fold, twirl a neat furl in a jiffy, and hand it back; going through the performance with a face of such portentous gravity, that Mr. Solomon Rout, the chief engineer, smoking his morning cigar over the skylight, would turn away his head in order to hide a smile, 'Oh! aye! The blessed gamp . . . Thank'ee, Jukes, thank'ee,' would mutter Captain MacWhirr, heartily, without looking up.[3]

The intentional humorous effects are surely obvious: the clothes looking 'a shade too tight'; the bowler hat, the suit, and the black boots, which illustrate MacWhirr's inability 'to grasp what is due to the difference of latitudes'; and that old comic standby, the umbrella. The climax of the paragraph also sets up the main comic structure of the story. It is based on the interplay of the three officers: young Jukes with his excessive concern with the social forms, who is ashamed of his captain's turnout for going into town; old Rout, vastly amused at the inappropriateness of young Jukes's 'portentous gravity'; and MacWhirr, simply but absent-mindedly grateful for Jukes's courtesy, and as totally unaware of Jukes's implied criticism of him as he is of its appeal to Rout's comic sense.

I

Throughout the first chapter everything that MacWhirr does and says makes him a figure of fun. 'Tom's an ass,' says his father, who treated him to chaffing 'as if upon a half-witted person' (5); and it is at least true that MacWhirr has a Lockean aversion 'against the use of images in speech' (25) and confesses to Jukes that 'I can't understand what you can find to talk about' (17–18). So it is very natural that we should agree with the narrator in expecting that he will die 'ignorant of life to the last' (19) and 'disdained by destiny or by the sea', which, we are told, 'had never put itself out to startle the silent man, who seldom looked up, and wandered innocently over the waters' (18).

This constantly mocking attitude to the protagonist is a little like the early chapters of Conrad's previous novel, *Lord Jim*; in both the language of the narrator expresses irony and contempt. But whereas Jim is young, complicated, and will develop, MacWhirr is middle-aged, apparently successful, and wholly set in his ways. Still, we soon learn that he is not 'disdained by destiny'. His first act in the chapter's narrative present is to observe that 'a barometer he had no reason to distrust' recorded so low a reading that it was 'ominously prophetic' (6). MacWhirr, however, draws from this only the conclusion that 'There must be some uncommonly dirty weather knocking about.' That record low reading initiates the theme denoted by the title; but in the whole first chapter there are only two references to the coming typhoon.

In the second chapter we have a description of the appalling heat and the terrible rolling of the ship, which gets so bad that Jukes decides that the ship really ought to be 'put head on to that swell' (30). He goes to suggest this to MacWhirr, but without success. Jukes speaks of the 'swell getting worse', to which, with his usual total literalness, MacWhirr returns, 'Noticed that in here . . . Anything wrong?' Then Jukes mentions 'our passengers', to which MacWhirr wonders gravely, 'what passengers?' – to him it seems a shockingly inappropriate term for the cargo of 200 coolies below deck. When Jukes hints more openly that the ship be headed east to face the heavy seas directly, MacWhirr is even more indignant: 'I've heard more than enough of mad things done in the world – but this . . . If I didn't know you, Jukes I would think you were in liquor.' Then MacWhirr goes on to say that he has been reading up 'the chapter on the storms' (32), but has decided not to follow the practice recommended there of trying to get out of the typhoon's way. He gives two very characteristic reasons for this: that nobody can know that a typhoon is actually there until he is actually in it; and that, if it is there, 'very well. There's your log-book to talk straight about the weather' (34).

In the whole of this conversation, the narrator says, MacWhirr has 'been making his confession of faith, had he only known it' (35). Two of its articles are that 'you don't find everything in books', and that 'A gale is a gale, Mr. Jukes . . . and a full-powered steam-ship has got to face it. There's just so much dirty weather knocking about the world, and the proper thing is to go through it with none of what old Captain Wilson of the *Melita* calls "storm strategy".'

That remains MacWhirr's fixed strategy throughout *Typhoon*, and in all matters. The reader, however, should not admire his decision to maintain his course directly into the typhoon. The official instructions, which MacWhirr should have learned for his Merchant Navy examinations, were very widely known. For instance, in *The Sailor's Hornbook for the Law of Storm*, which reached its seventh edition in 1889, Henry

Piddington supplied many examples of ships which had either encountered or avoided typhoons in the China Sea. He also stated that in those waters nearly all typhoons, or cyclones, come from the east, and that the center of the typhoon is eight points (that is 90 degrees) off the wind (as MacWhirr comments (33)).

In any case MacWhirr's argument against changing the ship's course is very weak. If the ship sails directly into the typhoon the expenses to the owners in repairs will be vastly greater than the 'pretty coal bill' which would be run up in dodging 'the bad weather' (34); and though the log would no doubt clear the captain of any wrong-doing, that seems rather a specious and unworthy argument from Captain MacWhirr, especially if one considers the human lives that his short-sightedness will – and does – endanger.

For Piddington then, MacWhirr would certainly have been a fine example of the kind of officer he attacks, the men of 'the old school' who 'do not like "new-fangled notions"', because they are 'too proud, too ignorant, or too indolent to take the trouble to learn'.[4] A vessel powered by steam is not as vulnerable to storms as a sailing ship, but it is clear that MacWhirr is wrong not to alter the *Nan-Shan's* course. On the other hand, this is by no means the only issue which affects our final judgement on MacWhirr.

Towards the end of the second chapter MacWhirr is having a nap in the chart-room when he is awakened by the sounds and movements which betoken the actual onset of the typhoon. There follow a variety of humorous episodes in which MacWhirr prepares for action – he catches one of his sea-boots skidding along the floor, kicks at the shoes he's discarded, jerks himself into his oilskins, and ties on his sou'-wester with all the deliberation 'of a woman putting on her bonnet before a glass' (36). Once out on deck he finds that Jukes has made all the possible preparations; 'Keep her at it as long as we can', MacWhirr shouts, but 'before had squeezed the salt water out of his eyes all the stars had disappeared' (38).

The main continuity of the third chapter comes from the actions and thoughts of Jukes. 'This is no joke', he thinks, when the full fury of the storm hits the *Nan-Shan*, and feels 'uncritically glad to have his captain at hand' (39). But when Jukes comments to MacWhirr that the sea has swept away two lifeboats, he is disappointed that MacWhirr merely remarks that losing things in such a storm 'stands to reason' (45). Jukes is privately convinced that 'She's done for'; in one relative lull he tries to 'outscream' the storm, and asks MacWhirr, who is holding on to him tight, 'Will she live through this?' He expects no reply, but 'after a while he heard with amazement the frail and resisting voice' of MacWhirr: 'She may!' (47–8). The narrative emphasis is on the word 'resisting'; and Jukes even hears snatches of further consoling reflections from his captain; they include, 'builders . . . good men . . . Rout . . . good man'. When MacWhirr removes his arm from him, however, Jukes, immediately lets 'himself sink slowly into the depths of bodily misery'. Then he feels something touching him at the back of his knees, and later exploring his 'person upwards with prudent, apologetic touches, as became an inferior'. It is the boatswain, who has come up on deck to report to his captain.

In Chapter Four, Jukes is sure that he will 'never see another sunrise', and is completely dominated by 'an overpowering dislike towards any other form of activity' than 'keeping his heart completely steeled against the worst' (51). But another more important activity is soon demanded of him. MacWhirr, who had earlier been anxious to know where the men have taken refuge, has now learned some very bad news from the boatswain. In the course of acceding to the crew's demand that they at least have 'some light to see each other by' (54), the boatswain had gone to the 'tween deck for a lamp, and discovered that, their boxes all having worked loose and got broken, the coolies were fighting each other for the seven years' pay they were taking home, and which was scattered with everything else on the deck. MacWhirr tells Jukes to go and see what the situation is: this is because his sense that he 'can't have . . . fighting . . . board ship' overpowers the contrary motive that he would 'much rather keep you here . . . case . . . I should . . . washed overboard myself' (60). MacWhirr's 'busy concern' sickens Jukes 'like an exhibition of blind and pernicious folly' (53); but very unwillingly he goes down to investigate. He is helped by the boatswain, who keeps cheerily yelling: 'What would my old woman say if she saw me now?' to which he imagines her answer: 'Serve you right, you old fool, for going to sea' (61).

Once Jukes gets as far as the bunker next to the coolies, he thinks of getting out again, 'but the remembrance of Captain MacWhirr's voice made this impossible' (62). So he opens the door, and glimpses the terrible scene of the coolies madly battling for their dollars. As ordered, Jukes immediately closes the door again, and makes his way to the engine room. There he tells the captain through the speaking-tube, that 'nothing could stop' the coolies now 'except main force'. Then he awaits the captain's order, hoping 'to be dismissed from the face of that odious trouble intruding on the great need of the ship' (72).

In Chapter Five the ship is swept from end to end. When that is over, Jukes, still in the engine room, hears MacWhirr tell him to 'Pick up all the money. Bear a hand now. I'll want you up here' (75). Jukes, hoping for sympathy, tells Rout: 'Got to pick up the dollars.' To this, Rout answers, 'I don't care', and adds, 'Go away now . . . You fellows are going wrong for want of something to do.' His ironic jocularity exemplifies the old animosity between the deck and the engine room, but it infuriates Jukes. His anger and the unacknowledged leadership of the boatswain combine to work a minor miracle. The two men collect the crew in the alleyway; they then lead them into the bunker, drive the coolies forwards to the end of the 'tween deck, collect all their belongings, including the money, and finally rig lifelines to give the coolies something to hang on to. This done, Jukes bolts the door again and makes his way back to the deck. There he sees the captain 'holding on to a twisted bridge-rail' and reports: 'We have done it, sir.' Captain MacWhirr merely returns: 'Thought you would', and then adds the dismissive comment – 'Wind fell all at once' (81).

Jukes, of course, feels that more attention should have been paid to the great risks he has just taken for the coolies, but MacWhirr merely repeats his reason: 'Had to do what's fair by them.' He is already brooding about his next problem as captain, and says to Jukes that: 'According to the books the worst is not over yet.' Leaving Jukes in charge, MacWhirr goes into the chart-room. It is very dark, but he can 'feel the disorder of that place where he used to live tidily' (83). He strikes one match to read the barometer, and then a second: 'There was no mistake. It was the lowest reading he had ever seen in his life.' The aneroid glass conveys the same gloomy message, and then, we are told, MacWhirr's 'feeling of dismay reached the very seat of his composure'. He is careful to put the matches back in their appointed place, but 'before he removed his hand it occurred to him that perhaps he would never have occasion to use that box any more'. 'For an infinitesimal fraction of a second', we read, 'his fingers closed again on the small objects as though it had been the symbol of all these little habits that chain us to the weary round of life.' MacWhirr lets himself fall on the settee; there he 'unsealed his lips' and, 'as if addressing another being awakened within his breast', says half aloud: 'I shouldn't like to lose her' (86). The combination of laughter and tears is the traditional hallmark of humour, and we certainly have it here.

At this point we might perhaps briefly consider the nature of Conrad's humour in the narrative tale as a whole. Thomas Mann sees Conrad's

The Secret Agent as rich in a 'humour' which is 'refreshingly comic' and at the same time 'ultramodern, post-middle-class'.[5] 'Modern art', he says, 'sees life as tragic-comedy, with the result that the grotesque is its most genuine style.' But in *Typhoon* there is surely something that is closer to the traditional English humour of character. There is grotesque in the description of the coolies; but most of the narrative is written in a straightforward and non-grotesque style.

MacWhirr towels himself down, and hears a voice say: 'She may come out of it yet.' He goes out on deck and tells Jukes the two things that are on his mind. First, MacWhirr says, 'We must trust her to go through it and come out on the other side'; and second, if it should happen that Jukes is 'left alone' and in charge, the Captain 'mumbling rather fast', says: 'Keep her facing it . . . You are a young sailor. Face it. That's enough for any man. Keep a cool head' (89).

MacWhirr mumbles 'rather fast' in embarrassment at speaking about his possible death, but Jukes, we are told, 'for some reason . . . experienced an access of confidence'. Then the blackness of the renewed onset of the typhoon strikes the *Nan-Shan*, and for the second time MacWhirr is 'moved to declare, in a tone of vexation, as it were: "I wouldn't like to lose her"'. The fifth chapter immediately ends with a very short paragraph: 'He was spared that annoyance.'

Before going on to the sixth and last chapter, two points should be made on that closing sentence. First, by omitting the climatic second part of the typhoon, a tactic typical of Conrad's love of ringing changes in his narrative method, he dramatically reverses the concentration of attention on the storm in the previous chapters. It thus prepares for the comic note of the concluding chapter; and so does the second point, the ironic downplaying of the threat to the *Nan-Shan* into a mere 'annoyance'.

II

The last chapter is largely devoted to strengthening the case for MacWhirr as a captain,[6] but in a highly comic way. Having finished with the typhoon, Conrad ends his tale in a series of narrative modulations which both amuse the reader and artfully delay the book's general thematic resolution.

'On a bright sunshiny day' the sixth chapter begins, carrying the cheerful assurance that the typhoon is over. First, there is a short scene showing the *Nan-Shan* arriving at Fu-chau, and how those at the quayside exercise their wits upon her catastrophic dilapidation. Next, the first arrival at the dockside, the second-mate, discloses that MacWhirr has paid him off but told him to get his breakfast ashore. The point of view shifts momentarily to MacWhirr, who is dutifully writing his monthly letter home, and then settles upon his wife, who is reading the letter. Feeling as she does that 'she couldn't be really expected to understand all these ship affairs', she skips most of what MacWhirr has written about the typhoon; consequently she is never to know that, as the steward had earlier read, and even passed on to the unbelieving cook, 'between 4 and 6 a.m. on December 25th, Captain MacWhirr did actually think that his ship could not possibly live another hour in such a sea, and that he would never see his wife and children again' (94). Mrs MacWhirr, provincial and self-centred, is much more interested in a sale at the local draper's, and soon goes out shopping. On the way she meets an acquaintance; at first Mrs MacWhirr voices her hypocritical regret, that 'It's very sad to have him away'; but she then explains that it is MacWhirr's choice – 'The climate there agrees with him.' It is, the narrator remarks, as if 'poor MacWhirr had been away touring in China for the sake of his health'.

The narrative next gives us Rout's letter to his wife, which she, in turn, discusses with Rout's mother. Captain MacWhirr, she reports, though 'a rather simple man . . . has done something rather clever' (96). But Rout doesn't exactly say what it was, partly because he soon turns to how the ordeal has brought home to him how much he misses his wife, and partly because, if Rout had tried, he would never have made her 'understand how much there was in it'.

What that 'something rather clever' was is still unknown to the reader, and telling it is left to the third and last of the letter-writers, Jukes. Jukes, we know, had assumed there would be real trouble with the coolies unless they were kept battened down under the hatches until the *Nan-Shan* gets to port; on the other hand, MacWhirr had already hinted that he feels he 'must plan out something that would be fair to all parties' (99). Jukes, however, is totally unprepared for MacWhirr's solution. He decides that if he left the coolies to claim what they had lost, they would all lie about how much it had been; on the other hand, if he left it to the Chinese authorities on shore, none of the money would ever wind up in the hands of the coolies. So MacWhirr decides that he is going to share 'all the cash we had picked up equally among the lot' (101). To do this, 'with his sea-boots still drawn up to the hips and in shirt-sleeves', MacWhirr summons up the coolies to hear his plan. Jukes hears from the steward that the coolies are on deck, and jumps to the conclusion that the worst has happened. He arms five of the crew and they go up on deck and charge the chart-room. But all is well there, and they find MacWhirr, who is very annoyed at the fuss: 'What the devil are these monkey tricks, Mr. Jukes?' Then he orders Jukes to disarm his band, and explains his plan of action. By nightfall the distribution of the money is peacefully completed. Rout says 'that this was plainly the only thing that could be done', but Jukes still does not understand. The book ends with Juke's own comment: 'I think that he got out of it very well for such a stupid man' (102). This light-hearted paradox places the emphasis where it belongs: on the irony of Jukes's resolute inability to understand or appreciate his captain.

One of the most standard devices of comedy is repetition of speech and action. In *Typhoon*, we notice, both the first and the last chapters end in the same way: the pattern is repeated, with each chapter containing a sequence of letters from MacWhirr, Rout and Jukes, letters which are interspersed by the reactions and commentary of their addressees. As to the repetition of speech, we notice that *Typhoon* is perhaps fuller of what must be calculated repetitions of characteristic mottoes than any other of Conrad's main works. Even Jukes's last remark echoes his summary of MacWhirr in the first chapter: 'He's too dense to trouble about, and that's the truth' (18).

The repetitions are also found in mere details; thus the crisis of the typhoon occurred on the early morning of Christmas day (94), but in the first chapter MacWhirr's early letters home contain the sentence, 'On Christmas day at 4 p.m. we fell in with some icebergs' (5). More importantly, some of the repetitions are used to organize the themes of the tale. Thus the most extended single incident in the first chapter concerns the transfer of the *Nan-Shan* to Siamese registration. Jukes takes the new flag, a 'ridiculous Noah's Ark elephant', as a personal affront; he speaks indignantly of it first to Rout and then to MacWhirr, without getting any satisfaction from either. Rout merely 'cleared his throat with the air of a man who knows the value of a good billet' (10); while MacWhirr, when Jukes says 'Queer flag for a man to sail under', at first just answers 'Seems all right to me'. Then, in a wholly characteristic – and irrelevant – exhibition of captainly caution, he goes to the chart room and consults the International Signal Code-book. Having done so, he reports to Jukes, 'There's nothing amiss with that flag . . . Length twice the breadth and the elephant exactly in the middle. I thought the people ashore would know how to make the local flag. Stands to reason.' MacWhirr's comical failure to understand Jukes's symbolic objection is itself symbolic: as is made clear when MacWhirr ingeniously adds that the crew should be very careful not to 'hoist the elephant upside down', because this would be 'understood as a signal of distress'. Completely defeated by his captain's misguided literalness, Jukes goes to tell Rout 'the old man's latest'; but, remembering that Jukes had earlier threatened to 'throw up the billet rather than sail under such a flag', Rout, greatly amused but impassive, merely asks Jukes, 'And did you throw up the billet?' To which Jukes answers – again repetitively – 'No . . . What's the good? I might just as well fling my resignation at this bulkhead. I don't believe you can make a man like that understand anything' (12).

There are a number of other references to the Siamese flag later, and they continue to develop the Jukes–MacWhirr contrast. Two of them occur in the last chapter. First, the second-mate says that he would have made trouble for MacWhirr 'if it wasn't for that damned Siamese flag' (92). This is a bluff to cover up his own disgrace at having lost his nerve in the typhoon, but the reader is surely led to wonder whether Jukes's conviction that the coolies should not be let loose is not undermined by illusory fear – similar to the second-mate's – that the crew is more vulnerable because the ship has 'been lately transferred to the Siamese flag' (98). Jukes concedes that: 'the skipper can't see that it makes any difference – "as long as *we* are on board"'; but by now the reader sees that Jukes, like the second-mate, is quite wrong on the issue; the flag is only a symbol, and MacWhirr is unthinkingly in command of his ship, whatever flag he happens to sail under.

The repetition of phrases in the final chapter is equally effective. For instance, Mrs MacWhirr quotes some of her husband's phrases which we already know, such as, 'Not in books' and 'Hope to have done the fair thing'; Jukes twice tells us that MacWhirr was concerned to do 'something that would be fair to all parties', and, in the novel's second to last sentence, reports his skipper's remark that 'There are things you find nothing about in books' (102). These formulae are already very familiar to the reader; and here they give the conclusion a combination of the humour which comes from the repetition of key stock phrases, with an increasing sympathy for MacWhirr, which comes from our understanding of the truth of the phrases as they apply to the later events of the story, and especially to his treatment of the coolies.

Did Conrad intend *Typhoon* as a whole to be a comedy? What little he
wrote about the book both at the time of writing and later offers rather
little help. His main discussion occurs in the 'Author's Note', which was
written in 1919, nearly twenty years after he had finished writing *Typhoon*.
Conrad tells how, 'casting about for some subject' that could be shorter
than the stories in the *Youth* volume, 'the instance of a steamship full
of returning coolies from Singapore to some port in northern China
occurred to my recollection'. When he had been in the China sea long
before, he remembered that people talked about the incident, 'the
interest of which for us was, of course, not the bad weather but the
extraordinary complication brought into the ship's life at a moment of
exceptional stress by the human element below her deck'.

Conrad's initial idea for *Typhoon*, then, came with the Chinese coolies;
but he soon realized that it was a 'mere anecdote', and that 'to bring
out its deeper significance . . . something more was required; a leading
motive that would harmonize all these violent noises, and a point of
view that would put all that elemental fury into its proper place' (vi).
That 'something more', he says, was, of course, Captain MacWhirr.
MacWhirr, Conrad affirms, was not based on any individual he had
ever met, but is the 'product of twenty years of life. My own life.' If
MacWhirr was the 'leading motive that would harmonise all these
violent noises', the 'point of view' which would 'put all that elemental
fury into its proper place' is not as easily identified; but the meiosis of
'in its proper place' suggests that it might be the humorous approach of
the narrative, especially in its treament of MacWhirr.

Conrad does not say this, however, but goes on to mention two
points which the critics had made at the time – that the story was a
'deliberately intended stormpiece', and that MacWhirr had a 'definite
symbolic intention'. This last possibility, incidentally, is strengthened
by what we know of the composition of *Typhoon*, where the passages
dealing both with the storm, and with Jukes, were cut down and more
attention was transferred to MacWhirr.[7] But Conrad does not pursue
either point, merely commenting that neither the idea of a stormpiece,
nor a symbolic intention for MacWhirr, was 'exclusively my intention',
although he adds that, like the other tales in the volume, *Typhoon* has
'more than one intention' (vii). Easily said, we may reflect.

Conrad does not mention the words 'comedy' or 'humour' in the
Author's Note for *Typhoon*. The closest he came to stating that this was

his aim occurred at the time of writing. In a letter to his agent, Pinker, he wrote that *Typhoon*, the first work handled by Pinker, was his 'first attempt at treating a subject jocularly so to speak'.[8] The intention of 'jocular treatment' finds some support in two of the early titles which Conrad considered for the tale – 'Equitable Decision' and 'A Skittish Cargo' – both of them obviously referring to the coolie side of the story.[9] Both suggest a much more light-hearted story than does the present, and more solemn, title of *Typhoon*.

We lack any other support from Conrad about his comic intention. Why? One possible reason is that he had become convinced that his friends did not admire this side of his writing. He may, for instance, have known even at the time of writing *Typhoon* that his fairly close friend, H. G. Wells, thought poorly of his comic talents. Wells was later to call the humour in *The Nigger of the 'Narcissus'* 'dismal'[10]; and in a personal episode of roughly the period of *Typhoon*, when Bernard Shaw had offended him, H. G. Wells pacified Conrad by saying 'It's humour', and adds, 'One would always baffle Conrad by saying "humour". It was one of our damned English tricks he had never learned to tackle.' Wells is not a wholly reliable witness, but it is certainly the prevalent critical wiew that Conrad, although admitted to be a master of irony, is not at his best when attempting anything more than incidental humour, and that he rarely attempted it in his later career.

There is, however, a small school of contrary opinion, especially for *Typhoon*. One of its reviewers, the distinguished writer Arthur Quiller Couch, wrote that it was 'a small masterpiece . . . built around a delightfully humorous character'.[11] Later, H. L. Mencken called it 'one of the curiosities of critical stupidity' to assume that Conrad was not a master of comedy.[12] Jocelyn Baines finds *Typhoon* somewhat exceptional; it is 'perhaps Conrad's most' cheerful tale, and in it, although 'humour, except for *Galgenhumor*, is rather rare in his work' Conrad can 'sometimes be delightfully funny as in the altercation over the Siamese flag between Captain MacWhirr and Jukes'.[13]

If we wish to pursue the idea that in *Typhoon* Conrad attempted comedy, we must ask with what 'deep conviction' Conrad 'approached the subject of the story', and whether it is consistent with a comic idea.

One simple way of putting it would be to say that *Typhoon* is about the corrections which experience administers to ideas. This, in one form or another, is a classic theme of intellectual comedy; and it would be consistent with Conrad's fiction in general, which normally exhibits a fairly critical attitude to theory as opposed to practice. 'No creed, in fact', as E. M. Forster put it, but 'only opinions, and the right to throw them overboard when facts make them look absurd'.[14] *Typhoon* stands out in the Conrad canon partly because its values are so completely dedicated to the triumph of fact. 'The China seas', we are told, are 'full of every-day, eloquent facts, such as islands, sand-banks, reefs, swift and changeable currents – tangled facts that nevertheless speak to a seaman in clear and definite language' (15). So MacWhirr, who has 'just enough imagination to carry him through each successive day, and no more' (4), is taciturn except for his duties. As the narrator puts it, 'the past being to his mind done with, and the future not there yet, the more general actualities of the day required no comment – because facts can speak for themselves with overwhelming precision' (9).

Conrad obviously uses MacWhirr's literal mindedness, and his monocular devotion to duty, as an extreme case, and in Jukes Conrad creates his opposite. Jukes, of course, has too much imagination, and this is allied with the inexperience of youth, and its disregard of ordinary realities. The conflict, as a result, is very different from that in *The Nigger of the 'Narcissus'*, to which *Typhoon* is often compared. Both captains, in the process of driving their ships hard, are responsible for the catastrophes which overtake them. Allistoun, however, is the ideal captain; he is almost superhuman in his understanding, and he also faces other appalling difficulties, especially the mutinous developments among the crew, for which he is not really responsible. MacWhirr is quite different; he seems to be below average in ordinary human understanding; and yet at the end he triumphs over his circumstances, and even teaches Jukes a great deal about command. Contrary to what some critics have said, MacWhirr also learns something from the typhoon, if only that he is mortal and may go down with the ship. But he is surely not a heroic figure in the same way that Allistoun is; much of what we are told about him, as opposed to Allistoun, emphasizes how he suffers the common tribulations of mortals, from an unfortunate marriage to the annoyances of having his tidy chart-room routines upset by the typhoon. MacWhirr, then, really is, as Conrad said, 'the product of twenty years of life. My own life.' As a young seaman, Conrad, as imaginative as Jukes, must have learned, with equal consternation and amazement, one of the hardest lessons of command, or rather of being commanded: the paradoxical fact that superiors who are in many respects inept can nevertheless be very good at the job; indeed, their very lack of interest or skill in conversation and books, the main values of verbal culture, may even have left them freer to do in a more single-minded way the one thing that they have trained themselves to do.

Conrad could not have done justice to his theme in merely showing this paradox in a straightforward way. The captain had to be exaggeratedly innocent of ideas, hostile to books, and devoid of emotional understanding, and yet he had to show that real, indeed essential, virtues can coexist without these traditional supports of civilized man. The comedy arose out of this conflict; and in it MacWhirr's imperceptiveness must be opposed by the contrasting character of his first mate. Jukes needs his captain badly in the typhoon; but he is too young to understand him. Thus he cannot imagine how MacWhirr can regard the boatswain as a 'first-rate petty officer' (49); that this is intended to reflect Jukes's youthful lack of judgment is emphasized by two earlier narrative parallels. First, there is the senior partner who thinks that MacWhirr is 'the very man' to command the *Nan-Shan*, while his young nephew asks, 'with faint contempt' 'What is it that you see in him?' (8) Second, there is the scene when the useless second mate eggs Jukes on to get MacWhirr to change course: the idea is good, but it is badly tarnished by this particular support.

Solomon Rout is very different from MacWhirr and Jukes. He is the shrewd observer whose humorous relish is suggested by his remark that 'the engineers that go down to the sea in ships behold the wonders of sailor nature' (16). He fights the typhoon in a pair of carpet slippers (69), but with dauntless tenacity; and we can surely trust what Rout says about MacWhirr: 'Give me the dullest ass for a skipper before a rogue' (16). Neither Jukes nor Rout is actually a close friend of MacWhirr; but they are forced to agree on MacWhirr's handling of the coolies: Rout says MacWhirr has 'done something rather clever'; and Jukes that he 'got out of it very well for such a stupid man'. These two judgements are alike in one respect: they place MacWhirr as a man in an illustrious comic tradition; he is the Innocent, the Natural, the Wise Fool, the man who is mocked by his fellows but who finally surprises them with a quite unexpected exhibition of real wisdom.

NOTES

1 Mario Curreli, 'Ugo Mursia: Una Vita per Conrad', in Ugo Mursia, *Scritti Conradiani*, ed. M. Curreli (Milan, 1983), pp. 10–11.

2 F. R. Leavis, *The Great Tradition* (London, 1948), pp. 183–5.

3 *Typhoon and Other Stories*, Dent's Collected Edition (London, 1950), pp. 3–4. Later quotations from *Typhoon* are given from this edition by page number

in the text. Where there are successive quotations from the same page, or immediately adjoining ones, only the first passage quoted is given a reference.

4 Henry Piddington, *The Sailor's Hornbook for the Law of Storms*, 7th edn (London, 1889), pp. 57–9, 107, 377.

5 Thomas Mann, 'Conrad's *Secret Agent*', *Past Masters and Other Papers* (London, 1933), pp. 231–47.

6 This is contrary to the view of some recent critics. Thus Paul Bruss argues that 'MacWhirr's fundamental unsuitability for life in Conrad's seas becomes the real focus of the narrator's concern' (*Conrad's Early Sea Fiction: The Novelist as Navigator* (Lewisburg, 1979), p. 124). William W. Bonney, in *Thorns and Arabesques: Contexts for Conrad's Fiction* (Baltimore, 1980), p. 35, sees MacWhirr as 'a product of the irresponsible commercial interests that fill the sea with steamships supervised by ill-trained officers'.

7 See H. T. Webster, 'Conrad's Changes in Narrative Conception in the Manuscripts of *Typhoon and Other Stories* and *Victory*', *PMLA*, 64 (1949), 953–4. I. P. Pulc argues that 'while the rendering of the storm in *The Nigger* is a magnificent triumph, the depiction of the hurricane in 'Typhoon' is almost a total failure' ('Two Portrayals of a Storm: Some Notes on Conrad's Descriptive Style in *The Nigger of the "Narcissus"* and *Typhoon*', *Style*, 4 (1970), 49–57).

8 Jocelyn Baines, *Joseph Conrad: A Critical Biography* (London, 1960), p. 258.

9 Frederick R. Karl, *Joseph Conrad: The Three Lives. A Biography* (New York, 1979), pp. 479, 497.

10 H. G. Wells, *Experiment in Autobiography* (New York, 1934), pp. 526, 530. John Galsworthy commented of Conrad that 'His sense of humour, indeed, was far greater than one might think from his work. He had an almost ferocious enjoyment of the absurd. Writing seemed to dry or sardonise his humour. But in conversation his sense of fun was much more vivid' (*Castles in Spain* (New York, 1927), p. 113).

11 *Conrad: The Critical Heritage*, ed. Norman Sherry (London, 1973), p. 156.

12 H. L. Mencken, 'Conrad Revisited', *Smart Set*, 69 (December 1922), 142.

13 Baines, *Conrad*, pp. 258–9.

14 E. M. Forster, 'Joseph Conrad: A Note', *Abinger Harvest* (London, 1946), p. 135.

CHAPTER 6

The political and social background of
The Secret Agent

The modern reader may find it useful to have some further information about the main historical source of *The Secret Agent*, the Greenwich Park explosion of 14 February 1894, and about Conrad's other sources for the novel.

This is not to imply that *The Secret Agent* is to be considered a novel about an actual historical event, in the sense that Josephine Tey's *The Franchise Affair*, say, is a fictional reconstruction of the mysterious Elizabeth Canning case in which Henry Fielding participated. For although Joseph Conrad's fiction nearly always started from some germ of reality – an anecdote, an historical event, an incident seen or a conversation overheard – by the time the work was finished it usually disclaimed any relation to actual persons, places or events. The germ of *Lord Jim*, for example, the desertion of the pilgrim ship, was a widely reported and notorious event; but in the completed novel Conrad tried to remove any details that tied it down to an identifiable place and time.

In *The Secret Agent* Conrad was hardly free to avoid specifying London and Greenwich as his locale; and he retained a good many of the actual details of the event. On the other hand, as the Author's Note says, after the initial challenge of his 'friend's' offhand remarks about the explosion, Conrad proceeded to develop the germinal cluster of ideas with the utmost imaginative freedom.

Conrad also steadfastly denied any detailed knowledge either of the explosion itself or of anarchism in general. As regards anarchism, Conrad's letter of 7 October 1907 to R. B. Cunninghame Graham is particularly explicit:

> . . . I am glad you like the *S. Agent. Vous comprenez bien* that the story was written completely without malice. It had some importance for me as a new departure in *genre* and as a sustained effort in ironical treatment of a melodramatic subject, – which was my technical intention. . . .

Every word you say I treasure. It's no use, I cannot conceal my pride in your praise. It is an immense thing for me, however great the part I ascribe to the generosity of your mind and the warmth of your heart.

But I don't think that I've been satirizing the revolutionary world. All these people are not revolutionaries, – they are shams. And as regards the Professor, I did not intend to make him despicable. He is incorruptible at any rate. In making him say: 'Madness and despair, – give me that for a lever and I will move the world', I wanted to give him a note of perfect sincerity. At the worst he is a megalomaniac of an extreme type. And every extremist is respectable.

I am extremely flattered to have secured your commendation for my Secretary of State and for the Revolutionary Toodles. It was very easy there (for me) to go utterly wrong.

By Jove! If I had the necessary talent I would like to go for the true anarchist, which is the millionaire. Then you would see the venom flow. But it's too big a job. . . .'

Conrad's emphasis here that anarchism in *The Secret Agent* is treated 'without malice' no doubt arises from his anxiety not to offend Cunninghame Graham's radical views. Yet there is much other evidence to show that Conrad did not think of *The Secret Agent* either as a serious study of anarchism, or even as a responsible reconstruction of the explosion itself. It is true that Conrad stated to Methuen that the story was 'based on the inside knowledge of a certain event in the history of active anarchism': but he also went on to insist that 'otherwise it is *purely a work of imagination*'. Nearly twenty years later Conrad repeated this qualification in a letter to Ambrose J. Barker, who had sent him a pamphlet about the Greenwich Outrage, presumably that by David Nicoll mentioned above. On 1 September 1923 Conrad replied:

Thank you very much for your letter and the pamphlet in which I was very much interested.

As a matter of fact I never knew anything of what was called, if I remember rightly, the 'Greenwich Bomb Outrage'. I was out of England when it happened, and thus I never read what was printed in the newspapers at the time. All I was aware of was the mere fact – my novel being, in intention, the history of Winnie Verloc. I hope you have seen that the purpose of the book was not to attack any doctrine, or even the men holding that doctrine. My object, apart from the aim of telling a story, was to hold up the worthlessness of certain individuals and the baseness of some others. It was a matter of great interest to me to see how near actuality I managed to come in a work of imagination.

I hope you will do me the pleasure to accept the book [*The Rover*] I am sending you – which is also a work of pure imagination though very different in subject and treatment from the *Secret Agent*.

P.S. I suppose you meant me to keep the pamphlet, which I would like to paste into my own copy of the novel.[2]

But if we must agree that *The Secret Agent* is not a novel about a particular event, and that its merits, therefore, do not depend upon the accuracy or insight with which the event is reconstructed, the opposite extreme also seems to me equally untenable. If *The Secret Agent* dealt with events, characters and ideas that had no basis whatever in the real world or human history, we should presumably have to read it as fantasy; but the novel surely enlists a quite different kind of credence, and makes more serious claims on our attention. More information about the background of *The Secret Agent* may help, then, not to test the authenticity of its interpretation of historical events, but to suggest what distance exists between Conrad's fictional world, and the actual time and *milieu* with which his novel deals.

It is impossible to establish with any precision how far Conrad's version departs from the facts about the Greenwich Observatory explosion, because these facts are still not fully known. This is really quite in the normal course of things for a not particularly important event in which the protagonist died, and in which secret police, double agents, and possibly foreign powers, were involved. Nevertheless, enough is known to make it possible to show that on some issues Conrad was close to the facts, and that on others he departed from them. There is, of course, a third category of matters on which there is insufficient evidence to make a judgement.

Norman Sherry has shown that Conrad's version was faithful in its general outlines to what the newspapers reported about the explosion in Greenwich Park, and how the anarchists reacted to it.

There is also some evidence to show that the Criminal Investigation Department was directly involved in the affair through a secret agent pretending to be an anarchist, who possibly inspired the Greenwich Outrage, and who almost certainly provided the explosives. Here the evidence comes from three main sources: from David Nicoll, whose two pamphlets on the matter are quoted above; from Ford Madox Ford; and from Sir Robert Anderson's memoirs.

Nicoll himself believed that Bourdin's brother-in-law, the former editor of an anarchist journal, *Commonweal*, H. B. Samuels, was a police spy who had sent Bourdin to his fate; and Samuels's loyalty to the movement was certainly questioned at the time by other anarchists. That the police had some informant about Bourdin's plans is obliquely confirmed by Sir Robert Anderson in a later memoir than the one Conrad quoted in his Author's Note. Anderson writes:

I never spent hours of greater anxiety than during one afternoon in February, 1894, when information reached me that a French tailor named Bourdin had left his shop in Soho with a bomb in his pocket. To track him was impracticable. All that could be done was to send out officers in every direction to watch persons and places that he might be likely to attack. His actual objective was the very last place the Police would have thought of watching, namely Greenwich Observatory. Travelling to Greenwich by tramcar, he entered the Park, and as he ascended the path leading to the Observatory he evidently took the bomb out of his pocket, and was preparing to use it, when it exploded in his hand, inflicting injuries from which he died after a few hours suffering.[3]

Anderson gives no further details – he is using Bourdin only as an illustration of how difficult it is 'to catch a criminal who works alone' and especially 'these fiends . . . the alien anarchist dynamiters'. If Samuels was in fact the informer, it sounds as though Samuels left Bourdin without knowing where he was going, so that he could not warn the police in time.

Nicoll mentions another police informer, Auguste Coulon, who started an anarchist journal on behalf of the police, and who was also watching Bourdin; but Anderson does not help establish what went wrong with the surveillance, and this aspect of the case remains a mystery. On other matters, however, Anderson is more helpful. In particular he confirms Conrad's picture of the conflict between a newly appointed Assistant Commissioner of Scotland Yard and such 'old departmental hands' as Conrad's Chief Inspector Heat. When Anderson moved from the political Secret Service to the Criminal Investigation Department he was, he tells us

not a little surprised . . . to find occasion to suspect that one of my principal subordinates was trying to impose on me as though I were an ignoramus. For when any important crime of a certain kind occurred, and I set myself to investigate *à la* Sherlock Holmes, he used to listen to me in the way that so many people listen to sermons in church; and when I was done he would stolidly announce that the crime was the work of A, B, C, or D, naming some of his stock heroes. Though a keen and shrewd police officer, the man was unimaginative, and I thus accounted for the fact that his list was always brief, and that the same names came up repeatedly. It was 'Old Carr', or 'Wirth', or 'Sausage', or 'Shrimps', or 'Quiet Joe', or 'Red Bob', &c. &c. one name or another being put forward according to the kind of crime I was investigating.[4]

It was actually only by an accident arising out of such conflicts within the police authority that the use of double agents by the Secret Service had come to public attention in the years previous to 1894. The matter is very fully set forth in the book of Anderson's which Conrad quotes in his Author's Note, *Sidelights on the Home Rule Movement*. Anderson had been in secret correspondence for over twenty years with one Major Henri Le Caron, the pseudonym of Thomas M. Beach, an Englishman who had risen high in the American Fenian movement, the Clan-na-Gael. Caron had given Anderson a great deal of important advance information about the bombing and other plans of the Fenians. Inevitably, in Anderson's view, Caron had acted as an *agent provocateur* in some of these cases.[5] The nature of Caron's activities became public during the Parnell case. In an interview with Parnell, Caron had learned of Parnell's general awareness of the plans for violence of the Irish Land League. This and other information about the relationships between the parliamentary and the revolutionary wings of the fight for Irish independence was eventually used, and falsified, in the 1887 *Times* articles on 'Parnellism and Crime'. In the Special Commission of investigation that followed, Caron appeared as a witness; and his testimony revealed both the extent to which the Government used double agents and *agents provocateurs*, and the way that they and their immediate superiors could influence public policy. As a result the secret use of Caron's evidence to support Conservative policy on Ireland was attacked by the Liberal leader Sir William Harcourt, who rightly believed that the alleged *Times* letter from Parnell to the dynamitard Patrick Egan was a forgery. Harcourt was also concerned at the way Anderson had employed Caron without even informing the then Home Secretary, Henry Matthews; and Anderson then defended the need to keep Caron's activities entirely to himself in a letter to *The Times*.[6]

In view of his letter to Barker it is perhaps wiser to assume that Conrad had not read Nicoll's pamphlets, and that his main informant for the background of *The Secret Agent* was Ford Madox Ford, the 'friend' mentioned in Conrad's Author's Note. In his memoir of Conrad written immediately after Conrad's death, Ford contradicts part of Conrad's version of their colloquy:

What the writer really did say to Conrad was: 'Oh that fellow was half an idiot: His sister murdered her husband afterwards and was allowed to escape by the police. I remember the funeral.' . . . The suicide was invented by Conrad. And the writer knew – and Conrad knew that the writer knew – a great many anarchists of the Goodge Street group, as well as a great many of the police who watched them. The writer had provided Conrad with Anarchist literature, with memoirs, with introductions to at least one Anarchist young lady who figures in *The Secret Agent*.[7]

There is no other evidence that Bourdin was 'half an idiot' or that his sister murdered her husband; and in any case Ford's testimony is suspect, if only because my own fairly prolonged frequentation of *The Secret Agent* has failed to discover even one 'Anarchist young lady' in it to whom Conrad might have been introduced.

Ford was probably thinking of his cousins, Helen and Olivia Rossetti. They did write a fictional memoir of their experiences as editors of an anarchist paper, *The Torch*, under the title *A Girl Among the Anarchists*, by Isabel Meredith (London, 1903). It gave, among other things, a thinly disguised account of the Greenwich explosion. The account is very close to Nicoll's as regards the role of Samuels (called Jacob Myers), and the supplying of sulphuric acid to Bourdin (called Augustin Myers) by Samuels from an anarchist called Dr Armitage, a Harley Street doctor (Macdonald in Nicoll). In 'Isabel Meredith's' account, however, Myers, the Verloc figure, accompanied by his wife, actually escapes to France to avoid giving evidence in the trial of two anarchists who are falsely accused of complicity in the outrage, and sentenced to five years' penal servitude.[8]

In *A Girl Among the Anarchists*, according to William Michael Rossetti, his daughters gave 'with fancy names and some modification of details, a genuine account of their experiences'.[9] Their account certainly tends to cast doubt on most of Ford's version where it differs from Nicoll's, except in two matters: Bourdin is shown as a rather simple enthusiast wholly under his brother's influence; and the brother's motives are suspect, though mainly for advocating irresponsible violence.

There is, then, no secure evidence for seeing Conrad's Verloc as being modelled on the historical Bourdin's brother or brother-in-law. Nor is it easy to find much beyond circumstantial evidence that the British Government of the period employed a secret informer who was both an anarchist leader and an *agent provocateur* for a foreign power. The general history of spying, however, shows that finding as many paymasters as possible is common, both among its important practitioners and even more among such marginal operatives as Verloc. Apart from Coulon there was another fairly close analogue to Verloc operating in London in 1895, Eugène Cottin, a French police spy pretending to be an anarchist. Cottin does not seem to have worked with the London police, however, and so his case only supports the general probability that since the communist and anarchist movements were international, and since England provided their main haven, foreign governments presumably met the threat in their usual ways. Thus the great outburst of terrorism in France from 1892 to 1895 probably explains the presence of both French anarchists and secret police agents in London which is often referred to by the press during the period.

The years between the Greenwich explosion and the writing of *The Secret Agent* were certainly the golden age of political *agents provocateurs*. The most picturesque example is that of the Russian Azev. On behalf of the Russian secret police he infiltrated the Socialist Revolutionary Party, became the head of its terrorist section, and there provided himself with impeccable subversive credentials by being involved in the assassination both of the Russian Minister of the Interior in 1904, and of the Grand Duke Sergei in 1905.[10]

Ford made Azev the instigator of Bourdin in two memoirs written long after Conrad's death. His most explicit account is in *Return to Yesterday*, and the passage is worth quoting at length for its no doubt over-coloured picture of the atmosphere surrounding the Russian anarchists and police in London at the time:

the fact that England was the international refuge for all exiles was not agreeable to the Russian police who filled the country with an incredible number of spies. There must have been at least one for every political exile and the annoyance that they caused in the country was extreme. I remember between 1893 and 1894 going home for longish periods almost every night from London University to a western suburb with Stepniak, Volkhovsky or Prince Kropotkin who were then the most prominent members of the Russian extreme Left and who were lecturing at the university on political economy, Russian literature and, I think, biology respectively. And behind us always lurked or dodged the Russian spies allotted to each of those distinguished lecturers. Stepniak or Volkhovsky dismissed them at Hammersmith station, as often as not with the price of a pint, for the poor devils were miserably paid, and also because, the spies and their purpose being perfectly well known in the district where the Russians lived, they were apt to receive very rough handling from the residents who resented their presences as an insult to the country. One or two quite considerable riots were thus caused in the neighbourhoods of Hammersmith proper and Ealing.

Those matters caused at one time a very considerable friction between the British and the Russian courts. The redoubtable Azev, who was the Russian chief spy-master and *agent provocateur*, conceived the fantastic idea that an outrage in England might induce the British Government and British public opinion to decree the expulsion of all political exiles from their shores, the exiles themselves being remarkably law-abiding. He accordingly persuaded a half-witted youth to throw a bomb into Greenwich Observatory. The boy, however, stumbling over a tree-stump in the Observatory Park was blown to pieces and the whole matter came to light. For diplomatic reasons, the newspapers made very little of it. But the Home Secretary, Sir William Vernon

Harcourt, made such caustic remarks over it to the Russian First Secretary of Embassy that Russian activities on the Afghan border became very marked for a considerable period.

I happen accidentally to know a good deal of these episodes. My own house was once – and my mother's twice – burgled by emissaries of the Russian Embassy in search of documents. In my case, I being the owner of *The English Review*, the above-mentioned scoundrel Azev sent me by one of his emissaries a volume of the diary of the late Tzar; he imagining that I might like to publish it – which I didn't. I didn't want to have it in my house for more than a minute and took it round to my bank for internment whilst I informed the police. In the interval between then and my return, a little after midnight my house had been carefully gone through and all my papers, which were very many, had been thrown all over the floor. In my mother's case, the same thing happened twice, during the time that Father Gapon, the heroic leader of the peasants to the Tzar's palace on Bloody Sunday, was being housed by her, my mother being very charitable but by no means interested in politics. Eventually Gapon was sandbagged outside the house and the burglar – a Russian – given a long term of imprisonment. The Embassy naturally denied all knowledge of or responsibility for him. I came in that way a good deal in contact with the Scotland Yard Inspector who had charge of that sort of case and he told me a great deal about not only the activities of the Russian spies but gave me an – I daresay highly coloured – account of what the Home Secretary had said to the Secretary of the Embassy.[11]

In *Portraits from Life* Ford is briefer, but his account is important for its explicitness about how he supplied Conrad with the material on revolutionaries for *The Secret Agent*:

The Secret Agent represents the anarchist-communists of London as being a pretty measly set of imbeciles, but it represents the *agent provocateur* – whom I knew well – as even more loathsome than the hideous Azev really was and the employer of that sad scoundrel as even more imbecile, if more sophisticated, than the shadows of Kropotkin, Stepniak, Volkhovsky, Bakunin, and the rest. And he had really made efforts to get behind the revolutionary mind. I supplied him with most of the material of that sort of book, and it was instructive in the extreme to see him react to those accounts of revolutionary activities.[12]

Both passages date from the 1930s, long after the events described; and they are demonstrably unreliable in some important matters. Asquith, not Harcourt, was Home Secretary at the time of the Green-wich explosion; and Ford's relationship with Azev, even by his own account, belongs to the period when he was owner of the *English Review*, that is, not before 1908, two years after Conrad wrote *The Secret Agent*, fourteen after the Greenwich explosion, and in the same year that Azev was finally exposed in a Russian revolutionary review, and forced to go into exile. Ford elsewhere allows for the difference of dates when, after an account of his connection with the anarchist paper *The Torch*, he writes in *Return to Yesterday* that the association

had one other curious literary offshoot. That was *The Secret Agent* by Joseph Conrad. In one of my visits to *The Torch* office I heard the inner story of the Greenwich Observatory outrage. It was subsequently confirmed and supplemented to me by Inspector French of Scotland Yard after first my mother's and then my own house had been burgled by a professional cracksman employed by the Russian Embassy. I happened to tell the story to Conrad shortly after my burglary and, since he detested all Russians, and the Russian Secret Police in particular, he made his novel out of it. In his attribution to me of the plot which will be found in the Preface to the book he says he is sure that the highly superior person who told him the tale could never have come into contact with Anarchists. I have recounted above how I did.[13]

Ford fairly obviously conflated three different periods: that of the Greenwich explosion; that immediately before the composition of *The Secret Agent* (Bloody Sunday, in which Father Gapon was involved, occurred on 22 January 1905); and that of Azev's exposure some years later. There are no doubt relics of the conflation of the first two periods in *The Secret Agent*; and so we must accept Ford's accounts as important sources for *The Secret Agent*, even if they are not accurate either as historical fact or as to what Ford actually told Conrad at any given time.[14]

As regards historical fact, for instance, the most convincing new detail in the last passage is highly dubious. The official reticence of Scotland Yard has so far yielded to the importunities of scholarship as to inform me that 'I am directed by the Commissioner to say that, on the particulars supplied, it has not been possible to identify Inspector French as having served at Scotland Yard.'[15]

For the purpose of estimating what Ford told Conrad before *The Secret Agent* was written, the version of the Greenwich affair given in Ford's earliest mention, the 1911 *Ancient Lights*, is probably the best guide. In it neither Azev nor the Russian Government is identified; but the Greenwich explosion is already seen as a foreign effort to force the British Government to stop harbouring revolutionaries:

I don't know where the crowds came from that supported us as anarchists, but I have seldom seen a crowd so great as that which attended the funeral of the poor idiot who blew himself to pieces in the attempt on Greenwich Observatory. This was, of course, an attempt fomented by the police agents of a foreign state with a view to forcing the hand of the British Government . . . so that they would arrest wholesale every anarchist in Great Britain. Of course the British Government did nothing of the sort.[16]

Again Ford erred. The new Tory Government did something of the sort by introducing a new Aliens Bill, and raiding the main anarchist meeting-places, the Autonomie Club and the office of *The Torch*. On the other hand the newspapers, and Nicoll's pamphlets, show that many anarchists agreed with Ford in thinking that the explosion was the work of an *agent provocateur* whose masters wanted to end the privileged asylum of foreign revolutionaries in England.

Conrad certainly had other sources besides Ford for the idea of secret but violent foreign interference in another country. He wrote in his letter to Cunninghame Graham of 7 October 1907: 'Mr Vladimir was suggested to me by that scoundrel, General Seliwertsow, whom Padlewski shot (in Paris) in the '90s. There were peculiar circumstances in that case'.

General Seliverskov was a former Russian Minister of Police who was suspected of spying on Russian nihilists in Paris. Some of these were arrested by the French police when making explosives in a village near Paris in the May of 1890; and six months later Seliverskov was murdered in his hotel by a Pole, Padlewski, who was helped to escape by some revolutionary French socialists.[17]

The parallel to Vladimir is not, of course, very close; but Seliverskov at least is one example of a high Russian police official spying on anarchists in a foreign country. That this also went on in England can plausibly be inferred from the fact that the Russian Ambassador in London for many years, Count Shuvalov, had formerly been head of the Russian political police.[18] On the other hand, since the foreign anarchists in general did not want to jeopardize their safety in England, and since there were consequently very few examples of anarchist terrorism in England, the instigation of such activities as the Greenwich explosion by Russian or other foreign governments must be regarded as on the whole unlikely, or at least highly exceptional.

Whether Bourdin in fact intended a demonstration against the Greenwich Observatory, either independently, or under the instigation of genuine anarchists, irresponsible *agents provocateurs* such as Samuels, or even a foreign power, cannot now be determined. The choice of such a target would not in itself have been exceptional. Anarchist extremism preached public gestures against public institutions, and self-immolation added resonance to the gesture. There is no anarchist parallel in England to the Greenwich case, but the Fenians provide several. Thus the Chicago Convention of 1886 determined to mount 'a pyrotechnic display in honour of the Queen's Jubilee' of 1887 – a projected dynamite explosion in Westminster Abbey; and in 1884 Mackay Lomasney was blown to pieces by his own dynamite in a demonstration against London Bridge.[19]

The Secret Agent, then, cannot be viewed as a reconstruction of the Greenwich explosion; and as regards Conrad's claim to Methuen, echoing Ford's to him, that it was 'based on the inside knowledge of a certain event in the history of active anarchism', we can accept it only with the proviso that, as we all know from reading the newspapers, the inside story is often false. There are, however, reasonably close historical analogues for the novel's general presentation of the activities of the anarchists, the police, and the British and foreign governments: so much so that, in his recent book *The Anarchists*, Joll calls *The Secret Agent* 'the classic description of the relations between anarchists and police'.[20]

Where Conrad increases the distance between fact and fiction is in two main areas. First, he creates a tighter domestic drama. Ford seems to be responsible for making Bourdin and therefore Stevie a half-wit, and for having the Samuels or Verloc in the case murdered. Conrad may have added the suicide of Winnie, though he was later under the impression that he got it from Ford. These changes also support the effect of the second and more political kind of departure from the original circumstances. Adding Vladimir, and omitting any attractive, impressive, or even merely English, revolutionaries, tended to under-line the irony of the picture, and to deepen what Conrad called the 'criminal futility' of the story. In short, although *The Secret Agent* is neither a historical nor a Naturalistic novel, its distance from reality, though varying, is never very great. It takes an initiated, slightly fanci-ful, and above all very selective, view of the *milieu* and the events out of which the story arose.

It is the nature of this selective perspective which is the basis of Irving Howe's objection that *The Secret Agent* does not give a fair picture of the anarchist movement as a whole. And, of course, Conrad did not intend to. Nor need we see Conrad's perspective as merely an expression of his own conservative prejudices, since it was much more difficult for anyone then to see the positive significance of anarchism than it is now, either for Howe or for us.

Conrad had certainly been an arch-reactionary in his early days. In 1885, for instance, he wrote to a Polish friend, Spiridion Kliszczewski: 'Where's the man to stop the rush of social-democratic ideas? The opportunity and the day have come and are gone! Believe me: gone for ever. For the sun is set and the last barrier removed. England was the only barrier to the pressure of infernal doctrines born in continental back-slums. . . .'[21] As the years passed, however, Conrad's political views became less frenetic and more objective. As a Pole born under Russian occupation he remained anti-Russian, and of course in his day anarchism was largely a Russian movement; but by 1905, as his important political essay 'Autocracy and War' shows, Conrad had come to see Russian despotism and Prussian militarism as the main dangers to the European order. At this time, at least, the threat of revolution seemed much less so – and with good reason.

After the split between Marx and Bakunin, and the dissolution of the First International in 1876, the revolutionary movement split into many factions. As regards anarchism, the great traditions of Godwin and Proudhon, continued by Bakunin and Kropotkin, were largely submerged by the terrorist tactics of Nechaev. This dominance of *propagande par le fait* was confirmed in 1881 when a conference of revolutionaries in London, including Malatesta and Kropotkin, agreed that revolution could only be brought about by illegal means. In the following decades anarchism was taken to mean terrorism; and all Europe was in fact terrified. There were innumerable attempts on the lives of prominent statesmen and royalty throughout Europe, and some were successful. Thus the assassinations of the Presidents of France and the United States, of the Prime Minister of Spain, of the Empress of Austria, of the King of Italy, were all attributed to anarchists.

What was most striking in all this to Conrad, we can assume, was the extraordinarily wide spectrum of persons and motives which composed the anarchist movement and its sympathizers. In every country they ranged from high-minded sympathizers who were mainly concerned with the degrading injustices of the current social order, to the most marginal criminals and psychotics who sought economic or emotional satisfaction in casual destruction. Even within the official anarchist movement itself there was a similar spectrum, from intellectual noblemen like Kropotkin to ruthless fanatics like Johann Most.

Conrad was in France at the height of the terrorist campaign early in 1894. There Vaillant, who had thrown a bomb into the Chamber of Deputies, was condemned to the guillotine despite the fact that no one had been killed. President Sadi Carnot refused clemency, and as he died Vaillant exclaimed: 'Long live Anarchy! My death will be avenged.' It was indeed, for on 24 June 1894 an Italian anarchist, Caserio, stabbed Carnot to death. In the ensuing prosecutions the wide following of the anarchists received great publicity. The writer Félix Fénéon, a civil servant in the Ministry of War, was prosecuted for forming a criminal association; and the subscription list of the main anarchist paper, *Le Révolté*, was found to contain the names of some of the most famous writers and artists of the day – France, Daudet, Leconte de Lisle, Signac, Seurat, Pissarro. When Mallarmé, who testified on Fénéon's behalf, was asked for his views on terrorism, he answered that 'he could not discuss the acts of these saints'.[22]

Anarchism had a similarly broad spectrum of adherents and sympathizers in England, from eminent intellectuals to the most feckless hangers-on. William Morris and Bernard Shaw were active supporters in the early 1890s; but it was difficult then to see what would come out of all the quarrelsome meetings and violent speeches. In some countries, as in Spain, anarchism was to become a viable tradition; in others, as in England, France and Russia, it was but one of many forces of protest which led to the creation and eventual victory of powerful socialist or communist parties. Many of the English anarchist sympathizers were concerned, in 1893, with the foundation of the Independent Labour Party; thirty years later one of its founding members, Ramsay Mac-Donald, would form the first Labour Government, and offer Conrad a knighthood.

Conrad, in *The Secret Agent* at least, seems blind to this historical perspective. One reason is probably that the political views and connections of his own immediate circle seemed to illustrate something that was both typical of the anarchist movement and very near to his own central concerns as a writer. The most aristocratic of his friends, Robert Cunninghame Graham, descended from the royal house of Scotland, and an MP, had spent six weeks in jail for 'assault of the police' when the authorities broke up a Trafalgar Square meeting of the Social Democratic Federation in 1887, which Kropotkin had also attended. Edward Garnett, a socialist, had a similarly varied set of connections: his father was an establishment figure, Principal Librarian of the British Museum; while his wife, Constance, was friendly not only with Kropotkin but with Stepniak, on whose behalf she went on secret business to Russia not knowing that Stepniak had earlier been a terrorist there and stabbed General Mezentzev.[23] In his youth Ford himself had been an anarchist; his sister married a Russian, David Soskice, who had recovered from his Siberian exile in the Garnetts' country home;[24] and most striking of all, Ford's mother's half-sister, though the wife of William Michael Rossetti, Secretary to the Board of Inland Revenue, nevertheless allowed her daughters to edit an anarchist journal, *The Torch*, in her own house.[25]

When Conrad, then, began to think about the tale which was to become *The Secret Agent*, he had already had close personal experience of the interpenetration of order and anarchy in the political and social order. That general conflict, together with individual isolation, were already his chosen themes; and they combined to provide an ironic perspective very different from the one in which secret agents were usually viewed. For Conrad we are all, one way or another, like Verloc: a little less conscious, no doubt, and a little less venal, but still secret agents torn between protecting and destroying the established order. Society seems unaware of the problem; but then society is really one vast conspiracy of blindness.

The fact that his locale was English, however, raised personal problems of a peculiar complexity for Conrad. Like the anarchists, he was himself a refugee from political oppression and, deeply grateful to England as he was, we may surmise that his elaborate notion of decorum made him averse to any direct political criticism of his adopted country. That there are no English anarchists in *The Secret Agent*, and that the anarchist theme is hardly allowed to have any serious domestic implications, may perhaps be regarded as in part an ironic tribute to his new country and his friends there. Unlike Conrad, neither his fictional English characters, nor his actual friends, seem able to imagine that there could conceivably be any serious threat to the continuance of their national life: in their insular security they treat politics as a game where, in the words of Sir Robert Anderson, 'the rules of the prize ring are held to apply to the struggle between the law and those who break it'.[26] In his heart, Conrad probably believed that trusting in such rules was just another example of Winnie Verloc's distaste for looking into things too deeply; but with courteous reticence he only said it in the most indirect and jesting way.

NOTES

1 Jean-Aubry, *Life and Letters*, II, 60. Conrad made several other similar denials. 'I know almost nothing of the philosophy, and nothing at all of the men', Conrad wrote in 1912 (*Letters of Joseph Conrad to Marguerite Poradowska, 1890–1920*, ed. John A. Gee and Paul J. Sturm (New Haven, 1940), p. 116); see also Elbridge L. Adams, *Joseph Conrad: The Man* (New York, 1925), p. 55.
2 Jean-Aubry, *Life and Letters*, II, 322.
3 Sir Robert Anderson, *The Lighter Side of My Official Life* (London and New York, 1910), pp. 175–6.
4 Sir Robert Anderson, *Criminals and Crime: Some Facts and Suggestions* (London, 1907), pp. 87–8.
5 Sir Robert Anderson, *Sidelights on the Home Rule Movement* (London, 1907), pp. 150–1.
6 See also David Nicoll, *The Greenwich Mystery* (Sheffield, 1897); Major Henri Le Caron's memoir, *Twenty-five Years in the Secret Service: Recollections of a Spy*

(London, 1892); and A. G. Gardiner, *The Life of Sir William Harcourt* (London, 1923) vol. II, pp. 244–50.

7 *Joseph Conrad: A Personal Remembrance* (London, 1929), p. 231.

8 Op. cit., pp. 39–73. The two anarchists are called Banter and O'Flynn (Cantwell and Quinn in Nicoll). Conrad's short story 'The Informer' deals with the same *milieu*; see James Walton, 'Mr X's "Little Joke": The Design of Conrad's "The Informer"', *Studies in Short Fiction*, 4 (1967), 322–33.

9 W. M. Rossetti, *Some Reminiscences* (London, 1906), p. 450.

10 See Boris Nikolajewsky, *Aseff the Spy* (New York, 1934).

11 Ford Madox Ford, *Return to Yesterday* (London, 1931), pp. 134–7.

12 Ford Madox Ford, *Portraits from Life* (Boston and New York, 1937), p. 66 (published in London in 1938 as *Mightier than the Sword*).

13 Ford, *Return to Yesterday*, p. 114.

14 The Azev case, for instance, was certainly a source of *Under Western Eyes* (1911); and Ford probably confused the details of his help on the two novels. The parallels are treated in Morton Dauwen Zabel's 'Introduction' to *Under Western Eyes* (New York, 1963).

15 Letter from The Secretary, New Scotland Yard, of 10 October 1960.

16 Ford Madox Ford, under the title *Memories and Impressions* (London and New York, 1911), pp. 135–7.

17 *The Times*, 20 and 25 Nov 1890.

18 See Anderson, *The Lighter Side of My Official Life*, pp. 246–8.

19 Anderson, *Sidelights on the Home Rule Movement*, pp. 284–5, 150.

20 James Joll, *The Anarchists* (London, 1964), p. 128.

21 Jean-Aubry, *Life and Letters*, I, 84.

22 Joll, *The Anarchists*, pp. 96–135.

23 David Garnett, *The Golden Echo* (London, 1954), pp. 10–14.

24 Ford, *Return to Yesterday*, p. 131.

25 *Ibid.*, p. 112.

26 Anderson, *Sidelights on the Home Rule Movement*, p. 127.

CHAPTER 7

'The Secret Sharer': introduction

Joseph Conrad wrote 'The Secret Sharer' with exceptional speed and pleasure. At the end of 1909 he had been struggling desperately to finish *Under Western Eyes*, harassed by sickness and debts. His depression was particularly severe in early November; but then, as he wrote to his old friend John Galsworthy, 'I took off last week to write a short story . . . and no gout so far.' Conrad said that this story – 'The Secret Sharer' – took him only ten days, but it probably took a bit longer. The stimulus to writing it was a happy one in two ways: Conrad received a letter, and later a visit, from Captain Carlos M. Marris, an adventurous trader in the Malayan archipelago. Marris renewed his memories of old times; and he also told Conrad that many seamen out there 'read my books', and 'feel kindly to the chronicler of their lives and adventures'. Conrad was happy to hear it, and at once decided that they 'should have some more of the stories they like'.

And so, after the years working on Western subjects – the South America of *Nostromo* (1904), the London of *The Secret Agent* (1907) and the Russia of *Under Western Eyes* (1911) – Conrad went to the fictional subjects of his earlier life, and his earlier writing career. 'The Secret Sharer' was the first written of these tales of the Eastern seas, and it was originally supposed to be placed first, although it eventually came second, in a volume of three tales called *'Twixt Land and Sea*. The book was dedicated to Marris, and appeared on 14 October 1912, in Conrad's largest first edition yet – 3,600 copies in England. It was very well received. One reviewer, Robert Lynd, singled out 'The Secret Sharer' as 'surely a masterpiece' which any doubter of 'Conrad's genius . . . will do well to read'; while the praise of his old friend Edward Garnett, moved Conrad to a burst of uncharacteristic self-congratulation: 'The Secret Sharer, between you and me, is *it*. Eh? No damned tricks with girls there. Eh? Every word fits and there's not a single uncertain note. Luck my boy. Pure luck.'

The tale's size – more substantial than a short story, but much shorter than a novel – is that of the 'nouvelle', which, as the poet John Masefield wrote in his review of 'The Secret Sharer', Conrad had 'always used . . . with fine effect', and which, Masefield thought, would 'perhaps become the usual literary form in the decades after this'. 'The Secret Sharer' is – on the surface – a simple but utterly convincing tale; but the last forty years or so of criticism, which have in general converted Conrad into a more modern and innovative writer than he was once thought, have also turned 'The Secret Sharer' into a work whose larger psychological and moral meaning has lent itself to considerable controversy.

Conrad himself had difficulties with the nouvelle's title. He considered 'The Second Self', 'The Secret Self', 'The Other Self', as well as 'The Secret Sharer'. This last title, Conrad thought, was 'maybe too enigmatic'; and it was his agent, J. B. Pinker, who finally decided for 'The Secret Sharer'. At the literal level, of course, the title is not unduly 'enigmatic'; the 'sharer' must be Leggatt, the fugitive from the law whom the unnamed captain and narrator picks up by accident and hides in his own cabin; and Leggatt is a 'secret' sharer because he must remain unseen by anyone else on the ship.

What else does the title imply? Some help may come from the tale's two main sources.

Most obviously, there is the actual occurrence on a famous teaclipper, the *Cutty Sark* (Scots for a 'short chemise'). In 1880 its chief mate, a Scot who went under the name of Sidney Smith, killed an incompetent black seaman called John Francis in a quarrel precipitated by Francis's insolent answer to a command during a change of course off the coast of South Africa. A week or so later, in Java, the mate, who had been confined to his cabin, was secretly allowed to escape by his captain. This exacerbated the anger of the crew, a near-mutiny occurred, and, as a result, the captain, a fine sailor, committed suicide by drowning. Two years later Smith was recognized, tried in London, found guilty of manslaughter, and given seven years penal servitude.

Conrad mentions the episode, which was rather well-known, in his 'Author's Note' to *'Twixt Land and Sea*. He says he had heard of it from 'the officers of the great wool fleet in which my first years in deep water were served'; and he later read about it in the newspapers. As many critics have pointed out, however, Conrad made many changes. In his version, when the death occurs there is a terrible storm and the mate is determined that for the ship to have any chance of surviving the crew must face the terrifying task of setting a reefed foresail. One sailor, 'half-crazed with funk', gives him some of his 'cursed insolence' whereupon the mate, under terrible strain, 'fells' the man 'like an ox'. The sea then almost submerges the ship for over ten minutes, and when the waters recede Leggatt is found to be still holding the dead man by the throat. He is locked in his cabin but before they arrive at Java he begs his captain to be allowed to escape; but although Leggatt had saved his ship, the captain refuses.

Conrad, then, gives his first mate a much more sympathetic role than Smith's; the death was accidental, and in a crisis for the whole ship; he did not cause the suicide of a fine captain, but on the contrary was victimized by the ridiculous and law-obsessed Archbold, captain of the *Sephora*; Leggatt then saves himself without any help, and by a great feat of swimming; and he is the son of a Norfolk parson, who was trained for the merchant navy on the *Conway*. The captain-narrator had also been a *Conway* boy a couple of years before; their immediate intimacy comes from this, and their both being gentlemen, and speaking the same language.

The second main source of the tale is Conrad's own experience. His first command had also come to him suddenly and unexpectedly, like that of his fictional captain, and in Bangkok, and on a ship that was new to him. Presumably Conrad himself, like the captain in the nouvelle, could have said, 'What I felt most was my being a stranger to the ship; and if all the truth must be told, I was somewhat of a stranger to myself.' Conrad may also, like the captain, have wondered if he would 'turn out faithful to that ideal conception of one's own personality every man sets up for himself secretly'. The captain's tense psychological state, which would have prevented him from sleeping anyway, is a plausible reason for his letting the exhausted crew turn in, and deciding that he alone will keep watch on deck that night. This violation of traditional nautical routine is essential to the narrative: the captain must be alone when he discovers Leggatt resting at the ship's ladder; if anyone else had discovered or seen Leggatt, he would have been arrested and handed over to the police. Leggatt is – for different reasons – at least as lonely as the captain. He is at the ship only because its riding-light was 'something to swim for'; then he feels a 'very unpleasant faintness', and sees the ladder. But he is still not thinking of going on board; he is there merely because he had 'a confounded lonely time', 'liked . . . being looked at', and wanted 'to talk with somebody, before I went on'.

Conrad later wrote a whole novel, *The Shadow-Line* (1917), that was based on his actual initiation as captain of the *Otago*. All that he uses of

his own experience in 'The Secret Sharer' is his own psychology when
he got his first command, and his first-hand knowledge of the setting of
what is now called the gulf of Thailand. The island of Koh-ring, for
instance, is mentioned in both works, and is the setting for the climax of
'The Secret Sharer'. There the captain performs a very dangerous
maneuver to bring the vessel closer to the island, and thus make a
conspicuous atonement for his sense of guilt at being forced to abandon
Leggatt to his fate. This idea of the captain's conspicuous risk-taking,
incidentally, may be a reflection of Conrad's own experience; having
asked permission of his owners, he had been allowed to take the *Otago*
through the very dangerous Torres Strait passage, between Australia
and New Guinea, to go from Australia to Mauritius. For both captains,
their risky maneuver on their first tour of duty would be an inward
demonstration that, despite their own fears and the doubts of others,
they had exceptional capacities as seamen.

The relationship of the captain and Leggatt in the narrative is shown
as deeply intimate but limited by circumstances. We are told that,
while Leggatt was still in the water, 'a mysterious communication was
established already between us two'; and also that the Captain found it
'strangely troubling to suspect' that perhaps Leggatt did not wish to
come on board. Once aboard, Leggatt puts on one of the captain's
grey-striped sleeping suits, which was 'just right for his size'; he wears it
all the time, and consequently he and the captain become virtual
lookalikes. The captain soon calls him 'my double', and from then on
there are some thirty or more references to the 'double', the 'secret self',
the 'other self', the 'secret sharer', to say nothing of the 'unsuspected
sharer of my cabin' and their 'secret partnership'. This emphasis must
be deliberate: 'the dual working of my mind' becomes an obsessive
feature of the captain's life; it makes him, for instance, in scenes of
macabre comedy, shout at the steward, whisper to the mate, and even
pretend to be hard of hearing so that Leggatt can hear the skipper of
the *Sephora*'s version of what had happened.

Narrative interest and psychological realism may well supply a sufficient reason for all these emphases on the captain's identification with
his 'other self'. At the same time the tale makes it clear that the secret
they share is their knowledge of, and feeling for, Leggatt's problem; there
is no evidence that the captain shares *his* secrets, such as his worries on
facing his first command, with Leggatt. This is easily explained; their
conversations are necessarily very limited, since for one word of them
to be overheard once would be fatal to them both. Nevertheless it is not

surprising that many critics have wished to see the close relationship of the two as having a larger and non-literal explanation or function.

Muriel Bradbook, I believe, was the first to suggest, in 1941, that Leggatt, in accord with Freudian and Jungian thought, comes out of and returns from the sea, and is dressed in 'a sleeping suit, the garb of the unconscious life'. This symbolic aspect of Leggatt was later developed to turn him into the representative of the captain's unconscious self. One of the earliest, and probably still the best, interpretations of the nouvelle which includes this idea, is Albert Guérard's *Conrad: The Novelist*. For him, 'The Secret Sharer', along with *Heart of Darkness* and *The Shadow-Line*, belong to 'the first and best . . . symbolist masterpieces in English fiction'; all three works belong to the archetypal category of the night journey, and in 'The Secret Sharer', this idea is 'unusually conscious'. It is certainly true that the story's wonderful opening and closing scenes happen at night. Guérard also argues that the 'relationship of the Captain and Leggatt is the whole story'; and more generally, he suggests that Conrad's essential subject is the problematic and temporarily crippling nature of the identification between the two men, a topic which Conrad had already treated in *Heart of Darkness* and *Lord Jim*.

There is no room here to give a full account of Guérard's argument, or of the many later interpretations developing this approach. Nor is there time to consider a variety of contrary views, of which Marvin Mudrick's was an extreme example. As early as 1954 he wrote that Conrad is 'not only anticipating psychoanalysis but showing how to vulgarize it'; and, Mudrick argues, Conrad thus effectively spoiled what he was really good at: 'a man who merely tells a tale'.

Conrad certainly tells his tale magnificently; the prose is on the whole economic, and yet eloquent; Guérard calls its prose, together with that of *The Shadow-Line*, his 'great triumph of a style plain and pure'. The reader can enjoy the narrative at its literal level, and must decide for himself how much more Conrad intends; and this must include why, if he intends Leggatt to represent the captain's unconscious, he makes him so conspicuously self-possessed.

Anyone who has ever harbored a stowaway on a ship, or merely hitchhiked for some time with a single driver, will have some idea of how intense a chance and relatively brief human identification can be; the literal experience of feeling dual is not itself particularly uncommon. What is certainly uncommon is that the union of these two officers undergoes a peculiar strengthening through their joint opposition to the law. This is not so much because the captain has thought that in the circumstances he, too, could have killed the 'ill-conditioned snarling cur', but because his initial and unthinking first favorable reaction to Leggatt at once puts him in a posture which is diametrically contrary to his duty. A ship's captain, of course, is the representative of the law on his ship; instead Conrad shows the two men establishing collusive kinship of understanding about the conflict between the spirit and the letter of the law; and this conflict is, as *Lord Jim* shows, one in which Conrad himself was deeply interested and morally divided.

For his part, Leggatt is aware of his great luck in having accidentally found, not only the captain of the ship, but one very different from Archbold. Towards the end he confesses: 'It's a great satisfaction to have somebody to understand. You seem to have been there on purpose . . . It's very wonderful.'

The wonders continue. The captain has risked his ship, and his naval future, because he feels that it is 'a matter of conscience to shave the land as close as possible'; but the whole crew is terrified. Eventually, however, the ship is saved by an unexpected twist of events. The captain, in another gesture of secret sharing, has given Leggatt his hat, to shield him from the sun after he is on his own. But, once overboard, the hat falls off Leggatt's head into the sea, and there acts as the captain's 'saving mark'. In the black proximity of Koh-ring, the hat alone can tell the captain that the ship has 'gathered sternway', and the captain can give the order to shift the helm; and the whole crew, which has been watching the dangerous maneuver in terror, can breathe again. Now the captain no longer 'shares' Leggatt; he can become a real captain and feel that 'no one in the world should stand now between us, throwing a shadow in the way of silent knowledge and mute affection, the perfect communion of a seaman with his first command'. As for Leggatt, he has gone into the water again 'to take his punishment'; but under his own terms, and having found a friend to strengthen his conviction that he had been right; he is now 'a free man, a proud swimmer striking out for a new destiny'.

The nouvelle's ending, then, gives us one reason Conrad thought he had been 'lucky'; 'The Secret Sharer' has a happy ending, and yet one that both he and his readers rightly feel, though hard-earned, was just.

CHAPTER 8

Conrad, James and Chance

'Think what English literature would be like without Conrad and James
... There would be nothing!'[1] Thus Ford Madox Ford; and we must at
least agree that there would be markedly less. The roles of Conrad and
James in the English tradition of fiction are parallel in many respects;
aliens themselves, they brought, and mainly from France, a view of the
novel form at once broader as regards subject-matter and more self-
conscious as regards form, than had been current in Victorian England;
and in so doing they became the recognized, perhaps the supreme, masters
of what we are still calling the modern novel. When one further considers
that James and Conrad knew each other fairly well for nearly twenty
years, one anticipates a relationship of quite exceptional human and
literary interest. Actually, though certainly not lacking an appropriately
ironic complexity, the relationship is above all elusive and obscure.

This is mainly for simple lack of evidence. Conrad habitually destroyed
his letters; James burned most of his papers before his death: and less
than a dozen letters survive from what must have been a fairly large
correspondence.[2] Even so, there was probably a good deal of ambiguity
in the relationship itself.

I

Conrad read and admired James rather early, while he was still at sea.
Once he had decided to become a professional writer, and his second
novel, *An Outcast of the Islands*, came out, he thought of sending it to
James; but it was very difficult to pluck up courage. In one letter (16
October 1896) Conrad writes to his first literary mentor, Edward Garnett:
'I do hesitate about H. James. Still I think I will send the book. After all
it would not be a crime or even an impudence.' Then, after two further
letters from Garnett, Conrad finally announces (27 October 1896): 'I have
sent *Outcast* to H. James with a pretty dedication; it fills the flyleaf.'[3]

Conrad's self-mockery about the 'pretty dedication' only partly pre-pares us for the lacerating embarrassment of the letter to James which accompanied the book. It begins

I address you across a vast space invoking the name of that one of your children you love the most. I have been intimate with many of them, but it would be an impertinence for me to disclose here the secret of my affection. I am not sure that there is one I love more than the others. Exquisite Shades with live hearts, and clothed in the wonderful garment of your prose, they have stood, consoling, by my side under many skies. They have lived with me, faithful and serene – with the bright serenity of Immortals. And to you thanks are due for such glorious companionship.[4]

The thanks continue, and the letter closes with Conrad asking James to accept his book and thus 'augment the previous burden of my gratitude'.

Psychologically one senses the paralysing apprehension of an insecure worshipper approaching a distant and redoubtable deity; or of a lover whose abject fear of rebuff almost invites humiliation. The laborious indirection of the prose has echoes of James's own reluctance to specify the referents of his pronouns; but the primary influence is French, not only in making 'children' stand for 'books', but in that special tradi-tion of abstract and hyperbolic magniloquence which gushes from the Immortals of the *Académie Française* on ceremonial occasions.

Some months after receiving this effusion, James reciprocated by sending Conrad his just-published *The Spoils of Poynton*, with the inscrip-tion: 'To Joseph Conrad in dreadfully delayed but very grateful ac-knowledgment of an offering singularly generous and beautiful'.[5] Then, a week later, on 19 February 1897, Conrad announced jubilantly to Garnett: 'I had a note from James. Wants me to lunch with him on Thursday next – so there is something to live for – at last.'

The meeting probably took place in James's London apartment at 34 De Vere Gardens, Kensington – it is there that Conrad later re-membered that he had chanced upon the Pepys epigraph for his next book, *The Nigger of the 'Narcissus'*. But Conrad was then living in Essex, and occasion for the two to meet very often was lacking. Eighteen months later, however, James and Conrad were brought closer together. In the summer of 1898 James became the lessee, and later the owner, of Lamb House, in Rye; and in October, the Conrads moved to the Pent, a Kentish farmhouse some fifteen miles to the east, and fairly close to Sandgate, where H. G. Wells was living. The Fords soon moved nearby, and there followed a period of quite close literary frequentation, of which many picturesque episodes have been recorded: Wells tells of

Conrad 'driving a little black pony carriage as though it was a droshky
and encouraging a puzzled little Kentish pony with loud cries and
endearments in Polish';[6] Mrs Conrad recalls Henry James taking the
Conrad's small son on his knee, and forgetting 'his existence, now and
then giving him an absent-minded squeeze', while baby Borys, with an
'instinctive sense of Henry James's personality . . . sat perfectly resigned
and still for more than half an hour';[7] and one also hears of James,
nearly sixty, accompanied by Edmund Gosse, bicycling some ten miles
across the marshes to have tea with H. G. Wells.[8]

Few of the friendships then formed were destined to survive; and there
is no Rye school of novelists to rival the Lake School of poets. Conrad's
feelings toward H. G. Wells cooled soon after he had dedicated *The Secret
Agent* (1907) to him, though the rupture was not as violent as that of Wells
and James, nor even as the earlier quarrels of Wells and Ford. James,
never very fond of Ford, broke with him completely at the time of his
conspicuously messy divorce (1910); Conrad's relationship with Ford
became a good deal less intimate after the years of collaboration; and
although there was no breach, Conrad saw very little of James after 1906.

The collaboration between Conrad and Ford on *The Inheritors* (1901)
and *Romance* (1903), and Ford's help on Conrad's fiction between *The
End of the Tether* (1902) and *Nostromo* (1904), is probably the most important, as it is certainly the best known, of the literary consequences of
these contacts. But it is worth considering what literary importance the
Conrad–James relationship may have had. James was fifty-four when
they met, and had been publishing for nearly thirty years, so the debt
would obviously be entirely on Conrad's side; and there is no question
of Conrad's profound reverence for James's achievement. Conrad
habitually addressed James, and James alone, as '*cher maître*';[9] one imagines that for Conrad the veteran who had been the friend of Flaubert
and Turgenev was a captain under whom he would willingly serve to
learn the final secrets of the novelist's craft. James, for his part, seems to
have been willing. He showed Conrad the prospectus of *The Wings of the
Dove*; this, for so secretive a writer as James, indicates a special kind of
confidence – Conrad was, as James later told Wells, the only writer
who had ever been permitted to read 'those wondrous and copious
preliminary *statements* (of my fictions that are to be)'.[10]

There was, then, an early period of considerable literary intimacy;
but although F. W. Dupee is not alone in viewing Conrad as James's
'greatest disciple',[11] as far as I know no one has investigated whether, or
how, Conrad may have learned from James.

There is, it is true, a very percipient comparison of 'James and Conrad' by E. K. Brown.[12] For Brown both novelists are alike, not only in their greatness, but in the fact that they focus our interest not on 'what will happen, but rather with what the happening will mean to the principal character or characters'; they differ mainly because James's subjective interest in the 'world within' tends, especially in the later novels, to place the characters in a void where the 'world without' hardly exists, whereas Conrad, is 'immensely strong' just where James is weak, in the representation of 'the visible world'; although Conrad's attempt to convey the internal, subjective world as well seems often to involve him in great technical difficulties.

Brown does not touch on the matter of influence; my own guess is that it was probably James's example which, more than anything else, helped Conrad to evolve his mature technique at a crucial stage in his development. Ford suggests – in the most generous spirit – that it was he who worked out with Conrad the new techniques of the Impressionist Novel,[13] which is itself an attempt to convey states of mind – E. K. Brown's 'world within' – through sense impressions of the visible world. But in 1898 Ford had written only one very youthful novel, whereas Conrad had read and admired James for many years before the collaboration began; and Conrad also met James some eighteen months before he met Ford.[14] It is significant that it was at this time, in the early years at Rye, that James, genial as never before, was producing the great works which precede *The Ambassadors* – *The Spoils of Poynton* (1896), *What Maisie Knew* (1897), and *The Awkward Age* (1898): novels in which the Jamesian method of narration through the registering consciousness of one or more narrators is already perfected. It may also be significant that these were the works which Conrad apparently most admired. Of *The Spoils of Poynton*, Conrad wrote to Garnett that 'the delicacy and tenuity of the thing are amazing' (13 February 1897); and although he then thought it only 'as good as anything of his – almost', Ford, who himself thought it 'the technical high-water mark of all James's work', reports 'the rapturous and shouting enthusiasm of Conrad over that story when we first read it together so that that must have been the high-water mark of Conrad's enthusiasm for the work of any other writer'.[15]

Ford's testimony is a little misleading – Conrad had read *The Spoils of Poynton* long before he met Ford; but it at least confirms Conrad's enthusiasm for a work which J. W. Beach calls 'the first absolutely pure example of the James method'.[16] The dates of this enthusiasm are significant: in February 1897 Conrad, after finishing *The Nigger of the 'Narcissus'*, was turning away from the French influence, notably that of Flaubert. James had moved away long before, his example and his teaching may well have helped Conrad to move in the same direction. At all events, in August 1897 Conrad completed 'The Return', a story with a somewhat Jamesian subject – 'the fabulous untruth' of a society husband's 'idea of life'; and in a letter to Garnett Conrad analyses the failure of the story in somewhat Jamesian terms – 'if I did see it [the reason for his failure] I would also see the other way, the mature way – the way of art'.[17] Then, after Conrad had failed to make any progress with his continuation of *An Outcast of the Islands*, *The Rescue*, partly because 'I seem to have lost all *sense* of style and yet I am haunted, mercilessly haunted by the *necessity* of style'[18] (29 March 1898), but still well before the meeting with Ford, Marlow made his appearance: 'Youth' was written in the summer; *Lord Jim* was begun; a story called 'Dynamite', the probable germ of *Chance*, was projected in May; and *Heart of Darkness*, the fourth of the Marlow stories, was written that winter, in the earliest days of Conrad's association with Ford.[19]

The significance of Marlow has been much analysed, and it certainly cannot be evaluated briefly. Very roughly, it seems to me that it was through Marlow that Conrad achieved his version of James's registering consciousness. Conrad's version is, of course, very different from that of James. In a sense it is technically more extreme, since where Marlow occurs, Conrad largely gives up the use of direct authorial narrative, which James usually retained; on the other hand Conrad's method is more expandable – there can be several narrators – and more suited to concrete visualization – Marlow tells us what he saw and heard, and we can see him doing it. With Marlow, in fact, the narrative point of view is wholly scenic, dramatized; and yet it's as completely adapted to the relation of inner states of consciousness as to descriptions of the external world.

Whether this change in Conrad's narrative direction was influenced by Henry James can hardly be proved; but if so Conrad must have been particularly pleased by a letter from James praising *Lord Jim*. The letter has not survived, but Conrad's delight at its tenor is evident in his report to Garnett (12 November 1900):[20]

I send you the H. J. letter. A Draught from the Fountain of Eternal Youth. Wouldn't you think a boy had written it? Such enthusiasm! Wonderful old man, with his record of wonderful work! . . . And to you alone I show it . . . P. S. Pray send the James autograph back – registered.

The friendship of James and Conrad, however, does not seem to have become any closer after 1900. The two men were never on christian-name terms; there are very few references to James in Conrad's correspondence after 1900; and even fewer references to Conrad in James's. One reason may be that James, long established in England, knew many more people, and inhabited a much grander and more fashionable world. One gets the sense of social distance very strongly from two letters of 1902[21] which James wrote to that complacent pillar of the Establishment, Edmund Gosse, about a plan to relieve Conrad's acute and endemic financial difficulties by an award from the Royal Literary Fund. In his covering private letter to Gosse James writes:

I lose not an hour in responding to your request about Conrad – whom I had not in the least known to be in the state you mention. It horrifies me more than I can say.

James can hardly bring himself to say 'poverty'; and it is perhaps because of James's special attitude to money that he was apparently one of the few friends Conrad did not tell about his recurrent financial crises; the acid test which distinguishes intimate friendship from cordial acquaintance often seems, sadly enough, to be the question: 'Would I turn to him, or he to me, for a loan if need arose?'

In his official letter of support James is certainly 'warm yet discrete', as he explains to Gosse, in his praise of Conrad's 'charming, conscientious, uncommon work' which has 'truly a kind of disinterested independent nobleness'. It is 'real literature, of a distinguished sort', and Conrad has been, for James, 'one of the most interesting and striking of the novelists of the new generation'. On the other hand the warmth of James's praise is curiously qualified by the distance of his tone.[22] However, it is always difficult to estimate the intention behind James's later style, if only because the use of abstract terms in personal relationships makes one suspect irony, or a defensive formality; so all one can be sure about from these two letters is that James admired and wished to help Conrad, but was not intimately involved in his affairs.

For his part Conrad not only gave James warm and perceptive praise in his letters to Garnett (13 February 1897) and Galsworthy (11 February 1899); he also wrote 'Henry James; An Appreciation' (1905) for the *North American Review*. The ceremonious grandiloquence of the essay's style hardly enables Conrad to come within sighting distance, of, as the saying is, 'the words on the page'; but it is a moving personal tribute, and at the same time suggests a profound inward understanding of James's moral world. As Conrad later wrote to John Quinn,[23] he intended only ' "An Appreciation"; nothing more – nothing less'; and more specifically, an appreciation of James's 'art in a large relation, as a fellow writer . . . the sheer great art of it, where not so much the mind as the soul finds its expression'.

Conrad begins by announcing that James's 'books stand on my shelves in a place whose accessibility proclaims the habit of frequent communion'; and he continues with jocose urbanity:

I do not know into what brand of ink Mr. Henry James dips his pen; indeed, I heard that of late he had been dictating; but I know that his mind is steeped in the waters flowing from the fountain of intellectual youth. The thing – a privilege – a miracle – what you will – is not quite hidden from the meanest of us who run as we read. To those who have the grace to stay their feet it is manifest. After some twenty years of attentive acquaintance with Mr. Henry James's work, it grows into absolute conviction which, all personal feeling apart, brings a sense of happiness into one's artistic existence.

Conrad's essay makes two main points about the nature of James's outlook: it is relativist and it is tragic. Relativist because

the creative art of a writer of fiction may be compared to rescue work carried out in darkness against cross gusts of wind swaying the action of a great multitude. It is rescue work, this snatching of vanishing phrases of turbulence, disguised in fair words, out of the native obscurity into a light where the struggling forms may be seen, seized upon, endowed with the only possible form of permanence in this world of relative values – the permanence of memory.

Conrad defines the tragic quality of James's work in the characteristic formula: 'Nobody has rendered better, perhaps, the tenacity of temper, or known how to drape the robe of spiritual honour about the drooping form of a victor in a barren strife.' The sphere of heroic action in modern times, Conrad concedes, has much diminished, for 'the earth itself has grown smaller in the course of ages'; but James is a heroic writer nevertheless:

the struggles Mr. Henry James chronicles with such subtle and direct insight are, though only personal contests, desperate in their silence, none the less heroic (in the modern sense) for the absence of shouted watchwords, clash of arms and sound of trumpets. James's vision denies the desire for finality, for 'which our hearts yearn'.

James's vision denies 'the desire for finality, for which our hearts yearn'; it asserts instead – and here Conrad places a familiar theme of later James criticism in a perspective that is at once highly general and deeply personal – the imperative of renunciation:

That a sacrifice must be made, that something has to be given up, is the truth engraved in the innermost recesses of the fair temple built for our edification by the masters of fiction. There is no other secret behind the curtain. All adventure, all love, every success is resumed in the supreme energy of an act of renunciation.

II

After 1905 James and Conrad seemed to have seen much less of each other, although they continued to exchange their works, usually adorned with magniloquent inscriptions, and usually acknowledged in equally lapidary style. But the resonance of full human reciprocity is absent; instead there sadly comes to mind E. M. Forster's phrase, 'a friendliness, as of dwarfs shaking hands, was in the air'. For instance, when Conrad sent *The Mirror of the Sea* to James in September or October of 1906, he wrote (in French) that he was 'very sure of the friendship with which you honour me'; nevertheless he also, as if not wholly sure of the book's welcome, repeated a deprecatory phrase he had used earlier in sending *The Nigger of the 'Narcissus'*: 'the book has at least the merit of being short'. James responded promptly (1 November 1906) with:

No one has *known* – for intellectual use – the things you know, and you have, as the artist of the whole matter, an authority that no one has approached. I find you in it all, writing wonderfully, whatever you may say of your difficult medium and your *plume rebelle*. You knock about in the wide waters of expression like the raciest and boldest of privateers.

Conrad, one surmises, may have winced at the faintly condescending colloquialism of 'knock about', and at the nautical metaphor, which had the effect of relegating him to a separate novelistic domain from James's. Yet we would be wrong to make too much of the implicit reservations: for James, a saucily colloquial trope was the fatal Cleopatra for which the world of explicit human communication was well lost; James certainly admired, and may have envied, Conrad's breadth of experience; and his praise is – for him – remarkably direct and unqualified, as he concludes with a uniquely impressive and eloquent tribute:

You stir me, in fine, to amazement and you touch me to tears, and I thank the powers who so mysteriously let you loose with such sensibilities, into such an undiscovered country – *for* sensibility. That is all for to-night. I want to see you again.

Early the next year, in 1907, the Conrads went abroad, and when they returned it was to move away from Kent into Bedfordshire. It is from there that Conrad's last published letter to James is written (12 December 1903), to thank him for the first six volumes of the New York Edition. Conrad 'gloats over the promise of the prefaces' and, after reading that of *The American*, tells how he 'sat for a long while with the closed volume in my hands . . . thinking – that's how it began, that's how it was done'.

In 1909 the Conrads moved back to Kent, to a house a dozen or so miles away from Rye, but there was no personal contact with James for some four years. The silence was apparently mainly on James's side; he was much preoccupied, saddened by the death of his brothers, gloomy about the public's neglect of his writings; and his visit to America, combined with a long and serious illness, meant that he remained out of touch even with close friends for several years. Conrad was not among the two hundred and seventy or so friends who presented James with a golden bowl on his seventieth birthday, 15 April 1913;[24] which may only mean that the sponsors did not think of him as a close friend, or that Conrad had failed to answer a letter.

Later that year, however, Conrad apparently made some friendly overture; and James responded, from London, in a supreme example of the later epistolary indirection (19 June 1913):

I always knew you were a shining angel, and now, under this fresh exhibition of your dazzling moral radiance (to say nothing of other sorts), my natural impulse, you see, is to take advantage of these sublime qualities in you up to the very hilt. Thus it is that I throw myself upon the use of this violent machinery [the letter was dictated and typed] for at last, and in all humility, approaching you; because I feel that *you* will feel how I must have some pretty abject personal reason for it. That reason, to deal with it in a word, is simply that, having so miserably, so helplessly failed to do what I was, during all the dreadful time, unspeakably yearning to – which was neither more nor less than to get again into nearer relation with you by some employment, however awkward, of hand or foot – I now leave each of these members as just damnably discredited and disgraced, and seek the aid of nimbler and younger and more vivid agents than my own compromised 'personality' has proved itself able to set in motion. In other (and fewer) words, I just sit here muffled in shame for the absolute *doom* of silence – in all sorts of directions too than the beautiful Kentish, and the insidiously Polish, and the triumphantly otherwise *magistrale* – that, beginning, horrible to think, something like four years ago at least, was so long to disfigure the fair face of my general and constitutional good intention. For the moment I merely lift the edge of the crimson veil of contrition to say to you, peeping, as it were, from under it, that I don't despair of helping you to lift it almost altogether off me when once we shall really be within mutual reach.

Not having yet exhausted the resources of syntax and metaphor to prolong the agonies of separation, James addresses himself to the possible modalities of reunion:

I hear with fond awe of your possession of a . . . miraculous car, the most dazzling element for me in the whole of your rosy legend. Perhaps you will indeed again, some July afternoon, turn its head to Lamb House, and to yours, my dear Conrad, and your Wife's all far more faithfully than you can lately have believed even by whatever stretch of ingenuity, Henry James.

Conrad paid a call; but he seems to have been told that the Master was not at home. There was nothing exceptional in the fact itself; Conrad himself apparently once had the great Lord Northcliffe turned away from his door when he had called uninvited;[25] as for James, though he delighted to receive his friends he was often away; and if he was busy, sick, or expecting guests, his servants were no doubt accustomed to shield him from the importunities of callers by the hallowed mendacities of social decorum.[26] After considerable delay James yet again proposed a meeting, in terms even more elaborately disingenuous (13 October 1913):

Will you conceive of me as approaching you as the most abject of worms, most contrite of penitents, most misrepresented – by hideous appearances – of all the baffled well-meaning and all the frustrated fond? If I could but *see* you for an hour all would become plain, and I should wring your heart with my true and inward history.

The cause of this particular 'reaching out' in what James terms 'the suppliant's flat-on-my-belly, the crawling with-my-nose-in-the-dust, posture' is to make amends for Conrad's

generous signal to me by your afternoon call of some weeks, horribly many weeks, ago. You will be able to say nothing, however, that will reduce me to softer pulp than I already desire to present to you every symptom of.

The combination of 'afternoon call' with the earlier phrase 'most misrepresented by hideous appearance', seems to exclude the simplest explanation – that James had actually been out; but no further explanation is given. Instead the baroque banter continues as James wonders if Conrad

mercifully and magnanimously can: come over to luncheon with me, by an heroic effort – and believe that I shall thereby bless you to the (perhaps not very distant) end of my days. If you tell me that this is impossible through the extremity of inconvenience, I will then arrange – that is, heaven forgive me! propose and aspire to – something less onerous to you.

There follows a review of possible methods of transportation: Conrad's fabled motorcar; that failing, James might 'recklessly procure one for the occasion myself'; and there are trains 'rather happily available'. Any specific proposal, however, is delayed until the postscript, which invites Conrad '*any* day after this week that you may kindly name for luncheon and if you can stay your stomach to 1:45'.

All things considered we might have expected James to consider waiving the customary lateness of his midday collation; but he was old and set in his ways. To anyone assured of James's regard, the letter as a whole would have been taken merely as one of James's increasingly elaborate jokes; and Conrad no doubt so took it. Writing after James's death he told John Quinn 'in our private relations he has been always warmly appreciative and full of invariable kindness. I had a profound affection for him. He knew of it and he accepted it as if it were something worth having. At any rate, that is the impression I have. And he wasn't a man who would pretend. What need had he? . . . even if he had been capable of it.'

One detects, alas, a note of guarded doubt: Conrad speaks of James 'accepting' Conrad's 'profound affection', not of his reciprocating it. This, taken with Conrad's apologetic deference in sending *The Nigger of the 'Narcissus'* and *The Mirror of the Sea*, and with the way that the delays in replying seem all to be on James's side, makes it likely that it was Conrad who sought to maintain the friendship, rather than James. It also seems probable that the elaborate formality of their intercourse, at least after the early days, had been a more-or-less conscious protection, by two proud but highly-civilized men, both against any overt acknowledgement of the inequality of their reciprocal sentiments, and against the intrusion of matters where they might disagree. Conrad for instance apparently felt that from *The Ambassadors* on, James had become the prisoner of his own technique;[27] while James must have had many reservations about Conrad's work, apart from *The Nigger of the 'Narcissus'*, *Lord Jim* and *The Mirror of the Sea*.

In any case the mere passage of time was bound to change their relationship. At first James had been able to see Conrad mainly as a curiosity – Wells reports that to James, Conrad was 'the strangest of creatures';[28] James referred to Marlow as 'that preposterous Master Mariner';[29] and although one cannot doubt the exceptional sincerity of James's praise in the passages cited, they are all concerned with Conrad as a seawriter or as an exotic (as in the letters about *Lord Jim* and *The Mirror of the Sea*). But, beginning with *Nostromo*, Conrad had increasingly encroached on the more normal and terrestrial domains of fiction; and by then Conrad's sales and reputation were steadily increasing, while James's continued to diminish. This contrast in their respective situations is vividly evoked in an interchange as early as 13 February 1904, related by Olivia Garnett: 'Conrad, for once gleeful, exclaimed: "I am at the top of the tree." H. J. replied: "I am a crushed worm; I don't even revolve now, I have ceased to turn".'[30]

By 1913 it had become apparent to many critics that Conrad was James's chief rival for the title of the greatest contemporary novelist; and then in *Chance* Conrad made his closest approach to a Jamesian novel.[31] John Cowper Powys, for example, comments that 'No work of Conrad's has so close an affinity with the art of Henry James . . . the disturbing vibration, the intense malice of provoked curiosity.' And – as we shall see – *Chance* has many other Jamesian elements; including the irony that Conrad's most Jamesian novel should have achieved a popular and financial success such as had for thirty years now eluded James, and at the same time provoked James to strike the last sad note in his dealings with Conrad.

III

We do not know whether Conrad finally had lunch with James, though the two men probably did meet again. But later that year James proposed to the *Times Literary Supplement*[32] an article which was to contain his only published critique of Conrad. It appeared under the title 'The New Generation' (19 March and 2 April 1914), and was reprinted in *Notes on Novelists* under the equally misleading title of 'The New Novel'.

The article – which is not James at his best, and which also provoked James's breach with Wells – divides the novelists into the very young, and the not-so-young. Among these latter James lists Maurice Hewlett, John Galsworthy, H. G. Wells, Arnold Bennett, and Conrad. All but the last of them are presented as following what James calls the 'fatal error' of Tolstoy, 'the great illustrative master-hand . . . of disconnexion of method from matter' – they all think only of their matter not of their art. Conrad, on the other hand, is presented as the prime – and unique – example of the other extreme:

It is doubtless fortunate that at the very moment of our urging this truth we should happen to be regaled with a really supreme specimen of the part playable, for our intenser interest, by a case of the exhibition of method at any price. Mr. Conrad's 'Chance' places the author absolutely alone as the votary of the way to do a thing that shall make it undergo most doing. The way to do it that shall make it undergo least is the line on which we are mostly now used to see prizes carried off; so that the author of 'Chance' gathers up on this showing all kinds of comparative distinction.

James's main objection to the narrative method of *Chance* is that it compromises the reader's sense of the reality of the events by drawing attention to the narrators rather than to the narrative: Conrad

sets in motion more than anything else a drama in which his own system and his combined eccentricities of recital represent the protagonist in face of powers leagued against it, and of which the *dénouement* gives us the system fighting in triumph, though with its back desperately to the wall . . . This frankly has been our spectacle, our suspense and our thrill; with the one flaw on the roundness of it all the fact that the predicament was not imposed rather than invoked, was not the effect of a challenge from without, but that of a mystic impulse from within.

This view of *Chance* seems to me not to take account of Conrad's aims, and since James singles out the novel's ending for special attention, I would like to suggest that the method of narration here is in fact a response to the 'challenge from without', to the imperatives of the story itself.

Very briefly, *Chance* is told through three major informants. The primary narrator, whose words constitute the novel, is an unnamed 'I' who reports his conversations with Marlow. Though technically a secondary narrator, it is Marlow who is chiefly responsible for assembling the stories of the fictional protagonists: the Fynes, Flora, her father, De Barral, and her lover, Captain Anthony; Marlow's interminable colloquies also interpret the psychological and moral dimensions of the story, in what James felicitously terms 'a prolonged hovering flight of the subjective over the outstretched ground of the case exposed'. Then there is the third narrator, Powell, who meets the first two narrators at the beginning by chance, and who was second mate of Anthony's ship when the events of the last half of the novel occurred.

In the denouement it is Powell who happens to observe De Barral putting poison in Anthony's nightcap of brandy and water. Powell warns Anthony in time; Anthony, totally misinterpreting the situation, and thinking Flora put the poison in, says he will let her off at the next port; Flora announces 'I don't want to be let off'; they embrace; out of jealousy De Barral drinks the poison himself; and Anthony, resolving that 'I am not going to stumble now over that corpse', at long last consummates his marriage with Flora while her father lies dead in the next cabin.

James, presumably, would have focused the whole narration on the sensibility of Flora, as he did with Fleda Vetch, Maisie Farange and Nanda Brookenham, who are in some ways similar figures – innocent and only superficially contaminated victims of adult corruption. But Conrad often used reciters, partly to avoid the posture of psychological omniscience, and partly to dramatize the difficulty of understanding human values and motives. In the present instance both these reasons seem particularly apposite; and in addition it is surely evident that the rather gamey melodrama of the final scene would be much too obtrusive if it were related through Flora's consciousness. Instead it comes to us indirectly, and very selectively, through the recital of Powell; having no knowledge of the events that led up to the harrowing emotional deadlock between the lovers, or of its final resolution, he merely reports a few surface manifestations whose real significance is reconstituted through Marlow's imagination and the reader's; nowhere, I imagine, can subject matter have called more strongly for externality and indirection of presentation.

But this scene, though the end of Powell's narrative, is not quite the end of the novel. For in the last few pages of *Chance*, we are surprised to discover the reason why Powell, four years after the death of Captain Anthony, is haunting the particular Thames-side inn where narrators one and two are doing a little holiday sailing. Since *Troilus and Criseyde* the remarriage of widows has called for supreme authorial tact; and in *Chance* Conrad has recourse to his 'eccentricities of recital' to bring about neatly postponed recognition and resolution combined. Marlow finally discovers that Flora lives nearby, which accounts for Powell's presence in the first place; and the two are going to marry. The system thus 'fights back in triumph' by relegating what might have been the anticlimax of Flora's remarriage into an artfully mundane, and structurally secondary, framework for the more vivid romantic colours of the central part of the story, the love of Flora and Anthony.

Much may be said against *Chance* and its narrative method: some obtrusive artificiality, a tendency to sentimentalize, and moments of fatiguing garrulousness; but the charge that its mode of recital is gratuitously imposed seems itself to be gratuitous.

James and Conrad must have looked at the treatment of *Chance* in the 'New Generation' essay from very different points of view. James would certainly have felt that he was innocent of envy or malice, and he could point to passages where Conrad was implicitly accorded a higher literary status than any other author treated: Conrad alone is called a 'genius'; and *Chance* is described as the work of 'a beautiful and generous mind' with 'a noble sociability of vision'. But, as Conrad must have seen, what James gives with one hand he takes away with the other, and in much more detail. Imperceptive about the reasons for the method of *Chance*, James, no doubt impelled by the rhetorical requirements of his polar opposition between Conrad's concentration on method, and the infatuation with mere matter of the other contemporary novelists, does not mention earlier works in which Conrad might have figured as offering happier examples of harmony between form and content. And it was surely stretching the prerogatives of age when, from the height of his 71 years, James placed Conrad, at 57, in the 'younger generation' (as he already had earlier in his 1902 letter to Gosse); especially when Conrad was actually nine years older than the next oldest novelist treated, H. G. Wells. It must also have been especially bitter to Conrad when James brought out his friend Edith Wharton, the only American novelist discussed, as his 'eminent instance ... most opposed to that baffled relation between the subject matter and its emergence which we find constituted by the circumvallations of *Chance*'. And when, finally, we notice that James cites his own *The Awkward Age* as a further salutary demonstration of how 'the novel may be fundamentally organised', only one conclusion seems possible: in what Edith Wharton noted as 'his increasing preoccupation with the structure of the novel',[33] James is leaving as his literary legacy: 'My life-work for the art of fiction has failed; nor can I acknowledge Conrad as a successor – even poor Edith Wharton has learned my lesson better.'

In a letter to John Quinn, Conrad wrote that James's treatment of *Chance* was 'the *only time* a criticism affected me painfully'.[34] But it did not alter their personal friendship which continued to the end: when, in the summer of 1915, James solicited a contribution for a war charity anthology, Conrad replied with all the old warmth to his '*cher maître*' (24 July 1915). But one understands how it must have hurt, not only that James didn't like *Chance* better, but that he went out of his way to say so in print, especially after his own public praise of James in the *North American Review*. For Conrad, rightly or wrongly, the obligations of friendship outweighed those of literary criticism: Curle tells of hearing Conrad 'say of some living author, "I like him and I don't want to talk about his books"'; in public, at least, if Conrad could not praise he preferred to remain silent.[35]

But, as Conrad knew, James was quite different; he had never been known to spare the critical rod even for his closest friends. With an

intimate, such as Edith Wharton, James had been savage enough in
private criticism:[36] for some reason – perhaps Conrad's devotion to him,
or his disarming politeness – James had not, probably, been as frank
with Conrad, and his reservations clamoured for expression somehow.
In the end it comes down to an invincible difference of temperament. The
impulse to love and be loved was not as close to the surface in James as
in Conrad; it was there, but always at the mercy of many other conflicting impulses; above all, the truth about what mattered most – the art of
the novel; and it was difficult to disentangle this felt truth completely
from other more personal impulses – the urge to dominate, to get other
people in your power, to achieve in fact the absolute satisfactions of the
Godhead, or of its latter-day embodiment, the critic. And this, in the
end, is surely the functional strategy of the later Jamesian style and point
of view: that formidable digestive instrument really does produce a
'baffled relation between the subject-matter and its emergence', because
the subject-matter – people – can only emerge in subordination to James's
detached analysis of them in abstract terms of his own choosing.

It was a subordination which came to dominate his life as well as his
fiction. 'Our poor friend' is the implied stance which James adopts for
Conrad, as well as for Strether and for his later fictional protagonists;
and it is difficult not to see it, ultimately, as a strategy of patronage: in
his last letters, Conrad as a person, and even James's feelings about
him, seem to have become merely pretexts for prose, artifacts to be
manipulated by an Omniscience with a capital 'O'.

It is not, I think, a question either of emotional insincerity or of
intentional patronage on James's part. To anyone at all self-conscious
about literary expression and personal relationships, the difficulty of
writing a letter increases in exact proportion to the writer's awareness
of the recipient's awareness of these things. James would have felt he
was insulting Conrad, as well as betraying his real self, if he remained
at the level of the usual epistolary banalities, from the opening 'Sorry
I haven't written before', through the central 'let's get together', to the
final 'regards to your wife'. Instead James felt bound to encompass in a
unified rhetorical structure everything from the immediate business at
hand – the hackneyed items of apology, invitation and salutation – to
the remoter and yet intimate presences of past relationship and present
feeling. So ambitious and all-enveloping a compositional imperative
inevitably pushes towards abstraction and indirection; and in the process
the sense of mutuality and naturalness is fatally compromised. As James
came to live more and more for his art, other people, in the letters, as

in the novels, became the victims, not of any conscious patronage, but, purely incidentally, of James's confidence in a finally-achieved stylistic mastery over his material.

Conrad's powerful critical mind may have proffered some such redeeming explanation; but the disappointment at what he called being 'rather airily condemned'[37] must have rankled. As Conrad had worked his painful way through the literary jungle it had been from James's voice that he most hoped for recognition; but when the voice finally spoke out it did not accept him as a peer.

The final muted footnote on the relationship follows closely enough along the lines of how Marlow, in *Heart of Darkness*, kept his own counsel after Kurtz's death. As an obituary tribute the *North American Review* reprinted[38] Conrad's 'Henry James: An Appreciation', though without his knowledge.[39] It is as if, in a final gesture of fidelity towards James, chance itself were enacting Conrad's affirmation in *Under Western Eyes*: 'A man's real life is that accorded to him in the thoughts of other men by reason of respect or natural love.'[40]

NOTES

1 Letter to Herbert Read, 19 March 1920 (*Letters of Ford Madox Ford*, ed. Richard M. Ludwig (Princeton, 1965), p. 127).

2 Of the six letters from Conrad to James known to me, two are published in *Lettres françaises*, ed. G. Jean-Aubry (Paris, 1929), and two in G. Jean-Aubry, *Joseph Conrad: Life and Letters* (London, 1927). I am indebted to Professor Frederick R. Karl, who is editing Conrad's letters, for copies of the originals; as also for his generous assistance and advice in other respects. I gratefully acknowledge the permission of the Trustees of the Joseph Conrad Estate to publish portions of these letters, and the gracious help of the Librarians of the Houghton Library at Harvard, the Beinecke Library at Yale, and the Academic Center Library at the University of Texas.

   Of James's letters to Conrad, three were published in *Twenty Letters to Joseph Conrad*, ed. G. Jean-Aubry (London: The First Editions Club, 1926); one of them is reprinted in *Selected Letters* of Henry James, ed. Leon Edel (London, 1956). I gratefully acknowledge Professor Leon Edel's help, and his permission, as editor of the James correspondence, to reprint portions of these letters here.

3 *Letters from Conrad, 1895–1924*, ed. Edward Garnett (London, 1927), pp. 50, 54. It seems likely that James was the only author whom Conrad singled out in this way.

4 The letter is dated 16 October 1896, the day of Conrad's first letter on the subject to Garnett; Conrad presumably kept it at least until 25 October, the date of his second letter to Garnett.

5　Jean-Aubry, *Life and Letters*, I, 201, n. 2.

6　H. G. Wells, *Experiment in Autobiography* (New York, 1934), p. 527.

7　Jessie Conrad, *Joseph Conrad as I Knew Him* (London, 1926), p. 48.

8　Wells, *Experiment in Autobiography*, p. 508.

9　*Lettres françaises*, pp. 34, 77.

10　15 November 1902 (*Henry James and H. G. Wells*, ed. Leon Edel and Gordon Ray (London, 1959), p. 83).

11　*Henry James* (London, 1951), p. 281.

12　'James and Conrad', *Yale Review*, 35 (1945), 265–85.

13　F. M. Ford, *Joseph Conrad: A Personal Remembrance* (London, 1924), pp. 174–215.

14　In September 1898 (Jocelyn Baines, *Joseph Conrad: A Critical Biography* (London, 1960), p. 215).

15　Ford Madox Ford, *Portraits From Life* (Chicago, 1960), p. 11.

16　Joseph Warren Beach, *The Method of Henry James* (New Haven, 1916), p. 233.

17　*Letters from Conrad*, pp. 94, 98.

18　*Letters from Conrad*, p. 127.

19　Baines, *Joseph Conrad*, p. 210; and *Joseph Conrad: Letters to William Blackwood and David S. Meldrum*, ed. William Blackburn (Durham, North Carolina, 1958), pp. 21, 36–7.

20　*Letters from Conrad*, pp. 173–4.

21　26 June 1902 (British Museum, Ashley MS 4792.) I am very grateful to David Thorburn for providing me with the transcripts.

22　There is a rather similar ambiguity towards Conrad in a letter James wrote to Gelett Burgess. James's price for 'a short tale' which Burgess has asked for, as an editor of *Ridgway's Militant Weekly*, had proved too stiff; but Burgess had acquired *The Secret Agent* for serialization; and in a postscript James commented: 'I rejoice for you in your having something from the interesting and remarkable Conrad!' (23 September 1906. I am grateful to Professor Joseph Backus for informing me of this letter, and for providing a transcript.)

23　24 May 1916. I am indebted to the Manuscript Division of the New York Public Library, and the Trustees of the Joseph Conrad Estate, for permission to quote this letter, from the John Quinn Papers, vol. 1.

24　I am indebted to the Colby College Library for photocopies of the correspondence and list of subscribers. Gosse's management of the affair caused 'the most awful fuss', according to Hugh Walpole (Rupert Hart-Davis, *Hugh Walpole: A Biography* (London, 1952), p. 99).

25　According to Joseph H. Retinger (*Conrad and His Contemporaries* (London, 1941), p. 68).

26　Jacques-Émile Blanche, indeed, speaking of how James protected himself from casual visitors, reports that much earlier Conrad had called without previous notice at the Reform Club, and been told that James was out (*Mes Modèles* (Paris, 1928), p. 176).

27　Richard Curle, *The Last Twelve Years of Joseph Conrad* (London, 1928), p. 119.

28　Wells, *Experiment in Autobiography*, p. 525.

29 Ford, *Joseph Conrad*, p. 161.
30 Cited by Simon Nowell-Smith, *The Legend of the Master* (London, 1947), p. 135, I am very grateful to Mr Nowell-Smith and to Professor Moser for giving me the date of this diary entry.
31 John Cowper Powys, 'Chance', *A Conrad Memorial Library* (New York, 1929), pp. 219–20.
32 Letter of James to Bruce Richmond, 19 December 1913 (*The Letters of Henry James*, ed. Percy Lubbock (London, 1920)), vol. II, pp. 350–2.
33 Edith Wharton, *A Backward Glance* (New York, 1934), p. 323.
34 24 May 1916.
35 Richard Curle, *Last Twelve Years of Joseph Conrad*, p. 16.
36 'His tender regard for his friends' feelings was equalled only by the faithfulness with which, on literary questions, he gave them his view of their case when they asked for it – and sometimes when they did not' (Wharton, *A Backward Glance*, p. 181).
37 Letter to Quinn, 24 May 1916.
38 April 1916.
39 In his letter to Quinn thanking him for sending the article, Conrad wrote that he had 'forgotten it completely' (24 May 1916).
40 Dent Collected Edition (London, 1947), p. 14.

CHAPTER 9

Story and idea in Conrad's The Shadow-Line

Reviewing Conrad's first masterpiece, *The Nigger of the 'Narcissus'*, Arthur Symons, though an admirer, complained that it had 'no idea behind it';[1] and since then this objection has been not uncommon. It was most memorably expressed by E. M. Forster, who reviewed Conrad's collected essays, and found that they, at least, suggested that 'the secret casket of his genius contains a vapour rather than a jewel; and that we need not try to write him down philosophically, because there is, in this particular direction, nothing to write. No creed, in fact. Only opinions'.[2]

'Opinions' certainly; and they are often disconcertingly typical of the main social rôles to which fate successively introduced Conrad – the Polish landowner, the French clerical *ultra*, the English quarter-deck martinet. 'No creed', equally certainly; the word implies theological sanctions which had no interest for Conrad; although his rather frequent use of a tone of sacerdotal commitment may explain why Forster misses in Conrad what he would surely deplore in anyone else: the only creed to which Conrad, a child of nineteenth-century scepticism, would freely have said 'Amen' was Forster's own – 'I do not believe in belief.' As for 'writing him down philosophically', Conrad certainly did his best to discourage any such enterprise: 'I don't know what my philosophy [of life] is', he once wrote sardonically to Edward Garnett, 'I wasn't even aware I had it.'[3] We obviously don't find in Conrad the persistent, overtly conceptualized, and often polemic, concern with philosophical issues which characterizes George Eliot or Meredith; nor are we aware of any continual pressure towards making us see the universe in a special way, as we are in reading Thomas Hardy, for example, or D. H. Lawrence. And yet we surely also sense in Conrad's narratives an intense and sustained thoughtfulness, whose larger tenor may indeed, as Forster says, sometimes seem obscure, but whose seriousness nevertheless persuades us that we are in the presence of something beyond mere 'opinions'.

Conrad's own statements on the kind of general meanings he attempted in his fiction do not compose a clear and systematic critical theory; what is most systematic about them, indeed, is their refusal to submit to the conceptual mode of discourse. Nevertheless their essential purport remained very consistent, from the time of their first enunciation in the Preface to *The Nigger of the 'Narcissus'*. The novelist's aim is defined there as 'by the power of the written word to make you hear, to make you feel – it is, before all, to make you *see*'; and the primarily descriptive nature of Conrad's purpose is then emphasized by his insistence that the aim of art is quite different from the 'clear logic of a triumphant conclusion' sought by the scientist or the philosopher. What follows, however, is less often quoted, and it shows that the impressionist rendering of the world of appearances was only a beginning; Conrad's final aim was to present the 'rescued fragment' of sense-impressions with 'such clearness of sincerity' that 'its movement, its form, and its colour, [would] reveal the substance of its truth'. 'The substance of its truth' has an ominously Platonic suggestion; but the nature of the ultimate 'truth' which inheres in sense experience is clarified when Conrad continues that 'at last the presented vision' should 'awaken in the hearts of the beholders that feeling . . . of the solidarity in mysterious origin, in toil, in joy, in hope, in uncertain fate, which binds men to each other and all mankind to the visible world'.

This explanation, in turn, helps to guide our interpretation of a literary aim which Conrad asserted almost as frequently as he denied having a philosophy: 'all my concern has been with the "ideal" value of things, events and people'.[4] We shall return to the problem of just what he meant by 'ideal values': for the moment we can at least relate it to the notion that the reader should apparently expect to discover in the way he is made to see the particular events and characters of the narrative, something much more general, something which stands for universal elements in man's relations to his fellows, and to the natural world.

Conrad's last masterpiece, *The Shadow-Line*, is one of his most typical works. The story – about how the young narrator suddenly throws up a satisfactory job as first-mate of a steamer trading in Eastern seas, only to find himself unexpectedly thrust into his first command, which turns out to be one of unique difficulty – is characteristic. Characteristic because its subject is a sea voyage; a voyage, moreover, that is, as Conrad wrote, 'exact autobiography',[5] an example, like *Heart of Darkness* and *The Nigger of the 'Narcissus'*, though even more literally so, of 'my personal experience . . . seen in perspective with the eye of the mind';[6] while the nature of the personal experience, moral initiation, is one of Conrad's dominant literary themes.

In general, *The Shadow-Line* is a by no means recondite piece of writing, and its main ideas are stated with such unusual explicitness that it hardly seems to call for analysis. But actually it was the lack of understanding with which *The Shadow-Line* was received that roused Conrad to complain that 'after 22 years of work, I may say that I have not been very well understood'. His friend Sir Sidney Colvin, for example, hesitated to review it on the odd grounds that he had no local knowledge of its setting – the Gulf of Siam;[7] while various other critics thought that it was a ghost story,[8] or merely an illustration of the 'taste for the morbid' of the *English Review*, in which it was serialized.[9] It was also about *The Shadow-Line* that Conrad made one of his most emphatic statements of intention: 'whatever dramatic and narrative gifts I may have are always, instinctively, used with that object – to get at, to bring forth *les valeurs idéales*':[10] and this, together with the story's own inherent interest and power, and the incidental fact that some of its recent commentators are also in considerable critical disagreement about it, may justify the present attempt at a further elucidation of 'the ideal values' in what Conrad 'admitted' to be 'in its brevity a fairly complex piece of work';[11] an attempt which may also serve to clarify the larger problem of the connection between story and idea in Conrad's work generally.

I

The first chapter of *The Shadow-Line* is mainly concerned with a petty intrigue at the Officers' Home between two of its derelicts – the Chief Steward and a permanently unemployed ship's officer named Hamilton – an intrigue aimed at preventing the narrator, a first mate, from receiving an urgent message from the Harbour Office about the command which awaits him. The slowness of this opening has often been criticized – most recently by Albert J. Guerard in his *Conrad the Novelist*:

The Shadow-Line, while written in part in the pure unpretentious prose of 'The Secret Sharer', is distinctly less perfect. It gets underway very slowly and uncertainly . . . Conrad apparently conceived of *The Shadow-Line* as dealing with the passage from ignorant and untested confidence through a major trial to the very different confidence of mature self-command. So conceived, the story ought logically to have reflected, in its first pages, a naïve and buoyant confidence.[12]

Actually, Conrad's deliberateness is necessary for several reasons. By the time we have observed how, on his way from the docks to the Officers' Home the narrator is indifferent alike to the glare of the sun and the pleasure of the shade, we have begun to participate in his state of mind on leaving the ship; a state of mind which has been defined retrospectively in the story's opening words:

> Only the young have such moments. I don't mean the very young. No. The very young have, properly speaking, no moments. It is the privilege of early youth to live in advance of its days in all the continuity of hope which knows no pauses and no introspection.
>
> One closes behind one the little gate of mere boyishness – and enters an enchanted garden. Its very shades glow with promise. Every turn of the path has its seduction. And it isn't because it is an undiscovered country. One knows well enough that all mankind had streamed that way . . .
>
> One goes on. And the time, too, goes on – till one perceives ahead a shadow-line warning one that the region of early youth, too, must be left behind.
>
> This is the period of life in which such moments of which I have spoken are likely to come. What moments? Why, the moments of boredom, of weariness, of dissatisfaction. Rash moments. I mean moments when the still young are inclined to commit rash actions . . . such as throwing up a job for no reason.

One way of refusing to see the shadow-line ahead is to rebel against all involvements: and so, as the narrator comments, he 'had never . . . felt more detached from all earthly goings on'. This fretful self-preoccupation – and the unconscious strategy it serves – had to be very firmly established before the reader could relish the irony of the scene where the narrator finally tells Giles that he has discovered that Hamilton and the Steward have kept him from receiving the message from the Harbour Office. But he is still blind to the implications of the message, and adds that it means 'nothing' to him:

> 'Nothing!' repeated Captain Giles, giving some sign of quiet, deliberate indignation. 'Kent warned me you were a peculiar young fellow. You will tell me next that a command is nothing to you – and after all the trouble I've taken, too!'
>
> 'The trouble!' I murmured, uncomprehending. What trouble? All I could remember was being mystified and bored by his conversation for a solid hour after tiffin. And he called that taking a lot of trouble.
>
> He was looking at me with a self-complacency which would have been odious in any other man. All at once, as if a page of a book had been turned over disclosing a word that made plain all that had gone before, I perceived that this matter had also another than an ethical aspect . . .
>
> . . . as soon as I had convinced myself that this stale, unprofitable world of my discontent contained such a thing as a command to be seized, I recovered my powers of locomotion.

When Guerard, then, complains that the narrator's 'irritability' 'at last becomes irritating to the reader',[13] it is surely because he doesn't see it as part of the novel's form and meaning that the reader should experience for himself the irritating obtuseness of the narrator's resistance to Captain Giles's well-meaning interference, a resistance whose narrative climax is the comically laborious double-take over his first command, but whose ultimate function is to exhibit for the reader the whole complex of conflicting emotions which characterize the onset of that penumbral transition from late youth to committed adulthood which is Conrad's professed subject.

As his title indicates. Conrad disliked titles that were 'too literal – too explicit';[14] but a shadow-line has just the right degree of suggestive mutability and indeterminacy of application to stand as a nautical metaphor for a transit through one of what Johnson called 'the climactericks of the mind'. A shadow-line is not a definite boundary that one crosses consciously, whether in space, like a line of longitude, or in time: Conrad isn't dealing with the rather obvious temporal indicators of adulthood – political or legal, like the 21st birthday, religious, like the first communion, or biological, like sexual maturity. The shadow-line is inward and social; approaching it one is only aware of some vague atmospheric change, and one may not know its cause; yet although it is mysterious and elusive, projected almost at random through the chance collisions of the individual with his endlessly varying environment, it has a compelling universality. The narrator, fleeing, as he puts it, from 'the menace of emptiness', is really fleeing from the shades of the prison house that lie ahead; and he tries to alter his course because pursuing the present one – his career as first mate – obviously involves renouncing many other aspirations; it means acknowledging an end to the youthful dream that one will, one day, be able to achieve everything; it means, alas, beginning to be like everybody else.

To have contemplated a successful struggle against the common fate may – in retrospect – seem a ridiculous form of self-confidence in the narrator. But the 'naïve and buoyant confidence' of youth is rarely as simple as Guerard seems to assume: jejune optimism alternates with equally intense indecision and self-doubt: the human mind will indulge in endless 'artful dodges', as Marlow put it in *Lord Jim*, 'to escape from the grim shadow of self-knowledge';[15] and one reason for refusing to be like everybody else is the fear that one may not even prove to be as good.

Conrad's slowness in the first chapter enables him to present all these perplexities concretely. And there are others, for the social perspective of the hero's situation is as important as the psychological; *The Shadow-Line*, as Carl Benson has written, is 'the communal counterpart' of 'The Secret Sharer';[16] and to present this in first-person narration, 'through the medium of my own emotions' as Conrad put it,[17] means that the larger representativeness and thematic coherence of the hero's personal relationships must be suggested through a fairly fully described sequence of encounters in which our understanding of the pattern of motives outstrips that of the narrator. We can then see that the narrator's three former colleagues on board the ship all attempted to understand and assist him in the light of their own characters: the misogynist second engineer, who gloomily suspected that sex was the great shadow-line which the narrator was approaching; the dyspeptic first engineer, for whom the 'greensickness of youth' could be cured by two bottles of a patent liver-medicine, which he generously offered 'out of his own pocket'; the more experienced captain, who showed greater insight in their parting interview, and added 'in a peculiar, wistful tone, that he hoped I would find what I was so anxious to go and look for'.

On ship, then, the narrator had encountered from society – but hardly noticed – a measure of helpfulness and sympathy; he is now equally blind to the series of warning examples which face him in the Officers' Home: the steward, who 'had been connected with the sea. Perhaps in the comprehensive capacity of a failure'; the comically supine officer from the Rajah's yacht, who was a 'nice boy' before he turned to indolence and debauch; and Hamilton's corrupt ineptitude, which – in a dangerous parallel to the narrator's own case – is masked by a defensive assumption of being above the common throng. But, as on the ship, there are also well-meaning friends; and Giles serves as a climactic reminder that the solemn rites of passage which youth must endure are comically protracted by the various attempts at help and understanding by which they are customarily attended, attempts whose purpose only the peculiar psychology of the protagonist at this stage of life prevents him from seeing as what they are.

II

The torpid vacillations of the first chapter, then, constitute a series of concrete enactments of the narrator's initial reactions to the ironic social and spiritual divisions which are Conrad's theme. The narrator next hurries to the harbour office, and is told to proceed that evening by steamer to Bangkok, and take over a sailing ship stranded there by the death of its captain. He meets all kinds of difficulties in getting the ship ready to sail, and even when he is clear of the harbour an unseasonable lack of wind makes it impossible for him to move out into the open sea. In these four central chapters the narrator gradually comes to realize that his new rôle as captain, which he had at first envisaged as the final, total, and, indeed, magical solution of all his life-problems, actually involves an intricate network of moral imperatives, psychological discoveries, and social responsibilities, which had until then been too abstract, too much in the future, to be real, but which now crowd thickly upon him: the shadow line has unsuspected depth; it can't be crossed easily, or quickly.

At first, we observe, the narrator pays as little attention to Giles's gloomy prognostications as to the later warnings of the friendly doctor at Bangkok; unreasonably but understandably he clings to the belief that once out of harbour all will be well because the sea is 'pure, safe and friendly'. Such security, however, is more than anyone should count on; the crew's health actually gets worse as the lack of wind makes it impossible to pass the island of Koh-Ring; and the nadir is reached at the end of the fourth chapter when the narrator discovers that the remaining five quinine bottles actually contain a worthless white powder. He informs the crew of the catastrophe, fully expecting to be overwhelmed by their anger and reproach: actually, the 'temper of their souls or the sympathy of their imagination' surprises him; and it is their stoic resignation, their refusal to see things personally, which does most to turn him away from his egocentric sense that all is merely a plot aimed against him personally – a plot by which he has been 'decoyed into this awful, this death-haunted command'.

Before then there had already been some signs of human interdependence, and of the narrator's growing awareness of it. In contrast to the moral intransigence he had showed towards the steward at the Officers' Home, he had listened to his sick first mate Burns's plea 'You and I are sailors', and allowed him, sick as he was, to come back from hospital on to the ship, even though Burns, like Hamilton, had been his rival for the command, and was now so broken in body and mind that his mere presence on board ship was a serious hindrance. But when the crisis comes, Mr Burns isn't wholly a dead loss: he steadies the narrator by telling him that it's 'very foolish, sir' to feel guilty about the quinine; and he unwittingly seconds Giles's earlier advice about keeping to the east side of the Gulf of Siam.

It is, however, to the clear-sighted persistence of Ransome that the protagonist is most indebted. In the fifth chapter, after two weeks of being virtually becalmed, Ransome points out 'a broad shadow on the horizon extinguishing the lower stars completely', and the narrator realizes that there are not enough fit men to prepare the boat for the coming squall. Overwhelmed by the depth of his 'contempt for that obscure weakness of my soul [under the] stress of adversity', he goes below in a state of paralysed remorse and confesses in his diary: 'What appals me most of all is that I shrink from going on deck to face it . . . I always suspected I might be no good.' Gradually, however, he becomes aware that Ransome is lingering 'in the cabin as he had something to do there, but hesitated about doing it'. Hesitates long enough to make the narrator ask 'You think I ought to be on deck', to which Ransome replies 'without any particular emphasis or accent: "I do, sir"'.

It is the final nudge into the realization that command means self-command. They go on deck, and the narrator finds in 'the impenetrable blackness' a sense of 'the closing in of a menace from all sides'.

It is in this crisis that we are closest to the Jungian analogy suggested by Guerard. The darkness of the night and the narrator's despair certainly receive sufficient emphasis to suggest a symbolic intent; and even to lend some support to the interpretation of *The Shadow-Line* as essentially concerned, like 'The Secret Sharer', with an 'archetypal . . . night journey'[18] which eventually causes the protagonist to subdue those aspects of his personality 'which interfere with seamanship'.

'The dark night of the soul' seems to be getting even more of a nuisance than the 'Dark Lady of the Sonnets' used to be. The objection is not that it doesn't exist – metaphors exist once they are made; but rather that the seductive concreteness of the phrase deludes its hierophants into thinking that they have gained more than they have when the analogy has enabled them to reduce the literary work to less than it is: in the present case, to find *The Shadow-Line* inferior to 'The Secret Sharer' primarily because, being much longer, it resists reduction to a single symbolic paradigm even more vigorously.

Actually, Conrad's emphasis in *The Shadow-Line* is not specifically on the forces which interfere with seamanship, but on something much more general – on 'an ordeal . . . which had been maturing and tempering my character'. It is true that the narrator often feels that he is a failure as captain: but this, and his consequent sense of guilt, is, as far as we can judge, a subjective – and typical – reaction to the difficulties of a first command; from the time that the doctor in Bangkok compliments him on his 'very judicious arrangements', we have no reason to doubt that the narrator is right in saying that 'the seaman's instinct alone survived whole in my moral dissolution'.

The darkness and immobility of the night do not, of course, in themselves require symbolic explanation. The increment of suspense and pictorial vividness would be justified for its own sake; it is in keeping with Conrad's frequent use of darkness for his narrative climax; and it may well have been dark when the actual events occurred which served as basis for the story. But if one looks for larger meanings, for symbolic representations of universal elements in man's relations to his fellows and to the natural world, there are several which are clearly relevant to the main implications of the narrative. The calm before the storm, and the intensified darkness that precedes dawn, are well enough established commonplaces of human experience: and here they derive a particular significance from the fact that the calm is the climax of the long period of calm since leaving port, and that the darkness is the climax of the longer inner darkness which began when the leading edge of the shadow-line began to trouble the narrator's youthful horizon.[19]

The calm, of course, has its psychological parallel in the narrator's prolonged inward lethargy, a parallel to which Conrad draws attention in the epigraph; in Baudelaire's sonnet 'La Musique' the poet's quest for 'ma pâle étoile' is most deeply menaced, not by tempests but by the 'calme plat' which is the 'great mirror of his despair'. More widely, the alternating rhythm of calm and storm is the equivalent in the natural order of a human perspective to which Conrad was uniquely attentive – the duality of rest and work; of the solicitations of inertia and the impulsions to action. In the beginning the narrator's deepest yearnings, in his inarticulate revulsion from the 'mortal coil',[20] were for repose; later, on his way to the harbour office, he found 'something touching about a ship . . . folding her white wings for a rest', and then heard that Captain Ellis had attributed his delay in coming to 'funking . . . too much work'.

Once at sea, the solicitations of the most extreme form of inertia, death, increasingly pervade the consciousness of the narrator. In the brilliant passage where he goes down to tell Burns about the quinine, for instance, he at first mistakes his glimpse of Burns trimming his beard with a pair of scissors as an attempt at suicide; and shortly afterwards Burns's ageworn look causes him to reflect: 'Enviable man! So near extinction'. Later, when Ransome comes to report on the darkening sky, the narrator thinks that the message must be that 'Someone's dead'; and when he finally goes up to prepare for the squall he welcomes the utter calm and darkness of the night as an image of death:

> When the time came the blackness would overwhelm silently the bit of starlight falling upon the ship, and the end of all things would come without a sigh, stir, or murmur of any kind, and all our hearts would cease to beat like run-down clocks . . . The quietness that came over me was like a foretaste of annihilation. It gave me a sort of comfort, as though my soul had become suddenly reconciled to an eternity of blind stillness.

It was this particular implication of the shadow-line which led Conrad's wife to object to his title on the grounds that it suggested the Psalmist's 'valley of the shadow of death'.[21] But death is only one of the terrors which occupy the narrator's mind as he waits in the 'blackness which had swallowed up our world' for the heavens to declare themselves; most obviously he experiences an unforgettable reminder of man's precarious exposure to the unpredictable power of the natural order as a whole; and the importance of this to the idea of the shadow-line was suggested in a letter which Conrad wrote to his relative and intimate friend Marguerite Poradowska: 'One always thinks oneself important at twenty. The fact is, however, that one becomes useful only on realising the utter insignificance of the individual in the scheme of the universe.'[22]

On the other hand, confronting his own 'utter insignificance' in the natural order heightens the narrator's awareness of his need for the support of his fellows. This is brought home, for instance, in the scene when, after the mainsail has been hauled up close and the mainyard squared, Ransome comes to report, and then, suddenly 'stepped back two paces and vanished from my sight' out of the light of the binnacle lamps. Shaken, the narrator

> moved forward too, outside the circle of light, into the darkness that stood in front of me like a wall. In one stride I penetrated it. Such must have been the darkness before creation. It had closed behind me. I knew I was invisible to the man at the helm. Neither could I see anything. He was alone, I was alone, every man was alone where he stood.

Here the vivid realization of complete human isolation is 'the darkness before creation', evokes the historical dimension of the theme of human solidarity; the narrator, having been deprived, first through the loneliness of command, and then through darkness, of the support of his fellows, is brought face to face with the long tradition of civilization since the creation, and his own utter dependence on it.

III

The historical perspective of the shadow-line has, of course, made its appearance much earlier in the narrative. For instance, as soon as the protagonist had boarded his ship, he had sat down alone in the Captain's chair, and it had occurred to him that: 'A succession of men had sat in that chair'; then, reflected in the cabin mirror, he had observed his own face 'rather with curiosity than with any other feeling, except of some sympathy for this latest representative of what for all intents and purposes was a dynasty; continuous, not in blood indeed, but in its experience, in its training, in its conception of duty, and in the blessed simplicity of its traditional point of view on life'.

F. R. Leavis, in a Conrad centenary address largely devoted to *The Shadow-Line*, comments that this passage 'very soon takes on in retrospect a profoundly ironic significance'. It is true that the preceding symbol of the nautical hierarchy soon proves to have completely betrayed it, acting with a complete disregard of his ship, its crew and its owners, and even selling the vital quinine so that he could 'cut adrift from everything' and pursue his own individual inclinations – sexual, in his squalid amour with the horrible female in Haiphong, and artistic, with his verse-writing and his final allegiance only to his violin. Ironical, therefore, it certainly is, that the narrator should look to this particular symbolic precursor for support. But Leavis is surely wrong in making the former captain an example of how the seaman's career had not in itself 'given him fulfilment';[23] he had failed it, not it him. In any case we should be careful before taking the irony too far, since although it is a sign of youthful illusion to expect more from its elders than they can give, it is also a sign of maturity not to reject the inheritance of the past merely because we have discovered the imperfections of its human representatives. Dynastic, like apostolic successions, must always make a distinction between the man and the rôle; and the traditional definition of the rôle represents a value about which Conrad was the last man to be ironical, however acute and indeed obsessive his awareness of the fullness with which its actual human representatives partake of the frailty of their kind.

The late captain's lurid defections enforce the point that the tradition of the past is not handed over purged of man's selfishness and weakness; and the idea is later reinforced by the eerie presence on deck of Burns's gibbering death's head when the squall finally comes and 'suddenly, the darkness turned into water'. Nevertheless the mind of the narrator is sustained, and the story as a whole enacts how the narrator finds 'his place in a line of men whom he did not know, of whom he had never heard; but who were fashioned by the same influences, whose souls in relation to their humble life's work had no secrets for him'.

One of F. R. Leavis's main aims in the essay is to emphasize that Conrad does not merely wish to preach the master mariner's 'glamorless routine doggedly taken'. Of course; but although Conrad would not have argued the equivalence of moral maturity and the acceptance of the seaman's code, he would surely have poured his wrath on anyone who proposed them as alternatives. Leavis tends to do so, in his wish to underline how Conrad stands for something more than 'any mere vocational ethos';[24] while, much more misleadingly, Guerard succumbs to the same dichotomy in an opposite direction by seeing 'the conclusion' as 'simply that . . . we cannot be good seamen, alone with our ships, until we have faced out, recognised, and subdued those selves which interfere with seamanship'.[25] But Conrad's presentation surely denies the relevance of such oppositions: the problems of the narrator's first command are not peculiar, essentially, to seamen; an awareness of the unsuspected multiplicity of reciprocal obligations is surely one in which all mankind partakes in its measure once it leaves youth behind, although most of all when it assumes responsibility for the lives of others; as Conrad suggested in his dedication: 'To Borys and all others who like himself have crossed in early youth the shadow-line of their generation'.

The terms of this dedication emphasize one aspect of the generality of the story's main theme. Conrad had long planned to relate his own first voyage as captain from Bangkok to Singapore in 1888; but when he came to write the story, nearly thirty years later, what had been personal, autobiographical, and particular took on so much larger a significance that it encompassed his own eighteen-year old son's taking up the dynastic inheritance as an officer at the front in the first World War: and what was originally to have been called 'First Command' became *The Shadow-Line*.

Conrad, then, is dealing with a particular version of a more general shadow-line which, under a host of different social and individual and historical circumstances, is traversed whenever youth's idealized image of the world, of itself and of its own destiny is penetrated and modified by its sense of solidarity with those who, in the past and in the present, continue man's struggle against all the powers of darkness and anarchy which pervade the natural, the historical, the social, and the personal order. And Conrad is being realistic rather than ironic – if the distinction be allowed – in presenting all the forces opposed to human solidarity so powerfully.

Burns, for example, stands for much more than the force of rivalry in advancement; his superstitious terror of the dead captain, lying in wait for the ship in latitude 8° 20′ (his place of burial), is no doubt the main reason why some critics thought that Conrad was invoking the supernatural; but in fact Burns makes a much more complex – and realistic – contribution to Conrad's theme: Burns's madness is a corruption of the legitimate power of the past over the present; his supernatural fears are a common enough caricature of a proper sense of what, in his 'Author's Note', Conrad called 'the intimate delicacies of our relation to the dead'; and, just as this superstitious awe is an indication of Burns's own incapacity, so it awakens uneasy echoes in the narrator's mind when he is obsessed with his own sense of powerlessness. Burns's conviction that no progress will be possible until they have passed the particular latitude where the captain was buried is itself a superstitious version of the shadow-line: one that Burns is afraid – and incompetent – to cross; while Burns's final diabolic laugh in the teeth of the squall is essentially only a melodramatic form of the hysteria in the face of impotence and terror which the narrator himself has just undergone.

The narrator, of course, needs these warning lessons: he must learn that neither the dynastic past – the dead captain – nor the present – his sick and demented first mate – live up to his ideal. But this discovery has by now been complemented by another – neither does he. Blame and regret, however, are equally futile, and in any case the reciprocities of inadequacy are not unqualified: in these depths of the narrator's self-accusation about the quinine it is the combination of Burns's pressure, the crew's understanding, and Ransome's direct intervention, which makes him shake off the sense of drifting impotence and betrayal; he determines: 'Remorse must wait. I must steer'; and steering, as Conrad had earlier reminded us, is 'a symbol of mankind's claim to the direction of its own fate'.

So, with only himself and Ransome able to handle the anchors, the ship eventually arrives at Singapore. Conrad's thought has altered a good deal from *Lord Jim*: conceit and error and guilt are universal, but their consequences, it seems, are not irredeemable; we are all in the same boat with them, and with sickness and death, but if we seize our fleeting and partial opportunities, we can steer.

Here, of course, it is Ransome's 'contained serenity' in the face of the most extreme physical disablement – a weak heart – which represents most fully the true dynastic inheritance. Ransome has learned to live with awareness of death, 'schooled himself into a systematic control of feelings and movements'; and later, for all his devotion to duty, he asserts, 'in a blue funk about [his] heart', that he 'has a right' to leave the ship. Thus the narrator glimpsed at the human level what the blackness of night had suggested at the natural level – the bitterest of all the lessons of the shadow-line – the reality of death; and death, in Sir Walter Raleigh's words, is 'he that puts into man all the wisdom of the world, without speaking a word'.[26]

Sickness and death, then, accompany the ship's final rush into port; and in the course of this severely qualified victory both the narrator and the reader experience intense and grateful recognition of the varied efforts that have enabled the ship, after all, to survive; a sense which overwhelms the narrator when his crew is carried off to hospital, but which he has already expressed to Ransome: 'I and the ship, and everyone on board of her, are very much indebted to you.'

The debt, however, is soon a matter of past history, and the narrator takes on another crew to continue his voyage. There is no heroic finality; and in the narrator's last interview with Giles we can find no warrant for believing that the shadow-line is crossed once and forever: we are never, as witness the late captain, in the clear; nor are the forces of inertia ever wholly vanquished. The narrator 'feels old'; he has learned Giles's lesson that there's 'precious little rest in life for anybody'; he can even confess that 'God only knows' whether he feels 'faint-hearted' or not. Further – and most troubling of all – he still cannot be absolutely sure that he has become a full member of the dynasty: as we see in the ironic resurgence of the earlier friction when, after he's told Giles that he'll be 'off at daylight tomorrow', and Giles has replied in his bluff, avuncular way, 'You will . . . That's the way . . . You'll do', the narrator feels 'irritated by his tone', and retorts – 'What did you expect?'

IV

Whether the ideas I have attributed to *The Shadow-Line* are true or interesting, and whether (and how) Conrad made them seem so, are not directly within my present purview. That they fit into Conrad's general thought could certainly be supported by reference to his other works, and to his correspondence; and one would also find evidence there for the view that Conrad is a symbolic writer only in the sense that his narratives have a larger meaning, though one which is not a matter of obscure and esoteric secrets, but only of extending and generalizing the implications of his 'things, events and people'. That is, Conrad deals in the kind of symbolism for which I have elsewhere[27] suggested the term *homeophoric* – 'carrying something similar', as opposed to *heterophoric*, 'carrying something else' – as the larger import of the tale's literal meaning. To interpret the story in terms of Jung, or of the supernatural, would be *heterophoric*; it would take us *away* to *another* meaning and would slight the literal one; whereas the homeophoric interpretation would be wholly consistent with the kind of expansion of particular narrative implications suggested by Conrad in his 'Author's Note': 'when we begin to meditate on the meaning of our past it seems to fill all the world in its profundity and its magnitude'.

Obviously many of the details in *The Shadow-Line* are there only because they were part of Conrad's memories of the past. But three decades of experience so guided the process of discovery, selection and emphasis that out of what Conrad himself called 'the mere material' of the story there arose a work which is perhaps the finest example of what Conrad meant by 'bringing out *les valeurs idéales*' – the French makes much clearer than does 'ideal values' in English that it is not, at least directly, a question of ethical ideals, but merely of trying to perceive and make visible the significance of a particular individual experience: trying to 'get the idea' and make us 'get it'.

In that sense Conrad must be considered a philosophic writer; and, although his frequent jests at those who tried to turn him into a philosopher once took the form – 'There is even one abandoned creature who says I am a neo-platonist.[28] What on earth is that?' – the analogy to Plato may serve to clarify Conrad's position. For in the end there is something Platonic about Conrad's concern with 'ideal values'; with his insistence, for example, in the case of *The Shadow-Line*, that the 'twilight region between youth and maturity' has certain features which are as universal as Plato's Forms. He does not, of course, make the metaphysical assertion that these universal features are part of a unified, harmonious, and timeless system; nor is he much concerned with the ethical preachment that we ought to devote our lives to trying to attain them. Indeed, since the narrator does not, after leaving the 'enchanted garden', achieve 'that special intensity of existence which is the quintessence of youthful aspirations', we are at liberty to see the shadow-line as only the process which age calls 'settling down' but youth calls 'selling out'. We misread Conrad if we see his recall of vanished youthful turmoil as sharing the vatic complacency of the initiate who has completed his analysis; the protagonist doesn't come out on the other side of the shadow-line into another 'enchanted garden'; 'experience', as he says 'means always something disagreeable, as opposed to the charm and innocence of illusions'; the loss of Eden brings painful exactions, not opportunities for realizing dreams. So, if Conrad gives the impression, as Virginia Woolf put it, that his characters are 'tested by their attitude to august abstractions'[29] it is not because he has a 'creed' but because that is his observation of what life does: everyone in *The Shadow-Line* is judged by the events. Conrad is not concerned to tell us that the various general features which he discerns in the experience of the narrator are inherently good or bad, but that they are there; and if we retort 'So what?', shrugs agreement.

Conrad's 'ideal values', then, are not intended to be ethical or normative; and the fact that he does not bridge the gap from 'is' to 'ought' is one reason why Conrad disappoints those who expect him to have a 'philosophy'; another reason is that his work falls far short of conceptual synthesis. This is not in itself inconsistent with the Platonic analogy: Plato thought you could not hope to describe the Ideas, but only to guide your hearers in such a way that they might eventually see them for themselves. But, of course, Conrad himself doesn't pretend to more than partial glimpses of any universals, and what Marlow says of Stein's wisdom in *Lord Jim* defines only one of the directions in Conrad's narrative: 'we had approached nearer to absolute Truth, which, like Beauty itself, floats elusive, obscure, half-submerged, in the silent still waters of mystery'.[30] Conrad's other major narrative direction, of course, lies in the vivid presentation of empirical reality; and that is perhaps why there are, as Forster puts it, 'constant discrepancies between his nearer and his further vision'. 'If', Forster remarks, Conrad 'lived only in his experiences, never lifting his eyes to what lies beyond them: or if, having seen what lies beyond, he would subordinate his experiences to it – then in either case he would be easier to read.'[31] Conrad lets us look beyond, but never in such a way as to subordinate actuality; and the actualities of life, especially as he learned to see them through English eyes, were to be respected, even if they fell short of more romantic and ideal expectations. He was, after all, a Platonist who fell among empiricists; a Pole cast among Anglo-Saxons.

Conrad, then, is like many great writers, a philosopher only in the sense that his own retrospective awareness of the continuities and discontinuities of human experience can enlighten ours: and *The Shadow-Line* is perhaps the most successful realization of Conrad's achievement in this direction. Many people, it may be hazarded, have stumbled, first with chagrin, and later, if they are fortunate, with re-assurance, on the discovery that most of their thoughts and deeds are not unique, but are linked in many ways with those of the dead and of those who are merely nearer death; that the reciprocity is real, even though we never receive, as we never bestow, the full measure of recognition; and that some elements of that reciprocity, however qualified, are still, to adapt Conrad's phrase on the title page, worthy of our mortal yet undying regard. In *The Shadow-Line* Conrad overwhelms us with these realizations; but he also accompanies them with various melancholy ironies: for one thing, the dynasties of experience are fragile, corruptible and intermittent; for another, despite the Existentialist version of the shadow-line, we do not choose our solidarities with the past and the present, but come to them – as we come into the world – involuntarily and unconsciously: are usually, indeed, dragged into them, screaming.

NOTES

1 *Saturday Review*, 85 (1898), 145–6.
2 'Joseph Conrad: a Note', *Abinger Harvest* (London, 1946), p. 135.
3 *Letters from Conrad, 1895–1924*, ed. Edward Garnett (London, 1928), p. 199.
4 G. Jean-Aubry, *Joseph Conrad: Life and Letters* (London, 1927), vol. II, p. 185.
5 *Life and Letters*, II, 181, 182.
6 'Author's Note', in *Collected Edition of the Works of Joseph Conrad* (J. M. Dent: London, 1950), p. vii.
7 *Life and Letters*, II, 185; II, 182.
8 See 'Author's Note', v; *Life and Letters*, II, 195.
9 *Ibid.*, II, 181.
10 *Ibid.*, II, 185.
11 'Author's Note', v.
12 Cambridge: Harvard University Press, 1958, p. 30.
13 *Conrad the Novelist*, p. 32.
14 *Letters from Conrad*, p. 298.
15 *Collected Edition*, p. 80.
16 'Conrad's Two Stories of Initiation', *PMLA*, 69 (1954), 46.
17 *Life and Letters*, II, 184.
18 *Conrad the Novelist*, pp. 30–1.
19 David Bone assumes a literal shadow-line – the 'darkling in the sea, the reflex of a wind in motion' which at last takes the ship out of the doldrums

– the lull between trade winds. (*A Conrad Memorial Library*, ed. George T. Keating (Garden City, New York, 1929), pp. 255–60.) But it is unlikely that anything so literal is intended: the narrator, for instance, speaks of how, ever since he set sail, 'all my life before that momentous day is infinitely remote, a fading memory of light-hearted youth, something on the other side of a shadow' (p. 106).

20 P. 73. This is, appropriately, but one of the many phrases from *Hamlet* in *The Shadow-Line*; e.g. 'undiscovered country', p. 3; 'stale, unprofitable world', p. 28; 'out of joint', p. 84.

21 *Joseph Conrad and his Circle* (London, 1935), pp. 193–4. The reference is to Psalm XXIII, 4.

22 *Letters of Joseph Conrad to Marguerite Poradowska, 1890–1920*, trans. and ed. J. A. Gee and P. J. Sturm (New Haven, 1940), p. 45.

23 'Joseph Conrad', *The Sewanee Review*, 66 (1958), 196, 197.

24 *Ibid.*, pp. 198, 193.

25 *Ibid.*, p. 31.

26 *The History of the World*, Book v, chapter 6, section 12.

27 'Conrad Criticism and *The Nigger of the "Narcissus"*', see pp. 76–8 above.

28 *Letters from Conrad*, p. 226.

29 'Mr. Conrad: A Conversation', *The Captain's Death Bed and Other Essays* (London, 1950), p. 76.

30 *Collected Edition*, p. 216.

31 *Abinger Harvest*, p. 137.

CHAPTER 10

The decline of the decline: notes on Conrad's reputation

There is a schism among the lovers of Conrad. It is, roughly, between those who find two opposed periods in his work, the good early and the bad late, and those who see his work from beginning to end as varying in quality, but as constituting nonetheless a good unified whole. This division of opinion is a common feature in criticism, with Wordsworth as a celebrated example. In the present case we will begin by looking briefly at Conrad's own opinion of the matter; then we'll go on to a brief review of the thoughts both of his contemporaries, and then of some later literary and critical historians of Conrad's works; and finally we will venture some not very resounding conclusions.

First, two obvious facts: there was no decline in the amount Conrad produced, or in its financial rewards. Seven novels were published between *Almayer's Folly* in 1895 and *The Secret Agent*, in 1907, and seven novels between *Under Western Eyes* in 1911 and *The Rover* in 1923: in each twelve year period Conrad completed an average of just under one major fiction in two years; there was only one major gap, of four years, between *The Secret Agent* and *Under Western Eyes*.[1] As for Conrad's financial fortunes, after the successive disasters of the very poor showings of *Nostromo*, *The Secret Agent* and *Under Western Eyes*, Conrad's sales went up very fast, and until his death. The publication of *Chance* in 1913 is widely regarded as a crucial turning point, although Najder points out that the collection of short stories *'Twixt Land And Sea* in October 1912 had a first printing of 3,600, which was more than that of *Under Western Eyes*, or indeed of any of his earlier works.[2]

Conrad said some words of praise for *Chance*, '*Of its kind*, it isn't a thing that one does twice in a lifetime!' But he also spoke of it with disgust: 'I have lost all belief in it,' he wrote; to Gide he said, 'I have written myself out'; most depressingly, perhaps, he wrote to Cunninghame Graham that, as regards the success of *Chance*, 'Now I can't even pretend I am elated. If I had Nostromo, the Nigger, or Lord Jim in my desk or only in my head I would feel differently no doubt.'[3] By an ironic compensation, then, Conrad's newfound economic success provoked Conrad into deeper disgust with his writing. Of the story 'The Planter of Malata', in *Within the Tides*, for instance, Conrad wrote to Galsworthy that it had 'earned eight times as much as "Youth", six times as much as "Heart of Darkness". It makes one sick.'[4]

Of course one shouldn't assume that Conrad only became a crybaby from senility; for, as we all know, his agonies in writing, and his disappointment with the results, were his trademarks from the beginning. Thus he wrote of *Lord Jim*, in a letter to Garnett of 12 November 1900: 'I've been satanically ambitious, but there's nothing of a devil in me, worse luck. The *Outcast* is a heap of sand, the *Nigger* a splash of water, *Jim* a lump of clay.'[5] Still, Conrad himself certainly felt, or thought he felt, a decline of his powers. It is of his later work that Conrad tells Ford that he no longer has 'the consciousness of doing good work', or instructs Henri Ghéon to tell Gide about *Chance*: 'Conrad has written a long (and stupid) novel since his visit. It's *disgusting* to even say it – try and imagine what it was like writing it! I have become disgusted with myself, with paper, with ink – with everything.'[6]

Edward Garnett, John Galsworthy, even Richard Curle, were among Conrad's old friends who expressed some momentary adumbration of his decline, but the theory was first expressed in more or less systematic form much later, by Douglas Hewitt, in his *Conrad: A Reassessment*, in 1952; after them came Albert Guerard, in his *Conrad the Novelist*, of 1958, and especially the classic and forthright study of Thomas Moser, *Joseph Conrad: Achievement and Decline* in 1957. The decline theory is also, to some extent, supported by the main modern biographers of Conrad, for instance by Bernard Meyer, *Joseph Conrad: A Psychoanalytic Biography* in 1967, by Frederick R. Karl, *Joseph Conrad: The Three Lives*, in 1979, and by Zdzislaw Najder in *Joseph Conrad: A Chronicle*, in 1983. Anyone wanting to dissent from the decline theory, therefore, has many people and much evidence to contest. The main critics who have opposed the decline theory are John Palmer in his *Joseph Conrad's Fiction: A Study in Literary Growth*, in 1968, and, more recently, Daniel Schwarz in his *Conrad The Later Fiction* in 1982.

The status of *Chance* is a key question. Henry James's extended consideration of that novel comes in his article on 'The New Generation' in the *Times Literary Supplement* on 19 March and 2 April 1914, which was published in *Notes on the Novelists* under the equally misleading title of 'The New Novel'. The essence of James's objection was that he saw Conrad as 'a really supreme specimen of the part playable in the novel' by 'method, blest method'. Mr Conrad's 'Chance', James continues, places the author 'absolutely alone as the votary of the way to do a thing that shall make it undergo the most doing'. The objection James finds is 'the fact that the predicament . . . was not the effect of a challenge from without, but that of a mystic impulse from within'.[7] I have argued elsewhere that in fact the method of *Chance* can well be regarded as a response to the 'challenge from without';[8] in literature the remarriage of widows has always called for supreme authorial tact. There had to be one witness, Powell, who begins the book, then tells the story of De Barral's suicide, and Flora's long delayed physical union with Captain Anthony, before being himself finally joined to Flora, at the end, after Anthony's death; but Conrad also needed Marlow for commentary. One can see why Conrad felt that he had been 'rather airily condemned';[9] and it was in any case odd to be treated as part of 'the new generation' since he was, after all, 57 years old. Still, we must not forget the more favourable aspects of James's essay; only Conrad is called a 'genius'; and James makes Conrad his major example of the remedy for the current 'disconnection of method from matter' which was the error of no less than Leo Tolstoy.[10]

Most of the contemporary reviews or comments on *Chance* were extremely laudatory. In the *Daily Telegraph* W. L. Courtney called Conrad, 'one of the marvels of our literature', and estimated that *Chance* was 'one of the best works which Mr. Conrad has written comparable with *Lord Jim* and *Nostromo*'; D. S. Meldrum thought 'one may well declare the latest to be the best of his books'; while Arnold Bennett sighed: 'This is a discouraging book for a writer, because he damn well knows he can't write as well as this.'[11] *Chance* has certainly remained on most critics' list of the canon of Conrad's major works. F. R. Leavis, for example, rates it one of the five great Conrad novels: '*Nostromo, The Secret Agent, Under Western Eyes, Chance* and *Victory* – it is an impressive enough tale of books.'[12]

Douglas Hewitt complained that *Chance* was full of 'clichés . . . defensive irony . . . imprecise rhetoric'.[13] We must concede there are a good many cases of these faults; but whether there are more than in 'Heart of Darkness' or *Lord Jim* is questionable. There are also some passages which Hewitt dislikes, but which seem quite acceptable to me. Here is one example from Marlow, near the climax of *Chance*:

if two beings thrown together, mutually attracted, resist the necessity, fail in understanding and voluntarily stop short of the – the embrace, in the noblest meaning of the word, then they are committing a sin against life, the call of which is simple. Perhaps sacred. And the punishment of it is an invasion of complexity, a torment, forcibly tortuous involution of feeling.[14]

The prose is not distinguished: after an overlong sentence, 'Perhaps sacred' is a redeeming brevity; but the last phrase is awkward and rather lame rhythmically; in any case, there should surely be an 'a' before 'forcibly'. But that is not Hewitt's objection. He writes:

There is no attempt to show any inherent inadequacy in Anthony; there is no suggestion of any deep inhibition of feeling in him. The 'involution' is entirely a temporary matter – a matter of this particular situation. As soon as Anthony and Flora realize they are in a false position, all can be well.[15]

No doubt it can be made 'well', and indeed it is; but since they are both orphans 'to a certain extent' in John Fyne's splendid phrase,[16] their inhibitions have been a part of their characters for a very long time; and they have surely been unprepared for the 'particular situation' on the *Ferndale*, or for anything remotely like it. Hewitt's criticism seems to me to be too easy.

Victory was very well received when it came out in September of 1915. Robert Lynd expressed the general opinion when he wrote that '*Victory* is, compared to *Chance*, an unambitious story', but 'it is the true gold of genius'.[17] The book was, the *Atlantic Monthly* thought, 'the finest thing that the season offers'.[18] On the other hand, Gerald Gould, despite much praise, concluded that Conrad 'does not quite bring it off'.[19] The outstanding opposition view was expressed very professorially by William Lyon Phelps: 'Despite many fine passages of description, it is poor stuff, and its author should be ashamed of Mr. Jones, who belongs to cheap melodrama.' He added that the work should be seen 'simply as one of the lapses of which nearly all great writers have shown themselves capable'.[20]

The later critics have been deeply divided; it has been seen favourably by several later critics, from F. R. Leavis to Harold Bloom. Harold Bloom's list of major novels is exactly the same as Leavis's; except that *Lord Jim* replaces *Chance*. Leavis, it should be explained, is not an enthusiast for *Lord Jim*, as an over-romantic sea tale.[21] Both these independent-minded critics agree in the fairly rare denigration of 'Heart of Darkness'.[22]

The main critical difference about *Victory* seems to arise from a basic disagreement about narrative modes. The standard new critical, and more generally modernist, assumptions seem to be twofold: first, that the author should not speak in his own voice, but present the larger meanings of the novel indirectly and objectively, through the complex associations of his imagery and metaphors: the text itself, and all its referents should be delusively simple and referential. With this goes an assumption that the ideological values of the literary work should be in some sense new; it should be new, that is, in forcing us to review our own too-conventional assumptions, attitudes and habits; the truths we are made to see should be unpleasant; they should make us wince. That, of course, is a parody; but there is surely a general truth behind it; modern criticism expects a radically new way of confronting our daily life as the significant element in literary experience; and, as we all know, today's kids at grammar school are all too complacently aware that they were born equipped with hearts of darkness.

Victory, rather different from Conrad's usual mode of writing, is claimed by John Palmer, in his *Joseph Conrad's Fiction: A Study in Literary Growth* (1968), as the chief work in what he describes as Conrad's third creative phase. The first phase dealt with individual problems, from *Almayer's Folly* to *Lord Jim*: the second with the individual in society, from *Nostromo* to *Under Western Eyes*; and the third phase takes up the problem of the metaphysical bases of moral commitment. Conrad, therefore, is less concerned with apparently realist narrative; he uses allegory as a technique, and metonymy, rather than metaphor, as the basis of his description.[23] As in *The Tempest*, the isolated extremity of a desert island is a fit setting for a relatively abstract treatment of the largest kind of human concern. On Samburan Conrad challenges the three 'good' figures with their evil opposites: the isolated intellectual Heyst is opposed to Jones; the sexual expert Lena versus Ricardo; and the savage Wang against the simian Pedro. Of course this allegorical confrontation may seem over-simple to modern taste, although we may note that metonymy has recently found favour in Paris, and Palmer, it should be noted, subtitles his chapter on *Victory*, 'The Existential Affirmation'. Conrad himself thought highly of *Victory*; at least he chose the last scenes of the novel for his only American reading, in 1923, at the gathering of notables in the Park Lane residence of Mrs Curtis James.

Conrad's next published work was *The Shadow-Line*, published in March 1917. *The Nation* wrote that 'Mr. Conrad is an artist of creative imagination, one of the great ones, not of the present but of the world.'[24] Not all reviews were wholly enthusiastic, but I cannot spend much time on the book since, at least since F. R. Leavis, it has come to be universally seen as a masterpiece which miraculously escaped from the indignity of Conrad's alleged decline. In this it shares the honour with Conrad's relatively late short story, 'The Secret Sharer', which was written in 1909 although only published in October 1912 in *'Twixt Land and Sea*. Conrad wrote to Garnett that the story 'between you and me, is *it*. Eh? No damned tricks with girls there. Eh? Every word fits and there's not a single uncertain note.'[25] 'The Secret Sharer' has also long been regarded as a masterpiece, as I can testify, having recently done an introduction to it for the Limited Editions club; in that edition Conrad's title was further honoured by being printed in gold on an inlay described as 'genuine Nigerian Oasis goat'.

Conrad's next novel was *The Arrow of Gold*, which certainly might be called 'a trick with girls'. Conrad wrote to Sidney Colvin that 'the first notices . . . are very poor, puzzle-headed, hesitating pronouncements; yet not inimical'.[26] The *New Statesman* wrote, in a review that delighted Conrad: 'If it is ever true of any book, then it should be true that a new novel by Mr. Conrad is an "event" – even if, as in the present case, the new book is something of a disappointment.' There are praises: the review says that it 'should be admired, if only for the gentle and valued persistence with which Mr. Conrad continues to teach English writers, who ought to be able to find out for themselves, how to manage their adverbs'. On the vitality of even the minor characters, the critic writes that 'It is hard to think of any other living writer capable of this endless prodigality of creation.'[27] Other reviews were definitely unfavourable, though usually respectful. W. L. Courtney complained that 'in this long-dragged-out romance there is a great deal that is tedious, while some of the conversations do not advance the narrative in the fashion of true and helpful dialogue'.[28]

I must confess that *The Arrow of Gold* seems relatively hard to defend very strongly; although both the scene of the events, and most of the characters, are very well presented. We should, however, mention some very favourable views. Graham Greene for example has written in his autobiography, *A Sort of Life*, about his early novel, *Rumour at Nightfall*:

Conrad was the influence now, and in particular the most dangerous of all his books, *The Arrow of Gold*, written when he had himself fallen under the tutelage of Henry James.[29]

We need not accept Greene's view of Conrad's tutelage here to Henry James; and we notice that in general Graham Greene is by no means an uncritical admirer of Conrad. But the influence was there; indeed

Greene recalls in *A Sort of Life*, that in 1932 'Never again, I swore, would I read a novel of Conrad's.'[30] He had abandoned Conrad 'because his influence on me was too great and too disastrous. The heavy hypnotic style falls around me again, and I am aware of the poverty of my own.'[31] Nevertheless Graham Greene also wrote in his essay on Conrad, that *Victory* is one of the two 'great English novels of the last fifty years'.[32]

Conrad's chief view of the next novel, *The Rescue*, which came out on 20 June 1920, was to rejoice that he had managed to at last finish the novel he had attempted, but failed, to write from 1896 to 1898: 'I am settling my affairs in this world', he wrote to Garnett, 'and I should not have liked to leave behind me this evidence of having bitten off more than I could chew. A very vulgar vanity. Could anything be more legitimate?'[33] The reviews were rather more favourable than those of *The Arrow of Gold*; for example, *Punch* thought *The Rescue*, 'probably the greatest novel of the year, one by which its author has again enriched our literature with work of profound and moving quality'.[34]

Virginia Woolf has been seen, by Norman Sherry and others, as an early supporter of the view that Conrad's work declined,[35] notably in the review of *The Rescue*. Her earlier views on Conrad were admiring. She began a review of the reissue of *Lord Jim* by complaining about the 'sad green colour' of the binding, and continues: 'it is not a question of luxury, but of necessity: we have to buy Mr. Conrad; all our friends have to buy Mr. Conrad'.[36] Elsewhere Virginia Woolf writes that 'There is no novel by Mr. Conrad which has not passages of such beauty that one hangs over them like a humming-bird moth at the mouth of a flower.'[37]

To return to *The Rescue*, Virginia Woolf begins by asking 'in what directions can we expect Mr. Conrad to develop?' 'There were signs that the inevitable changes were taking place', but 'there was nothing to regret; and it could easily be held that in *Chance* and *Victory* Mr. Conrad was advancing, not in the sense of improving, but in the sense of attacking a problem that was different from those magnificently solved before'. The first part of *The Rescue* is praised; the man and his brig is 'founded on truth. And it is only Mr. Conrad who is able to tell us.' When we get to the resolution, however, 'we cannot deny that we are left with a feeling of disappointment'.[38] The difficulty is with Mrs Travers, and her relationship to Lingard. She was, *The Rescue* says, to have found 'the naked truth of life and passion buried under the growth of centuries'.[39] But when 'the moment comes, . . . they cannot take

advantage of it. It seems as if they had lived too long to believe implicitly in romance, and can only act their parts with dignity and do their
best to conceal the disillusionment which is in their hearts.' This ad-
verse judgment is treated fairly gently. Virginia Woolf also writes: 'It
need scarcely be said that Mr. Conrad provides out of his great riches
all sorts of compensation for what we have called the central deficiency.
If he were not Mr. Conrad we should sink all cavil in wonder at the
bounty of his gift. Here are scenes of the sea and of the land, portraits
of savage chiefs and of English sailors, such as no one else can paint.'
Still, Virginia Woolf concludes that 'Mr. Conrad has attempted a
romantic theme and in the middle his belief in romance has failed
him.'[40]

My own view is that, although there is a lack both of narrative and
emotional movement in many of the scenes between Lingard and Mrs
Travers, their relation in general and the final farewell scene on the
sandbank seem convincing. We would, of course, prefer them to make
a fuller commitment to their love; and we are perhaps entitled to
expect it from the early parts of the novel; but both protagonists are
middle-aged; one is married, and the other feels embittered by an
awareness that, for his love of Mrs Travers, he has failed in the darling
project of his life, to restore Hassim and Immada to their kingdom.
Conrad's sense of human reality surely allowed him very little choice;
and disillusionment is a real subject.

The last novel that Conrad completed was *The Rover* which came out
on 3 December 1923. It received mixed reviews. Raymond Mortimer
in the *New Statesman* found it 'downright bad'; but the *Manchester Guardian*
wrote with real appreciation: 'The tale races to its close in as fine a
piece of direct narrative as Mr. Conrad has ever written.' The *Glasgow
Evening News* commented that 'Than Mr. Conrad there is no writer in
English who can make human beings live more vividly in print'; and
the *Times Literary Supplement* comments that 'we are "inside" Peyrol
because the whole manner and physique of him, and the very ground
he treads on, are felt with a tangible vividness'.[41]

Conrad himself was pleased with the story. He welcomed a letter of
praise from Edward Garnett: 'As I have not claimed to be more than
only half-dead for the last month, I feel, after reading your letter, like a
man with wings.' He goes on to explain that 'This was perhaps my only
work in which brevity was a conscious aim. I don't mean compression.
I mean brevity ab initio, in the very conception, in the very manner of
thinking about the people and the events.' At the end of a longish letter,

mainly defending Scevola ('a pathological case'), he repeats his 'secret desire to achieve a feat of artistic brevity, once at least, before I died'.[42] Both Peyrol and Conrad are united in the quest for a youthful former self. This was an appealing theme for the aged Conrad; as he writes to Galsworthy on 22 February 1924: 'I am glad you think well of *The Rover*. I have wanted for a long time to do a seaman's "return" (before my own departure).' He goes on to talk about *Suspense*, and mentions that in his view '*The Rover* is a mere "interlude".'[43]

Several reviewers commented on the lack of interest in Conrad by the younger generation. Leonard Woolf said that 'the younger or youngest generation see only this eternal sameness in him so that they tend to see nothing in him'; and Courtney opined that 'Conrad is no longer popular with the younger school of writers.'[44]

This was probably true in England; Ford Madox Ford and Graham Greene are his main disciples; neither Joyce nor Lawrence nor Forster were great admirers, although T. S. Eliot was. On the other hand the American younger writers certainly were. It is nice to remember the story that Scott Fitzgerald and Ring Lardner, deprived of the opportunity of meeting a writer they much admired, planned to do an informal dance to honour Conrad on the lawn of his American host, Nelson Doubleday; sad to relate, the only person who noticed them was the caretaker, who naturally turned them off the property.[45] Much has been written about the Conrad influence on William Faulkner; and although Hemingway was somewhat less enthusiastic, he at least paid Conrad, and *The Rover*, a memorable tribute.

It was in an obituary notice in the *Conrad Supplement* of Ford's *transatlantic review*. He begins by challenging the low repute of Conrad among his friends. 'It is agreed by most of the people I know that Conrad is a bad writer, just as it is agreed that T. S. Eliot is a good writer.' Hemingway then goes on to pronounce with obvious irony: 'If I knew that by grinding Mr. Eliot into a fine dry powder and sprinkling that powder over Mr. Conrad's grave Mr. Conrad would shortly appear, looking very annoyed at the forced return, and commence writing I would leave for London [he was then in Paris] early tomorrow morning with a sausage-grinder.' This final comment was, no doubt, rude (and very personal); but it was surely what newspaper men used to call 'a grabber'. And the basis of the grabber, was Hemingway's recalling how he read *The Rover* all through the night in his hotel room. Then, 'when morning came I had used up all my Conrad like a drunkard . . . and felt like a young man who has blown away his patrimony. But, I thought, he will write lots more stories. He has lots of time.' But now Conrad had gone, and Hemingway affirmed, again with heavy irony: 'I wish to God they would have taken some great, acknowledged technician of a literary figure and left him to write his bad stories.'

Hemingway wrote his tribute in a hurry, with Ford waiting for it to be done; and later he somewhat repented. 'I cannot reread them [the novels]. That may be what my friends mean by saying he is a bad writer. But from nothing else that I have ever read have I gotten what every book of Conrad has given me.'[46]

Hemingway, then, was a Conrad addict. And if we glance at another Conrad obituary, in the *Times Literary Supplement*, we shall find little talk of declining powers either. It is by Virginia Woolf. She had not been popular for her review of *The Rescue*, as she makes clear in her diary: 'I was struggling . . . to say honestly that I don't think Conrad's last book a good one. I have said it. It is painful (a little) to find fault there, where almost solely, one respects.'[47] But now, perhaps because of the obituary occasion, the tribute to Conrad's memory is touching in its grace and sincerity. The beginning is particularly lovely: 'Suddenly, without giving us time to arrange our thoughts or prepare our phrases, our guest has left us; and his withdrawal without farewell or ceremony is in keeping with his mysterious arrival, long years ago, to take up his lodging in our country.' How fine is the appropriately mocking formality of the opening, and how delicate the wording, notably the word 'lodging' with its connotation of impermanence.

Virginia Woolf next addresses Conrad's literary stature: 'His reputation of later years was, with one obvious exception [presumably Hardy], undoubtedly the highest in England; yet he was not popular.' Why? After all, he had readers who were people of the most opposite ages and sympathies, 'from fourteen year old schoolboys' to the most fastidious. One reason for his lack of popularity, she surmises, lay 'in his beauty. One opens his page and feels as Helen must have felt when she looked in her glass and realized that, do what she would, she could never in any circumstances pass for a plain woman.' For Conrad 'it seemed impossible for him to make an ugly or insignificant stroke of the pen'. Virginia Woolf then goes on to discuss the changes in the nature of Conrad's inspiration; going from the sea stories to the land, and thus closer to the narrative direction of Henry James. These later works, '*Nostromo, Chance, The Arrow of Gold*', are those 'which some will continue to find the richest of all', she concedes. But Conrad, she asserts, 'never believed in his later and more highly sophisticated characters as he had believed in his earlier seamen'. The old beliefs are inculcated in the newer works, 'beautiful always', Virginia Woolf writes, 'but now a little wearily reiterated, as if times have changed'. Virginia Woolf, therefore concludes that 'though we shall make expeditions into the later books and bring back wonderful trophies, large tracts of them will remain by most of us untrodden. It is the earlier books – *Youth, Lord Jim, Typhoon, The Nigger of the "Narcissus"* – that we shall read in their entirety.'[48]

Virginia Woolf, then, sticks to her preference; but whether that remains a position that supports the general belief that Conrad's work declined, is rather a different question; we note her great respect for *Chance* and *The Arrow of Gold* which are placed alongside *Nostromo*. The decline theorists, then, are not agreed when it began.

Douglas Hewitt begins Conrad's decline in *Under Western Eyes*, but *Chance*, he thinks, 'bears, more clearly than *Under Western Eyes*, the marks of the decline in his art'. *Victory* is somewhat better, but not very much so when we look at its rhetoric, and the lack of real development of the plot. *The Shadow-Line* is much better; it is a simpler tale which does not raise the questions which cause Conrad 'uneasiness and evasion'; still, he finds 'an inability to sustain the tension set up by that awareness of corruption and loneliness which give such force to his best work' – that is, 'Heart of Darkness', *Nostromo, The Secret Agent*.[49]

Thomas Moser, in the classic work *Joseph Conrad: Achievement and Decline*, seems to have established the notion of a pre-ordained determinism of failure in Conrad criticism through the very phrase of the title. He ventures a relatively simple causal explanation of the decline. The first chapter has the title 'The Early Conrad's Anatomy of Moral Failure', and awards the highest standing to *The Nigger of the 'Narcissus', Lord Jim, Typhoon* and *Nostromo*. The later works are almost entirely summed up in the title of chapter two: 'The Uncongenial Subject: Love's Tangled Garden'. This includes the two apprentice Malayan novels, and the early short stories in *Tales of Unrest*. Their trite and unconvincing handling of the theme of love can also be traced in the defects of the later novels, and yet Moser does not argue for a neat chronological decline; some of the short stories are affected throughout Conrad's career, and parts of many novels.

Moser also suggests that the thematic and structural weakness of the novels is allied with the poverty of the expression; Conrad's later prose becomes less satisfactory.[50] Here one must agree that many of the passages cited support Moser's case; the best defence is that – contrary to Virginia Woolf's view – Conrad was quite capable of occasional sloppiness or over-complication in his prose, but it was throughout his career; 'Heart of Darkness', and *Nostromo* and *The Secret Agent* are no more immune than *Chance* or *The Rescue*.

There is a somewhat similar defence to be made against the charge that Conrad's work declined because he turned to an emphasis on women characters, and the love theme generally, because he thought this would make his novels popular. This is no doubt true; but there is one chronological difficulty: Conrad had always wanted to make more money. For example, he wrote hopefully of *The Secret Agent* that 'there is an element of popularity in it . . . my mind runs much on popularity now'.[51] Nevertheless Conrad wrote the novel in a style and with an evaluative attitude which was the reverse of those in popular fiction; the novels did not, finally, prove popular. Indeed from *Almayer's Folly* to *The Rover* one sees Conrad dealing with possibly popular topics on the one hand, and then treating them in a very characteristically ironic way which trod hard on romantic and optimistic attitudes.

We still have to accept the fact that many of Conrad's critics see *Under Western Eyes*, *Chance* and *Victory* as major works; while some major writers, such as Graham Greene and Hemingway, have been entranced by *The Arrow of Gold* and *The Rover*.

I will now advance my own very tentative hypothesis. It is that some positive qualities are also found fairly uniformly throughout Conrad's writing career.

First the style. To read any page of Conrad, whenever written, is surely to become aware of a recognizable and highly personal mode of expression. This is no doubt why Hemingway, although he found it difficult to read or reread Conrad, and paid little attention, apparently to the plot, nevertheless said that 'From nothing else that I have ever read have I gotten what every book of Conrad has given me.'[52] Conrad's unique cultural background somehow found expression in a unique style. It is why Graham Greene, despite his various objections, could write of Conrad's 'heavy hypnotic style', and go on to confess that it reminds him of 'the poverty of my own'.[53] Virginia Woolf has suggested in her own way that with Conrad the style is, to an exceptional degree, the man. We must surely agree that whether he is at the top, or even at the bottom, of his form, Conrad has created his own individual voice.

Second, this individual voice has a moral component; it is itself an expression of human values. As Virginia Woolf put it in the same essay, 'Mr. Conrad: A Conversation', 'The beauty of surface has always a fibre of morality within. I seem to see each of the sentences you have read advancing with resolute bearing and a calm which they have won in strenuous conflict, against the forces of falsehood, sentimentality and slovenliness. He could not write badly, one feels, to save his life.'[54]

Third. The sense of scene. In the review of *Lord Jim*, after quoting Marlow's remark that he saw the French lieutenant 'as though I had never seen him before', Woolf comments that Conrad 'expounds his vision, and we see it too'.[55] Conrad, we may conclude, writes uniformly in accord with his aim in the Preface to *The Nigger of the 'Narcissus'*: 'My task . . . is, by the power of the written word to make you hear, to make you feel – it is, before all, to make you *see*.' Emphasis is not only on '*see*' but on the thrice repeated 'make'. Part of Conrad's spell as a writer is the literal way in which he *makes* us see; the person, the time of day, the place. It is what the *T.L.S.* called his 'tangible vividness'. And this pressure to visualize the characters and the scene is found throughout his work, from Almayer in his rotting Folly to the people and the terrain of Escampobar in *The Rover*.

Lastly, Virginia Woolf also points out that Conrad's gift is not just that of conveying sensory perceptions; it is always, or very often, a matter of going beyond them. She remarks in a letter, of *The Shadow-Line*: 'It is very beautiful and very calm. I wish I knew how he gets his effects of space.'[56] Don't we all. We cannot know exactly how, but we can tell Conrad is trying by the way that he writes; that way evokes much larger dimensions of experience; and it, also, is Conrad's permanent possession.

An individual voice, its moral component, a sense of scene and its suggestion of larger meanings – these are surely enduring qualities of all Conrad's writing. We can see all these, to take a crucial example, in his unfinished novel *Suspense*. A good deal has been written about Conrad's dependence on the *Memoirs* of the Comptesse de Boigne for much of the plot and the characters,[57] and the slowness of development of the story. On the other hand I do not think that the 80,000 words of the text show any signs whatever of failing powers. The presentation of the setting, the basic action, the convincing characters, the smoothness of the flashback transitions from one scene to another, surely convey a powerful sense that we are in the hands of a master who knows just what he is doing: Genoa, with its harbour tower, Cantelucci's hotel, and the Palazzo Brignoli, have a wonderful solidity, and so do the characters, Cosmo Latham, Adèle Armand, Count Helion, Martel and Attilio; while the settings and its denizens collaborate to create a mysterious atmosphere of puzzling suspense, which surely make the reader regret that we do not have the whole novel. *Suspense* is, as Richard Curle wrote, 'a fragment that will take its place among the recognized masterpieces'[58] of Conrad.

I believe, then, that Conrad is a writer to whom the decline theory does not really apply; and to accept it as true may deter us from the deep pleasures afforded by reading the later works. Granted, we all hate change; *Lord Jim* may remain our preferred favourite; we may even regret that Conrad did not write more *Lord Jim*s; but if he had, would we have liked them as much? Surely, even if his basic ideas, and the essence of his technique did not change, his subjects did, and they had to. There are less than perfect works all along the way of Conrad's career; but there are remarkable triumphs too, and they, also, are to be found all along the way. One can, perhaps, object that the continuity is all a question of Conrad's manner; but manners maketh man.

NOTES

I gladly thank various people who have helped me on this project: C. W. E. Bigsby and the hearers who heard the first version of this essay at the Lausanne meeting of the International Association of University Professors of English on 21 August 1989; also Steve Danzig, Gloria Escobar, George Light, Meg Minto and Zdzislaw Najder.

1 Zdzislaw Najder, *Joseph Conrad: A Chronicle* (New Brunswick, N.J., 1983), pp. 335–6, quotes an earlier count by Conrad.
2 *Ibid.* pp. 380, 390.
3 *Ibid.* pp. 385, 391.
4 *Ibid.* p. 407.
5 *Letters from Conrad, 1895 to 1924*, ed. Edward Garnett (London, 1928), pp. 172–3.
6 Najder, *Conrad*, p. 375.
7 Henry James, *Literary Criticism: Essays on Literature, American Writers, English Literature* (New York, 1984), pp. 147, 150.
8 In 'Conrad, James and *Chance*', see p. 145 above.
9 Letter to Quinn, 24 May 1916, cited 'Conrad, James and *Chance*', p. 319.
10 James, 'The New Novel', pp. 151, 134.
11 Norman Sherry, ed., *Conrad: The Critical Heritage* (London, 1973), pp. 282, 281, 276.
12 F. R. Leavis, *The Great Tradition: George Eliot, Henry James, Joseph Conrad* (London, 1948), p. 225.
13 Douglas Hewitt, *Conrad: A Reassessment* (Cambridge, 1952), p. 89.
14 *Chance*, Dent Collected Edition (London, 1949), pp. 426–7.
15 Hewitt, pp. 94–5.
16 *Chance*, p. 60.

17 Sherry, *Critical Heritage*, p. 287.

18 *Ibid.* p. 298.

19 *Ibid.* p. 299.

20 *Ibid.* p. 303.

21 F. R. Leavis, *The Great Tradition*, pp. 189–90.

22 Harold Bloom, ed., *Modern Critical Views: Joseph Conrad* (New York, 1986), pp. 4, 3. Leavis, *Great Tradition*, pp. 174–82.

23 John A. Palmer, *Joseph Conrad's Fiction: A Study in Literary Growth* (Ithaca, 1968), pp. xii, 45, 170, 197.

24 Sherry, *Critical Heritage*, pp. 304–5.

25 Garnett, *Letters from Conrad*, p. 263.

26 Sherry, *Critical Heritage*, p. 314.

27 *Ibid.* pp. 321, 322, 324.

28 *Ibid.* p. 325.

29 Graham Greene, *A Sort of Life* (New York, 1971), p. 154.

30 *Ibid.* p. 212.

31 Graham Greene, *In Search of a Character: Two African Journals* (London, 1961), p. 48.

32 Graham Greene, 'Remembering Mr. Jones', *Collected Essays* (New York, 1969), p. 184.

33 Garnett, *Letters from Conrad*, pp. 287–8.

34 Sherry, *Critical Heritage*, pp. 343, 336.

35 *Ibid.* p. 35. 'The wave of reaction to Conrad began with some delicately expressed criticism in TLS.'

36 Virginia Woolf, *Collected Essays* (London, 1987), vol. II, p. 140.

37 *Ibid.* III, p. 174.

38 *Ibid.* III, pp. 229, 230, 230.

39 Joseph Conrad, *The Rescue*, Dent Collected Edition (London, 1949), p. 153.

40 Virginia Woolf, *Essays*, III, pp. 231, 231–2, 232.

41 Sherry, *Critical Heritage*, pp. 358, 350, 356, 354.

42 Garnett, *Letters from Conrad*, pp. 330, 331, 333.

43 G. Jean-Aubry, *Joseph Conrad: Life and Letters* (London, 1927), vol. II, p. 339.

44 Sherry, *Critical Heritage*, p. 36.

45 André Le Vot, *F. Scott Fitzgerald: A Biography*, trans. William Byron (New York, 1983), p. 123.

46 Ernest Hemingway, *By-Line, Selected Articles and Dispatches of Four Decades* (New York, 1967), pp. 132–3.

47 Virginia Woolf, *Diary* (New York, 1978), pp. 49, 51.

48 Virginia Woolf, *Essays*, I, pp. 302, 302, 302, 302–3, 306, 307, 307.

49 Hewitt, *Conrad*, pp. 89, 117, 117.

50 Thomas Moser, *Joseph Conrad: Achievement and Decline* (Cambridge, Mass., 1957), pp. 44, 51. There is much of interest, including a rejection of the view that Conrad was a misogynist, in 'Conrad Criticism Today: An Evaluation of Recent Conrad Scholarship', by Jan Verleun and Jetty de Vries, in *English Literature in Transition, 1880–1920*, 29 (1986), 241–75.

51 Jean-Aubry, *Life and Letters*, II, p. 49.

52 Hemingway, *By-Line*, p. 133.

53 Greene, *A Sort of Life*, p. 206.

54 Virginia Woolf, *Essays*, I, p. 312.

55 *Ibid.* II, p. 142.

56 *Ibid.* II, p. 149.

57 Jocelyn Baines, *Joseph Conrad: A Critical Biography* (London, 1960), pp. 436–8 and notes.

58 Joseph Conrad, *Suspense: A Napoleonic Novel*, Dent Collected Edition (London, 1954), p. vi.

CHAPTER 11

Around Conrad's grave in the Canterbury cemetery — a retrospect

I begin with a letter written to me long ago. The text has three interesting stylistic features and makes two points concerning what, somewhat portentously, we may call my research methods.

24th Oct/55   No 10 not 8 Sudbury Avenue
                                Westgate Court Estate
                                Canterbury

Dear Sir referring to my knolage of the late Joseph Conrad he was buried on the 7th Aug 1924 his wife Buried on 9th Dec 1936 I having been employed at the cemetery for 30 years was helping with both funerals previous to Joseph Conrad dying he used to walk round and have a few words with us men at our work after his Death Mrs Conrad for the Anaversery sent an very large wreath to be put on his grave at that time she was living at the Top of Mill lane Canterbury but she Died in Hospital in London but with regard to knowing much about them I am afraid I cannot tell you very much about them so with this small bit of Information
> I close hoping this meets with
> your Approvall
> I am yours Etc

         Mr Albert R Smith
         10 Sudbury Avenue
         Westgate Court Estate
         Canterbury

(After you saw Mr Beeching at the Cemetery you must have gone to the Wrong house)

Stylistically this is not badly composed for a gravedigger, which its author was. Still, it is the only letter I have ever received without any single mark of punctuation from beginning to end; its spelling is remarkable – an extraordinary effort to reproduce each difficult word's sound apparently *de novo*; and lastly, the author is not unaware of how his text should try to honor in its style the majesty of death: he gives a capital letter 'D' both to 'Death' and to 'Died,' though not to 'dying'. As to my own scholarly idiosyncrasies, I note that Albert R. Smith, despite his no doubt sincerely intended show of proper humility to an educated gentleman, feels he must correct my sloppily attributing to him the house number '8' instead of '10'. Nor does he let pass without notice that, with a familiar lapse, I had had difficulties in following directions, and had 'gone to the wrong house'. By no means, I must confess, for the first or the last time.

Hm. An informant possibly offended, and a research opportunity missed. Yet I must confess that I do not remember anything about either the informant or the wrong house. Still, I will totter down memory lane to see what comes up.

As a boy I lived outside Dover at River, and so Canterbury was only some dozen miles away. I do remember having bicycled to Bishopsbourne with my sister and brother when I was about twelve; and we had even stopped to look at 'Oswalds', where Conrad had lived from October 1919 until his death. My father had a copy of *Lord Jim* in the house, so I had set myself early on the Conradian path. But I don't think we went to the cemetery that trip; it would have been several miles more to cycle; and I can't remember ever having gone there before the war at all. Yet I must have done so, because I have a vivid memory of a day, as a Japanese prisoner of war on the Kwai, when I had suddenly thought: 'There was no mention of Jessie on Conrad's grave; but she had died in 1936. Why? There must have been a bad quarrel or misunderstanding of some kind between Joseph and her.' I'd often wondered, even then, how Conrad could have married so dull and unintellectual a person.

That memory, I now realize, explains why, within the first ten days or so of my return from captivity, when I was back at Dover, I had gone on a splendid walk to Canterbury. It was a clear October day in 1945; the green Kentish landscape was still beautiful; and I'd even picked some mushrooms. Then I had gone to have a look at Conrad's gravestone, and discovered that yes, I had been right: there was no mention of Jessie on it even now.

Unfortunately, I was very rarely at Dover; I lived at Cambridge and then at Berkeley. My next visit to Dover must have been in 1955, the date of Smith's letter. My mother was ill, and I had gone for a quick visit from Berkeley. Research on Conrad had hardly begun – I was still revising *The Rise of the Novel*. But I had managed to visit Conrad's second son, John, at the lovely brick house he had built, Broome Quarry House, only six or so miles away. There was a Polish national carving over the front door, and from the garden a fine view of the valley down the Nail Bourne, stretching to Bishopsbourne some two miles away; the Bourne even flowed through 'Oswalds'.¹ We had a very good talk, and I finally dared to ask him if Jessie was buried in Conrad's grave. 'Yes', he said, 'she was', and thus gave a resounding 'No!' to my speculations.

True, there was no inscription. But that was for a significant reason. In her will Jessie had left instructions that a very lavish memorial tribute to her should be placed on the gravestone; the effect would have been that Joseph's simple inscription – his name, his dates, and two lines from Spenser – would be lost; he would, in effect, figure merely as 'the husband of the above'. Joseph Conrad's executors, Richard Curle and Ralph Wedgwood, had very properly objected; and the deadlock had stopped any action being taken on Jessie's proposed inscription for nearly twenty years. Their difference on this, I gathered, had for a time divided John from his brother Borys. Fortunately, John said, the differences had now been patched up, and a simpler inscription for Jessie would soon be carved on the grave. As it has been.

I come back now to 'Mr. Beecher', or, as my rather rough note spells it, 'Beauchamp'. I no longer remember the meeting, but I have the note. I apparently spoke to him in early September 1955. He was then in charge of the records of the Canterbury Cemetery on Westgate Court Avenue. It is a large city affair for all comers, not a parish churchyard. On August fifth, two days after Conrad's death, Mrs Jessie Conrad had bought four plots, two large, and two small. She had bought two more plots on 28 December 1924. Conrad was buried on 7 August, four days after his death. There was a Roman Catholic mass for Conrad at Saint Thomas's church in Canterbury; the officiating cleric was Father E. H., or possibly F. H., Sheppard. Beecher also told me that even if Conrad had been a Catholic or an atheist, he could have been buried in the parish churchyard of Bishopsbourne, if he wished. It therefore looks as though Conrad himself had deliberately chosen to be buried in Canterbury. There he could have a mass, and then be buried in the part of the Canterbury cemetery specially reserved for Roman Catholics, and with their usual burial service. His grave is still surrounded by Italian names such as Salvatore and Megliococca. Conrad 'used to walk round' the cemetery according to Albert Smith; this seems faintly possible, I suppose, and if so, would benefit our memory with a picturesque image.

Jessie Conrad had died in Guy's Hospital, London; she was buried next to Conrad on 9 December 1936, by a cleric called Middleton, who, Beecher thought, was probably the rector of Bishopsbourne.

There, no doubt, we should leave them undisturbed. But, of course, in research, after dealing with its usual questions, 'Who did?', and 'Did what?', there is always the third question, 'What of it?' One possible answer is that my initial mistake is common enough. As Henry James put it in the Preface to *The Princess Casamassima*, 'it seems probable that if we were never bewildered there would never be a story to tell about us'. The whole investigation had started in my silly and prejudiced error, but behind the error was a genuine fact; and this fact had illustrated the undeniable truth that authors have posthumous lives: so one sad theme of Conrad's posthumous life seems to have been illuminated by my mistake.

In one of my interviews with David Garnett, at the Reform Club on 7 September 1955, he had contrasted Henry James, who thought about 'nothing but money', with Conrad, who, 'in his way – thought about nothing but honour'. Conrad assumed that the people round him thought likewise about honour and lived accordingly. But it was not so: his honour was betrayed on every side. In the two books on her husband, *Joseph Conrad As I Knew Him* (1926), and *Joseph Conrad and his Circle* (1935), Jessie had shown a rather inordinate sense of her own importance. She presented her life as one long martyrdom to an impossible husband. It was her stupid vanity that had later created her ridiculous demands for the gravestone, and which then led to there being no inscription on it for more than twenty years.

When I asked Richard Curle in London, 57 Queensborough Terrace, on 16 September 1955, about the rumours that Jessie had been broke in her later years at Canterbury, he answered that she had been left very well-off; Conrad's will gave her three-fifths of the residuary income from his considerable estate. But, Curle said, she 'had gambled'. I asked, 'Was it the Stock Exchange?' Curle laughed: 'She didn't have the intelligence to know about that. It was horses.' In his *Times Remembered*, John Conrad, incidentally, blames his mother for having sold the collection of books and manuscripts that Conrad had intended for him, to the American collector, George Keating; she needed the money. John writes: 'It never occurred to me that my father's wishes would be ignored . . . My mother was, relatively, well provided for but she never discussed with me the sale of any object; in fact it was all done without my knowledge so I was presented with a *fait accompli* about which nothing could be done' (168). Conrad, then, had been right to protect Jessie and his family by acting on his suspicions and tying up his capital in a trust.

As for Borys, he had presumably supported his mother's wishes for her grave. There had been something of a quarrel with Jessie after his marriage, but it was made up, according to Borys.[2] Borys was later brought to court for having, as David Garnett put it, 'swindled his best friend', on the false pretence of having access to Conrad manuscripts. The facts as reported in the *Times* are that 'Alfred Borys Conrad, 29, a motor engineer, of Hythe road, Ashford, Kent, arrested on a warrant, was remanded on £600 bail by the Marylebone Magistrate yesterday [i.e. 9 June 1927] charged with fraudulently converting to his own use and benefit £1,100 entrusted to him on March 10, 1926.' The 'borrowed' money, Borys claimed, was to be added to £2,900 which he possessed, and this £4,000 would be sufficient to enable him to buy Joseph's manuscripts, which could at once be sold for £5,000. Of course Borys never had the £2,900, nor any knowledge of either the alleged owner, or the purchaser, of the Conrad manuscripts. Garnett may have exaggerated in calling the lender of the money, a Mrs Dorothy Bevan, Borys's 'best friend'; but there was no doubt of Borys's guilt, and he was eventually sentenced to one year's imprisonment. Earlier, in his father's lifetime, Borys had already exploited his father's fame by assuring his creditors that his father had invested £1,000 on his behalf in the United States.[3]

I was, and remain, much influenced by the view of David Garnett and Richard Curle, neither of them, admittedly, very well disposed to Jessie. But there were other events which dogged the posthumous story of the Conrads' betrayal. John seems to have been the only loyal member of the family; but he was subject to an outrage by the Kent County Council. In a sublime example of – to put it mildly – tactlessness, it was decided to build what used to be called a 'lunatic asylum', but is now, no doubt, to be more properly termed a 'residential institution for the mentally challenged', on the down side of the road from John Conrad's house, so as to block his view of Bishopsbourne and 'Oswalds'. He moved out. There was another building outrage at 'Oswalds' itself. The owner of Bourne Park, to whom it belonged, tore down the drawing room and ploughed up the Dutch Garden, which was turned into just a field. The reason? Being no longer rich, and unable to live in the main house, the owner wanted 'Oswalds' reduced in size and status, so that his own smaller house would still be grander.[4]

A fine example of petty spoliation. And in another sense, 'Oswalds' is no more; it has been renamed 'The Rectory'.

Complete diplomatic secrecy on these matters was kept both in Borys Conrad's *My Father: Joseph Conrad* (1970), and Conrad's *Joseph Conrad: Times Remembered* (1981); there is no indication whatever in their memoirs of the divisions I've been talking about. So we can find a bright side: in its own way time heals wounds. The bold grey granite monolith of Conrad's grave still stands out defiantly from the surrounding crosses. But there are other names on it now: Jessie Emmeline Conrad Korzeniowski (her Polish enthusiasm had not gone so far as to spell her husband's second forename, Teodor, correctly – her version on the tombstone is 'Teador'; the tombstone also anglicizes the original Józef to Joseph, and Konrad to Conrad); John's two sons, Peter Stewart Thaddeus Conrad Korzeniowski and John Richard Teodor Conrad Korzeniowski, are in the grave; and now, Alfred Borys Conrad Korzeniowski and John Alexander Conrad Korzeniowski have also died, alas! and been buried there too. It is a wry, though belated, triumph for family solidarity over its opposite.

NOTES

1 John Conrad, *Joseph Conrad: Time Remembered* (Cambridge, 1981), p. 133.
2 Borys Conrad, *My Father: Joseph Conrad* (1970), p. 158.
3 Jeffrey Meyers, *Joseph Conrad: A Biography* (1991), p. 353.
4 John Conrad interview (BBC, 16 November 1947); Borys Conrad, *Joseph Conrad's Homes in Kent* (1974), p. 12.

CHAPTER 12

'The Bridge over the River Kwai' as myth

The Kwai is a real river in Thailand, and nearly thirty years ago prisoners of the Japanese – including myself – really did build a bridge across it: actually, two. Anyone who was there knows that Boulle's novel, *The Bridge on the River Kwai*, and the movie based on it, are both completely fictitious. What is odd is how they combined to create a world-wide myth, and how that myth is largely the result of those very psychological and political delusions which the builders of the real bridges had been forced to put aside.

THE REAL BRIDGES

The origin of the myth can be traced back to two historical realities.

Early in 1942, Singapore, the Dutch East Indies, and the Philippines surrendered: and Japan was suddenly left with the task of looking after over two hundred thousand prisoners of war. The normal procedure is to separate the officers from the enlisted men and put them into different camps; but the Japanese hadn't got the staff to spare and left the job of organizing the prison-camps to the prisoners themselves; which in effect meant the usual chain of command. This was one essential basis for Boulle's story: prisoners of war, like other prisoners, don't normally command anyone; and so they don't have anything to negotiate with.

The other main reality behind the myth is the building of that particular bridge. Once their armies started driving towards India, the Japanese realized they needed a railway from Bangkok to Rangoon. In the summer of 1942 many trainloads of prisoners from Singapore were sent up to Thailand and started to hack a two-hundred-mile trace through the jungle along a river called the Khwae Noi. In Thai, *Khwae* just means 'stream'; *Noi* means 'small'. The 'small stream' rises near the Burma border, at the Three Pagodas Pass; and it joins the main tributary of the Me Nam, called the Khwae Yai, or 'Big Stream', at the old city of Kamburi, some eighty miles west of Bangkok. It was there that the Japanese faced the big task of getting the railway across the river. So, early in the autumn of 1942, a large construction camp was set up at a place called Tha Makham, about three miles west of Kamburi.

Like the hundred of other Japanese prison camps, Tha Makham had a very small and incompetent staff. To the Japanese the idea of being taken prisoner of war is – or was then – deeply shameful; even looking after prisoners shared some of this humiliation. Consequently, most of the Japanese staff were men who for one reason or another were thought unfit for combat duty; too old, perhaps, in disgrace, or just drunks. What was special about Tha Makham and the other camps on the Kwai was that they were also partly controlled by Japanese military engineers who were building the railway. These engineers usually despised the Japanese troops in charge of running the camps almost as much as they despised the prisoners.

The continual friction between the Japanese prison staff and the engineers directly affected our ordinary lives as prisoners. Daily routine in the camps in November 1942, when work on the Kwai bridge began, normally went like this: up at dawn; tea and rice for breakfast; and then on parade for the day's work. We might wait anything from ten minutes to half an hour for the Korean guard to count the whole parade and split it up into work groups. Then we marched to a small bamboo shed where the picks, shovels and so on were kept. Under any circumstances it would take a long time for one guard to issue tools for thousands of men out of one small shed; the delay was made worse by the fact that the tools usually belonged to the engineers, so two organizations were involved merely in issuing and checking picks and shovels. That might take another half hour, and then we would be reassembled and counted all over again before finally marching off to work.

When we had finally got out on the line, and found the right work site, the Japanese engineer in charge might be there to explain the day's task; but more probably not. He had a very long section of embankment or bridge to look after and perhaps thirty working parties in widely separate places to supervise. He had usually given some previous instructions to the particular guard at each site; but these orders might not be clear, or, even worse, they might be clear to us, but not to the guard.

There were many organizational problems. For instance, in the early days of the railway the total amount of work each man was supposed to do – moving a cubic meter of earth or driving in so many piles – was quite reasonable under normal circumstances. But the task often fell very unequally: some groups might have to carry their earth much further than others, or drive their teak piles into much rockier ground. So, as the day wore on, someone in a group with a very difficult, or impossible, assignment would get beaten up: all the guard thought about was that he'd probably be beaten up himself if the work on the section wasn't finished: so he lashed out.

Meanwhile, many other prisoners would already have finished their task, and would be sitting around waiting, or – even worse – pretending to work. The rule was that the whole day's task had to be finished, and often inspected by the Japanese engineer, before any single work party could leave the construction site. So some more prisoners would be beaten up for lying down in the shade when they were supposed to look as though there were still work to do in the sun.

At the end of the day's work an individual prisoner might well have been on his feet under the tropical sun from 7 in the morning until 7 or 8 even 9 at night, even though he'd only done three or four hours' work. He would come back late for the evening meal; there would be no lights in the huts; and as most of the guards went off duty at 6, he probably wouldn't be allowed to go down to the river to bathe, or wash his clothes.

So our lives were poisoned, not by calculated Japanese brutality, but merely by a special form of the boredom, waste of time, and demoralization which are typical of modern industrial society. Our most pressing daily problems were really the familiar trade-union issues of long portal-to-portal hours of work, and the various tensions arising from failures of communication between the technical specialists, the personnel managers, and the on-site foremen – in our case the Japanese engineers, the higher prisoner administration, and the guards.

The people best able to see the situation as a whole were probably the officer-prisoners in charge of individual working parties. (This was before officers had been forced to do manual work.) These officers, however, normally dealt only with the particular guards on their section of the line; and back at camp headquarters neither the Japanese prison staff nor the senior British officers had much direct knowledge of conditions out on the trace. But since – mainly because of a shortage of interpreters – most of the Japanese orders were handed down through Allied officers, who were in fact virtually impotent, everything tended to increase the confusion and mistrust in our own ranks.

At first the difficulties in the Bridge Camp of Tha Makham were much like those in all the others. But soon they began to change, mainly because of the personality of its senior British officer.

Colonel Philip Toosey was tall, rather young, and with one of those special English faces like a genial but sceptical bulldog. Unlike Boulle's Colonel Nicholson, he was not a career officer but a territorial.

Toosey's previous career had been managerial. Now a cotton merchant and banker, he had earlier run a factory, where he had experienced the decline of the Lancashire cotton industry, strikes, unemployment, the Depression; he'd even gone bankrupt himself. This past training helped him to see that the problem confronting him wasn't a standard military problem at all: it had an engineering side, a labor-organization side, and above all, a very complicated morale side affecting both the prisoners and their captors.

Escaping or refusing to work on a strategic bridge were both out of the question. Trying either could only mean some men killed, and the rest punished. We had already learned that in a showdown the Japanese would always win; they had the power, and no scruples about using it. But Toosey had the imagination to see that there was a shade more room for manoeuvre than anybody else had suspected – as long as the manoeuvres were of exactly the right kind. He was a brave man, but he never forced the issue so as to make the Japanese lose face; instead he first awed them with an impressive display of military swagger; and then proceeded to charm them with his apparently immovable assumption that no serious difficulty could arise between honorable soldiers whose only thought was to do the right thing.

The right thing from our point of view, obviously, was to do everything possible to increase food and medical supplies, improve working conditions, and allocate the work more reasonably. Gradually, Toosey persuaded the Japanese that things like issuing tools or allocating the day's tasks to each working party more evenly would be better handled if we did it ourselves. He also persuaded the Japanese that output would be much improved if the duties of the guards were limited entirely to preventing the prisoners from escaping. We would be responsible for our own organization and discipline. The officers in charge of working parties would supervise the construction work; while back at camp headquarters, if the Japanese engineers would assign the next day's work to Colonel Toosey, he and his staff would see how best to carry it out.

The new organization completely transformed our conditions of life. There was much less waste of time; daily tasks were often finished early in the afternoon; weeks passed without any prisoner being beaten; and the camp became almost happy.

Looked at from outside, Toosey's remarkable success obviously involved an increase in the degree of our collaboration with the enemy. But anybody on the spot knew that the real issue was not between building or not building the bridge; it was merely how many prisoners would die, be beaten up, or break down, in the process. There was only one way to persuade the Japanese to improve rations, provide medical supplies, allow regular holidays, or reduce the brutality of the guards: to convince them that the work got done better our way.

Toosey's drive and panache soon won him the confidence of the Japanese at the camp: they got about the same amount of work out of us, and their working day was much shorter too. At the same time Toosey was never accused by his fellow prisoners – as Boulle's Colonel Nicholson certainly would have been – of being 'Jap-happy'. Some regarded him as a bit too regimental for their taste; but, unanswerably, he delivered the goods. Eventually, in all the dozens of camps up and down the River Kwai, Toosey became a legend: he was the man who could 'handle the Nips'. His general strategy of taking over as much responsibility as possible (often much more than the Japanese knew), was gradually put into practice by the most successful British, American, Australian and Dutch commanders in the other camps. Even more convincingly, in 1945, when the Japanese saw defeat ahead, and finally concentrated all their officer-prisoners in one camp, the vast majority of the three thousand or so allied officers collected there agitated until various senior commanding officers were successively removed and Colonel Toosey was put in charge. He remained in command until the end of the war in August 1945, when, to general consternation, all kinds of ancient military characters precipitately emerged from the woodwork to reclaim the privileges of seniority.

THE MYTH BEGINS

But Toosey, like all the other heroes – and non-heroes – of our prisoner-of-war days, would normally have been forgotten when peace finally broke out. That he left any mark on the larger world is only because a Free-French officer, Pierre Boulle, who had never known him, had never been near the railway, and was never a prisoner of the Japanese, wrote a novel called *Le Pont de la Rivière Kwai*.

The book was not in any sense intended as history. Though he took the river's real name, Boulle placed his bridge near the Burmese frontier, two hundred miles from the only actual bridge *across* the Kwai, the one at Tha Makham. And, as Boulle recounted in his fascinating but – on this topic – not very explicit autobiographical memoir, *The Sources of the River Kwai* (1966), Colonel Nicholson was based, not on any prisoner of war but on two French colonels he had known in Indo-China. Having been Boulle's comrades in arms until the collapse of France in 1941, they then sided with Vichy, and eventually punished Boulle's activities on behalf of the Allies as treason, quite blind to the notion that it was they, and not Boulle, who had changed sides.

In his novel Boulle made Nicholson's 'collaboration' much more extreme: he built a better bridge than the one the Japanese had started, and in a better place. Boulle may have got the idea from the fact that the Japanese actually built two bridges over the Kwai at Tha Makham: a temporary wooden structure, which no longer survives; and another begun at the same time and finished in May, 1943, which was a permanent iron-trestle bridge on concrete piers, and still stands. Both bridges showed up clearly on Allied aerial photographs; and Boulle may have seen these photographs when he was a Free-French Intelligence officer in Calcutta during the last year of the war.

Boulle's main aim in the novel was presumably to dramatize the ironic contradictions which he had personally experienced in Indo-China. First, Nicholson embodied the paradox of how the military – like any other institutional – mind will tend to generate its own objectives, objectives which are often quite different from, and may even be contrary to the original purposes of the institution. Secondly, there was the political paradox – the total reversals of attitude which continually occur, almost unnoticed, in our strange world of changing ideological alliances. To drive this point home Boulle also invented the Allied commandos who were sent to blow up the bridge with exactly the same patient technological expertness as had been used by their former comrades in arms who had built it.

The book's interest for the reader comes mainly from the similar but opposite efforts of the commandos and the prisoners. Like Nicholson we forget about aims because the means are absorbing; we watch how well the two jobs are being done, and it's only at the end that we wake up and realize that all this marvellous technological expertness harnessed to admirable collective effort has been leading to nothing except death; Nicholson sabotages the saboteurs, and then dies under the fire of Warden's mortar. So, finally, we see that the novel is not really about the Kwai, but about how the vast scale and complication of the operations which are rendered possible, and are even in a sense required, by modern technology tend finally to destroy human meanings and purposes. The West is the master of its means, but not of its ends.

This basic idea was lost, of course, in the movie; but there were many other elements in Boulle's narrative which gave it a more universal appeal.

First, there was the character of Nicholson, which was very little changed in the movie: an amiable fellow in his way, but egocentric; admirable, but ridiculous; intelligent, but basically infantile. Here we come back to a very ancient French myth about the English character, a stereotype which was already fully established in a book written about an English colonel by a French liaison officer after the first world war – in André Maurois's *The Silences of Colonel Bramble*. The infantile and egocentric side of Nicholson's character is essential to the plot; the book is after all about a monomaniac who falls in love with a boy's hobby: to build a bridge, but not with an Erector set, and not for toy trains.

The audience, of course, gets caught up in the hobby too; perhaps because it fulfills the greatest human need in the modern world: being able to love one's work. Along the Kwai there had been a daily conflict between the instinct of workmanship and disgust with what one was being forced to do: people would spend hours trying to get a perfect alignment of piles, and then try to hide termites or rotten wood in an important joint. These sabotage games weren't really very significant; but they expressed a collective need to pretend we were still fighting the enemy, and to resist any tendency to see things the Japanese way. We were always on the lookout for people becoming what we called 'Jap-happy'; and if anyone had started talking about 'my bridge', like Nicholson, he'd have been replaced at once.

Neither the novel nor the film even hint at these conflicting impulses; and so the question arises, 'How can Boulle's shrewd and experienced mind ever have imagined that Nicholson could plausibly get away with his love affair for a Japanese bridge?'

There are at least three possible reasons. First, Boulle himself was born in Avignon, site of the world's most famous ruined bridge. Secondly, he was trained as an engineer and presumably shared the mystique of his profession. These were two positive motives for loving bridges; and there was also the general intellectual and political context of the post-war world. Boulle's first collection of short stories, *Tales of the Absurd,* expressed not only a sense that history had arrived at a meaningless dead-end, but the whole Existential perspective on the human condition in general; all political causes and individual purposes were equally fictitious and ridiculous. Boulle certainly intended *The Bridge on the River Kwai* to have the same implication; as we can see from his epigraph, taken from Conrad's *Victory*: 'No, it was not funny; it was, rather, pathetic; he was so representative of all the past victims of the Great Joke. But it is by folly alone that the world moves, and so it is a respectable thing on the whole. And besides, he was what one would call a good man.'

THE MOVIE

Boulle's book was published in 1952 and sold about 6,000 copies annually in France until 1958. That year sales leaped to 122,000 – the movie had come out. Later, the film's success caused the book to be translated into more than twenty languages, and to sell millions of copies; it also, of course, created the myth.

Hollywood has been a great creator of myths, but they have usually been personal – myths of individual actors, such as Charlie Chaplin or Humphrey Bogart, or of character-types, such as the cowboy or the private eye. The Hungarian producer, Sam Spiegel, and the English director, David Lean, turned a little river in Thailand that is not marked in most atlases into a household word.

So great a success obviously presupposes a very complete adaptation to the tastes of the international cinema public: and this adaptive process can be seen in the differences between the book and the movie, which is even further from what really happened on the railway. Of course, one can't fairly blame the movie for not showing the real life of the prisoner-of-war camps along the Kwai, if only because that life was boring even to those who lived it. On the other hand, using the name of an actual river suggested an element of authenticity; and the movie's version of events at the bridge certainly seemed to the survivors a gross insult on their intelligence and on that of their commanders. When news of the film's being made came out, various ex-prisoner-of-war associations, led, among other people, by Colonel Toosey, protested against the movie's distortion of what had actually happened; since the name of the river was fairly well known, people were bound to think there was an element of truth in the film. But history had given Sam Spiegel a lot of free publicity, and he refused even to change the film's title. This was vital, not only for the aura of historical truth at the box-office, but for the growth of the myth; since, in the curious limbo of mythic reality, collective fantasies need to be anchored on some real name of a place or a person.

The movie's air of pseudo-reality was also inevitably enforced by its medium. No one reading Boulle could have failed to notice from his style alone that the book aimed at ironic fantasy, rather than detailed historical realism; but the camera can't help giving an air of total visual authenticity; and the effect of this technical authenticity tends to spread beyond the visual image to the substance of what is portrayed. Every moviegoer knows in some way that – whenever he can check against his own experience – life isn't really like that; but he forgets it most of the time, especially when the substance of what he sees conforms to his own psychological or political point of view.

Politically, the movie gave no inkling of the unpleasant facts about the terrible poverty and disease along the real river Kwai. Instead, the audience must have taken away some vague impression that the poor jungle villagers of South-East Asia all have perfect complexions, and fly elaborately lovely kites. They don't. Equally unrealistically, the movie suggested that beautiful Thai girls don't have any boyfriends until some handsome white man comes along. Much more dangerously, the movie incidentally promoted the political delusion – less common now than in 1958 – that the people of these poor villages are merely marking time until they are given an opportunity to sacrifice their lives on behalf of the ideology of the Western powers. All these are examples of the colonialist attitudes which were also present in the central idea of the novel: although the Japanese had beaten the Allies in a campaign that, among other things, showed a remarkable command of very difficult engineering and transport problems, Boulle presented them as comically inferior to their captives as bridge builders. Both the novel and the movie, in fact, contained as a primary assumption the myth of white superiority whose results we have seen most recently in that same Vietnam that Boulle had known.

In the movie the bridge itself, of course, also had to be transformed into a symbol of Western engineering mastery. The form and color of those two giant cantilevers had a poised serenity which almost justified Nicholson's infatuation; but it was totally beyond the technical means and the military needs of the actual bridges over the Kwai; and its great beauty soon made one forget the sordid realities of the war and the prison camp. What actually happened was that the movie-makers went to Thailand, took one look at the Kwai, and saw it wouldn't do. The area wasn't particularly interesting – too flat, and not at all wild; there was already a bridge over the river – the real one; and in any case there wasn't any accommodation in the little provincial town of Karnburi to match the splendors of the Mount Lavinia Hotel in Ceylon, where most of the movie was eventually shot.

All this is a normal, perhaps inevitable, part of making movies; and one's only legitimate objection is that ultimately the pseudo-realism of Hollywood has the accidental effect of making millions of people think they are seeing what something is really like when actually they are not.

The biggest departure of the movie both from history and from the novel was the blowing up of the bridge, which distorted reality in a rather similar direction. The movie credits read 'Screenplay by Pierre Boulle, Based on His Novel'. Actually, though Boulle got an Oscar for the screenplay, he took only a 'modest' part in the preliminary discussions of the screenplay with Spiegel and Lean: and the real writer – who couldn't then be named – was Carl Foreman, who had been black-listed by Hollywood during the McCarthy era. Pierre Boulle eventually approved their final version; but only after he'd objected to many of their changes, and especially to the one which contradicted his whole purpose: that in the movie the bridge was blown up. He was told that the audience would have watched the screen 'for more than two hours . . . in the hope and expectation' of just that big bang; if it didn't happen 'they would feel frustrated'; and anyway it was quite impossible to pass up 'such a sensational bit of action'. So, on 12 March 1957, a beautiful bridge that had cost a quarter of a million dollars to build was blown up with a real train crossing it.

Building a bridge just to blow it up again so that the movie public won't feel frustrated was an unbelievably apt illustration of Boulle's point about how contemporary society employs its awesome techno-logical means in the pursuit of largely derisory ends.

Boulle's readers had been made to think about that; not so the moviegoers. Their consciences were kept quiet by a well-intentioned anti-war message – the killing of the terrified young Japanese soldier, for example – while they were having a rip-roaring time. But, as we all know, you can't have it both ways. You can't turn an exotic adventure-comedy into a true film about war just by dunking it in blood. The film only seemed to take up real problems; at the end a big explosion showed that there was no point in thinking things over – when things will work out nicely anyway, why bother?

In the movie of the *Bridge on the River Kwai*, then, historical and political and psychological reality became infinitely plastic to the desires of the audience. All over the world audiences gratefully responded; and in the end they even caused the myth to be reincarnated where it had begun.

REINCARNATION ON THE KWAI

The decisive phase of a myth is when the story wins a special status for itself; when people begin to think of it, not exactly as history, but as something which, in some vague way, really happened; and then, later, the fiction eventually imposes itself on the world as literally true. The earliest signs of this are normally the erection of shrines, and the beginning of pilgrimages; but the process of reincarnation is only complete when whatever is left of the truth which conflicts with the myth's symbolic meaning is forgotten or transformed. All this has begun to happen to the myth of the Kwai.

After the war ended, in August 1945, and the last train had evacuated the sad remnants of the Japanese army in Burma, silence at last descended on the railway. Robbers furtively stole the telegraph wire; termites ate away the wooden sleepers of the line and the timbers of the bridges; the monsoon rains washed away parts of the embankment; and sensing that all was normal again, the wild elephants (which few prisoners had ever seen) once again emerged from the jungle, and, finding the railway trace a convenient path, leaned against whatever telegraph poles inconvenienced their passage. By the time that, in 1946, the Thai government bought the Kwai railway from the Japanese for about $4,000,000, its track was on the way to being derelict.

Eventually it was decided to keep the railway going only as far up as a place called Nam Tok, some hundred miles above the bridge over the Kwai. Nam Tok was probably chosen as terminus because there are beautiful waterfalls nearby, waterfalls that are very famous in Thai history and legend. In 1961 the whole area was scheduled as a National Park; and now three trains a day carry villagers and tourists up to see the sights.

When I visited Nam Tok in 1966 I found that, just at the end of the embankment, the local villagers had set up a little shrine. On the altar table, in front of the little gilded image of the local tutelary deity, or *Chao Tee*, there were the usual propitiatory offerings, flowers, incense-sticks, fruit, sweets, candles, paper garlands; but in the place of honor were two rusty old iron spikes – the kind we had used to fasten the rails to the wooden ties.

There are also other and much vaster shrines near the Tha Makham bridge: an Allied cemetery for 6,982 Australian, British and Dutch prisoners of war; a Roman Catholic chapel just opposite; a Chinese burial ground for a few of the Asiatic forced-laborers of whom over a hundred thousand died along the Kwai; and a Japanese Memorial to all the casualties of the railway, including their own. All these shrines are much visited, as the fresh flowers and incense sticks testify: the Japanese Ambassador regularly lays a wreath at the Japanese Memorial; and there is an annual commemoration service in the Allied cemetery.

There are also other kinds of pilgrim. In Bangkok, 'Sincere Travel Service', for instance, advertises

Tour No. 11 Daily: 7:30 a.m. Whole day soft drinks and lunch provided. The Bridge over River Kwai and the notorious 'Death Railway' of World War fame is at Karnburi. The tourists will definitely have the joy of their life when cruising along the *real River Kwai* on the way to pay a visit to the Chungkai War Memorial Cemetery, then follows a delicious lunch by the Bridge Over River Kwai and see the real train rolling across it. All inclusive rate: US $20. – per person minimum 2 persons.

The world-wide diffusion of Boulle's novel through the cinema, then, has left its mark on the Kwai. Outside the Karnburi cemetery there stands today a road sign which reads: 'Bridge over the River Kwai 2.590 kilometres'. It points to a real bridge; but it is only worth pointing to because of the bridge the whole world saw in the movie.

In a recent pictorial guide to Thailand there is an even more striking example of how the power of the myth is beginning to transform reality. The book gives a fine photograph of what is actually the Wang Pho viaduct along a gorge some fifty miles further up the line; but the caption reads 'Bridge on the River Kwai'. Some obscure need, disappointed by the failure of the real bridge *over* the river Kwai to live up to the beauty of the one in the movie, has relocated the home of the myth, and selected the most spectacular view along the railway as a more appropriate setting.

THE MYTH AND THE REALITY

The myth, then, is established. What does it mean?

When *The Bridge on the River Kwai* was first televised it drew the largest TV audience ever recorded. Millions of people must have responded to it because – among other things – it expressed the same delusions as are responsible for much unreal political thinking. There was, as I've already said, the colonial myth – the odd notion that the ordinary people of South-East Asia instinctively love the white strangers who have come to their lands, and want to sacrifice themselves on their behalf. There was also the implication of the blowing-up of the bridge

– however muddled we may be about our political aims, advanced high-explosive technology will always come out on top in the end. The Big Bang theory of war, of course, fitted in very nicely with the consoling illusion of a world of Friendly (and militarily backward) Natives.

The theory, and the illusion, have one fatal weakness: they clash with what Sartre calls '*la force des choses*'.[1] What happened to the real bridge illustrates this very neatly.

In the summer of 1944 the new American long-range bombers, the B 29s, started flying over the Kwai, and bombing the bridges. To anyone who knows any military history, what happened was absolutely predictable. Quite a lot of people, mainly prisoners, were killed; but eventually the bombers got some direct hits, and two spans of the steel bridge fell into the river. While it was being repaired, the low wooden bridge was put back into use; and when that, too, was damaged, it was easily restored by the labor of the prisoners in the nearby camps. Japanese military supplies weren't delayed for a single day. If you can build a bridge, you can repair it; in the long run, bombing military targets is only significant if the target can later be captured and held.

The Allied command in Ceylon know this very well. They bombed the Kwai railway then because their armies were advancing in Burma and preparing to attack Thailand: but this vital context is absent from the novel and the film. Actually there were also Allied commandos in the bridge area at the time: not to blow up the bridge, though, but to link up with the Thai resistance, and help liberate prison camps once the invasion started. Boulle probably knew this, since he called his commandos Force 316, whereas the real ones were Force 136. Still, Boulle's novel certainly undercuts the Big Bang theory, and one imagines that he found in its blind destructive credulity a folly that wasn't exclusively military. Since 1866, and Nobel's invention of dynamite, all kinds of individuals and social groups have attributed magical powers to dynamite; they've refused to see that the best you can expect from explosives is an explosion.

The Big Bang theory of war is rather like the colonial myth, and even the schoolboy dream of defying the adult world; all three are essentially expressions of what Freud called the childish delusion of the omnipotence of thought. The myth of the Kwai deeply reflects this delusion, and shapes it according to the particular values of contemporary culture.

Hollywood, the advertising industry, Existentialism, even the current counter-culture are alike in their acceptance or their exploitation of the delusion of the omnipotence of thought. From this come many of their other similarities: that they are ego-centered, romantic, anti-historical; that they all show a belief in rapid and absolute solutions of human problems. They are all, in the last analysis, institutional patterns based on the posture of anti-institutionalism.

These basic assumptions of the myth are perhaps most obvious in the kernel of the story, which the movie made much more recognizable as a universal fantasy, the schoolboy's perennial dream of defying the adult world. Young Nicholson cheeks the mean old headmaster, called Saito: he gets a terrible beating, but the other students kick up such a row about it that Saito just has to give in. Confrontation tactics win out; and Nicholson is carried back in triumph across the playground. In the end, of course, he becomes the best student-body president Kwai High ever had.

I don't know if anything like this – total rebellion combined with total acceptance – has ever occurred in any educational institution; but I am forced to report that nothing like it ever happened in the prison-camps along the Kwai. There, all our circumstances were hostile to individual fantasies; surviving meant accepting the intractable realities which surrounded us, and making sure that our fellow prisoners accepted them too.

No one would even guess from the novel or the film that there were any wholly intractable realities on the Kwai. Boulle proposes a simple syllogism: war is madness; war is fought by soldiers; therefore, soldiers are mad. It's a flattering notion, no doubt, to non-soldiers, but it happens not to be true; and it's really much too easy a way out to delude ourselves with the belief that wars and injustices are caused only by lunatics, by people who don't see things as we see them.

Neither the novel nor the film admits that certain rational distinctions remain important even under the most difficult or confusing circumstances. They seem instead to derive a peculiar satisfaction from asserting that in a world of madness the weakness of our collective life can find its salvation only in the strength of madmen. There is no need to insist on the authoritarian nature of this idea, but it does seem necessary to enquire why these last decades have created a myth which totally subverts the stubbornness of facts and of the human will to resist unreason.

The basic reason is presumably the widespread belief that institutions are at the same time immoral, ridiculous, and unreal, whereas individuals exist in a world whose circumstances are essentially tractable. A prisoner-of-war camp has at least one thing in common with our modern world in general: both offer a very limited range of practical choices. No wonder the public acclaimed a film where, under the most limiting circumstances imaginable, one solitary individual managed to do just what he planned to do. Of course his triumph depended on making everything else subservient to his fantasy; and if our circumstances on the Kwai had been equally pliable, there would have been no reason whatever for Toosey or anybody else to act as they did.

It's probably true that at the beginning of our captivity many of us thought that at last the moment had arrived for revolt, if not against the Japanese, at least against our own military discipline and anything else that interfered with our individual liberty. But then circumstances forced us to see that this would be suicidal. We were terribly short of food, clothes, and medicine; theft soon became a real threat to everyone; and so we had to organize our own police. At first it seemed too ridiculous, but not for long. When cholera broke out, for instance, whole camps of Asiatic laborers were wiped out, whereas in our own camps nearby, with an effective organization to make sure everyone used the latrines and ate or drank only what had been boiled, we often had no deaths, even though we had no vaccine.

In the myth, then, the actual circumstances of our experience on the Kwai were overwhelmed by the deep blindness of our culture both to the stubbornness of reality and to the continuities of history. It was surely this blindness which encouraged the public, in accepting the plausibility of Nicholson's triumph, to assert its belief in the combined wickedness, folly, and unreality of institutions – notably of those which were in conflict on the Kwai: the Japanese and their prisoners.

It isn't only on the walls of the Sorbonne that we can see the slogan 'It is forbidden to forbid.' It is written on all individuals at birth, in the form 'It is forbidden to forbid me'; and this text has been adopted to their great profit by the movie and advertising industries: by Hollywood, in the version 'You don't get rich by saying no to dreams', and by Madison Avenue in the version 'Tell 'em they're suckers if they don't have everything they want.'

The movie, incidentally, added one apt illustration of this slogan which had no basis whatever in Boulle or reality. No one wants to be a prisoner; you don't have to be; and so William Holden escapes, easily. On the Kwai, hundreds tried; most of them were killed; no one succeeded.

Among today's pilgrims to the present cemeteries on the Kwai, an increasing number come from the American forces in Thailand and Vietnam. When I leafed through the Visitors' Book, one entry caught my eye. A private from Apple Creek, Wisconsin, stationed at Da Nang, had been moved to write a protest that made all the other banal pieties look pale: 'PEOPLE are STUPID.'

Stupid, among other things, because they are mainly led by what they want to believe, not by what they know. It's easier to go along with the implication of the movie, and believe that a big bang – anywhere – will somehow end the world's confusion and our own fatigue. It would undoubtedly end it, but only in larger cemeteries for the victims of the last Great Joke.

Vietnam has been a painful lesson in the kinds of mythical thinking which *The Bridge on the River Kwai* both reflected and reinforced; we seem now to be slowly recovering from some of the political forms of the omnipotence-of-thought fantasy. Recently, I observed that the main audience reaction to the movie was ironical laughter.

If we can accept the notion that in all kinds of spheres some individual has to be responsible for the organization and continuity of human affairs, we should perhaps look again at the man without whom the myth would not have come into being. Along the Kwai, Colonel Toosey was almost universally recognized for what he was – a hero of the only kind we could afford then, and there. For he was led, not by what he wanted to believe, but by what he knew: he knew that the world would not do his bidding; that he could not beat the Japanese: that on the Kwai – even more obviously than at home – we were for the most part helpless prisoners of coercive circumstance. But he also knew that if things were as intractable as they looked, the outlook for the years ahead was hopeless: much death, and total demoralization, for the community he found himself in. The only thing worth working for was the possibility that tenacity and imagination could find a way by which the chances of decent survival could be increased. It was, no doubt, a very modest objective for so much work and restraint – two of Conrad's moral imperatives that Boulle didn't quote, incidentally; but in our circumstances then on the Kwai, the objective was quite enough to be getting on with; as it is here, now.

NOTE

1 The force of things as they are.

Index